"Fascinating, comprehensive, and clearly explained, *Sexed Up* leads the reader through a radically sensible analysis of what sexualization is and how it happens. (Hint: You're soaking in it!) As we work to create a sex-positive culture, we'll reference this vitally important book again and again."

—CAROL QUEEN, PhD, author of *Exhibitionism for the Shy* and cofounder of the Center for Sex & Culture

"Julia Serano acutely speaks to many nuances in gender and sexuality that unjustly dictate the safety, value, and autonomy of marginalized genders. Immersive and precise, she traces enduring stigmas to their illogical roots."

—KOA BECK, author of *White Feminism*

"Julia Serano has done it again, taking an idea you thought you understood and unfolding depths to it you never knew were there. *Sexed Up* is the sexualization rethink you didn't know you needed."

—JACLYN FRIEDMAN, author of *What You Really Really Want*

"Julia Serano is a razor-sharp observer and a generous, compassionate, and liberatory thinker. *Sexed Up* is a wise, nuanced, and unapologetic guide to understanding what goes on under the hood of sexualization in American culture."

—DR. HANNE BLANK BOYD, historian and author of *Straight*

SEXED UP

UP

How Society Sexualizes Us,
and How We Can Fight Back

JULIA SERANO

SEAL PRESS

NEW YORK

Seal Press
Hachette Book Group
1290 Avenue of the Americas, New York, NY 10104
www.sealpress.com
@sealpress

Printed in the United States of America
First Edition: May 2022

Published by Seal Press, an imprint of Perseus Books, LLC, a subsidiary of Hachette Book Group, Inc. The Seal Press name and logo is a trademark of the Hachette Book Group.

The Hachette Speakers Bureau provides a wide range of authors for speaking events. To find out more, go to www.hachettespeakersbureau.com or call (866) 376-6591.

The publisher is not responsible for websites (or their content) that are not owned by the publisher.

Print book interior design by Linda Mark.

Library of Congress Cataloging-in-Publication Data
Names: Serano, Julia, author.
Title: Sexed up : how society sexualizes us, and how we can fight back / Julia Serano.
Description: New York, NY : Seal Press, [2022] | Includes bibliographical references.
Identifiers: LCCN 2021045851 | ISBN 9781541674806 (hardcover) | ISBN 9781541674790 (ebook)
Subjects: LCSH: Sex—Social aspects—United States. | Gender identity—United States. | Transgender people—United States. | Sexual minorities—United States.
Classification: LCC HQ18.U5 S445 2022 | DDC 306.70973—dc23
LC record available at https://lccn.loc.gov/2021045851
ISBNs: 9781541674806 (hardcover), 9781541674790 (ebook)

LSC-C

Printing 1, 2022

JUL 1 3 2022

for Rynn
thank you for your love, friendship, and support
especially over these last two trying years
and to all the fun times
we'll share together moving forward

CONTENTS

INTRODUCTION

Human sexuality is such a vast and complex subject that it's impossible to cover it in its entirety within a single book. So instead, authors usually examine these matters from a specific angle or focus on a particular subtopic.

A biologist might frame the subject strictly in terms of anatomical or neurological differences between the sexes. An endocrinologist might focus on the role that hormones play in driving sexual behaviors, while a geneticist might explain those same behaviors in terms of evolutionary pressures. A sexual minority of one stripe or another might pen a memoir that delves into aspects of sex and desire that fall outside most people's purview. A psychiatrist might describe those behaviors as sexual "deviations" or "dysfunctions," and speculate about what supposedly "goes wrong" in such individuals to make them turn out that way.

A philosopher might question the underlying belief systems that lead us to deem sexual behaviors either "right" or "wrong" in the first place. A historian might analyze changes in sexual norms that have occurred over time, while an anthropologist might chronicle differences in sexual identities and practices that exist from culture to culture.

And so on. Each of these perspectives has the potential to provide important insights, but they inevitably tell only part of the story.

I have been researching and writing about gender and sexuality for over two decades now, and I am quite familiar with all the aforementioned perspectives. But from my vantage point, one crucial piece of the puzzle is almost always missing from these narratives. Namely, they tend to portray sex and sexuality as things that individuals "do" or "possess" without giving much, if any, thought to how we *see* and *interpret* these aspects of people.

I first recognized the importance of these issues back in 2001, when I had a formative experience that relatively few people ever have. After having spent the first thirty or so years of my life being perceived as male, I transitioned to female. Most mainstream accounts of transgender people tend to place all the attention on the ways that *we* change: our identities, personal journeys, and physical transformations, and how our transitions impact our relationships with others. But having lived through that experience firsthand, what *I* found most fascinating was the way *the rest of the world seemed to change*. Small exchanges and mundane interactions at the grocery store, in restaurants, on public transit, and elsewhere suddenly shifted as people began to see and treat me differently.

Of course, going into my transition, I was well aware of the existence of sexism, and knew that I would likely face discrimination once people started perceiving me as female (and this did come to pass). But what I was not prepared for were the countless—sometimes subtle, sometimes major—ways in which people interpreted my body and actions differently. Behaviors that would have elicited a particular reaction back when I was perceived as male suddenly went unnoticed or else provoked an entirely different response. People began to make all sorts of new presumptions about my history, interests, preferences, abilities, and motives, as well as how I would (or should) act, or react, in a given situation. In other words, while my body had taken on a new shape, mostly it just took on new meanings.

In addition to being transgender, I also happen to be bisexual—that is, I am attracted to people of the same gender, as well as people whose genders differ from mine. Over the years, I've dated a wide range of people: Some were women and others men; some were transgender and others cisgender; some identified as queer and others as straight.

Discussions about sexual orientation are often framed in terms of "attraction to women" or "attraction to men," as though such attractions are entirely disembodied and divorced from our own identities, thought processes, and cultural meanings. I suppose that for people whose bodies, genders, and desires are more fixed and unchanging over time, whom they are "attracted to" might seem like the most relevant criterion, given that everything else remains relatively constant.

But for me, in addition to whether I find a potential partner attractive, I need to be able to anticipate the varied gendered and sexual expectations that they may be projecting onto me because I am a woman, or because I am bisexual or transgender. If we do become involved, then what form does our relationship take, and how do we interpret our similar or differing bodies and identities (are we a lesbian couple? a bisexual pairing? a trans woman dating a cis man? a binary-shattering trans relationship? etc.)? And just as important, how do we *feel* about that relationship (proud? ashamed? dirty? subversive? normal?), and do those feelings positively or negatively influence how we act and what we do together? In addition to all those internal feelings are the relentless external expectations of outsiders: Are we perceived as a straight couple or a queer couple? Is it safe for us to hold hands or express affection in public?

Because these sexual expectations and meanings are constantly shifting for me, I have spent a lot of time contemplating and questioning them, trying to understand where they come from and why we project them onto certain people, relationships, and desires but not others. In this book, I will elucidate these sexual double standards for readers and provide explanations for how they arise and function.

Far and away, the most difficult sexual double standards that I've had to grapple with involve *sexualization*: when an individual is reduced to their sexual body or behaviors rather than viewed as a whole person. Admittedly, this too was something I did not fully comprehend prior to my transition. Back when people perceived me as male, there were occasions when someone expressed sexual interest in me or told me they found me attractive, but it always felt more empowering than invalidating. The reason seems obvious in retrospect. Such occurrences were relatively rare for me, so they felt special rather than ordinary or annoying. And they always happened in an appropriate setting—typically when I was out on a date with the person, or sometimes while at a party or a bar. Most crucially, these expressions of sexual interest never once denied my humanity or autonomy—the people in question found me attractive because of who I was as a person, and it was always clear that I was free to decline their proposition.

But as soon as I transitioned, I was suddenly subjected to the many manifestations of sexualization that often plague young women in our culture: Strange men in public settings would sometimes aggressively stare at me, or make comments about my body and what they'd like to do to me. In an early Google self-search, I discovered a message board where someone had posted a photo of me from my website, and (knowing that I was trans) all the commenters were debating whether or not they would "fuck" me (their word).

If these and other experiences of sexualization had been once-in-a-blue-moon occurrences, perhaps I could have dismissed or ignored them. But they were pervasive and relentless. They became routine. And I found myself changing my behaviors accordingly. Some days I'd purposefully dress down or take an alternative route to work in an attempt to mitigate the street harassment I regularly faced. When I began dating men as a woman, typically through personal ads or dating websites, I always left their contact information with a friend, just in case something awful happened—a precaution I had never thought to take back when I had gone on dates *as* a man. And when attending the same sorts of bars and parties where I used to move about unencumbered, I found myself keeping my guard up in order to avoid being cast in a role that I had never auditioned for.

Given how greatly sexualization has personally impacted my life, I find it astounding that most books about human sexuality never even mention it, or raise the issue only in passing. To date, the subject has been largely relegated to feminist writings and research focusing on how women are often sexualized in our straight male–centric culture.

Currently, the standard model for understanding sexualization within feminist discourses is the "rape culture" paradigm. Feminists who forward this paradigm are concerned primarily with the ways in which sexual violence against women is normalized in our society and often view less extreme manifestations of sexualization—objectification, slut-shaming, sexual harassment, and sexism more generally—as enabling or perpetuating rape.

While this model has played a critical role in raising awareness and addressing sexual assault, I believe it fails to account for many other forms of sexualization. For instance, when people discover that I am a transgender (rather than a cisgender) woman, they often sexualize me in a host of other ways: viewing me as sexually deviant, or predatory, or hypersexual, or desperate, or undesirable, or exotic, or as a "fetish object." Notably, some of these additional forms of sexualization are projected onto other minority groups, including other LGBTQIA+ folks, people of color, and people with disabilities. In fact, as I will show, all marginalized groups seem to be sexualized to some degree, although the specific stereotypes they encounter may vary considerably.

In other words, sexualization is a more general tactic to delegitimize and dehumanize people. This helps to explain why there is often so much shame, reluctance, and secrecy surrounding discussions of sexuality, as even broaching the subject can lead a person to become stigmatized. For those of us who are routinely targeted by sexualization, its constant presence complicates our sexual experiences, often leading us to not act upon our desires or to feel conflicted or ashamed if we do. In other words, it can profoundly affect our sexual tendencies and histories. Over the course of the book, I will reflect upon the many ways in which undue sexual attention, scrutiny, and condemnation have shaped my experiences and how they alter the way that many of us move through the world.

While this book is not organized into discrete sections, it is roughly arranged according to specific themes. Over the course of the first five chapters, I will describe a series of unconscious mindsets that help shape our perceptions and interpretations of other people, and that give rise to many commonly held double standards regarding sex, gender, and sexuality.

For explanatory purposes, I will often speak generically about "men" and "women" in these chapters, peppering them with some of my own personal experiences both pre- and post-transition, in order to highlight some general differences in how these groups are often perceived and treated. But of course, no one is a "generic" member of a particular gender, as we all possess countless other attributes that influence how others may view us. In my case, in addition to being a bisexual trans woman, I'm a white, middle-class, able-bodied, "Generation X" person who was in her early thirties and living in a major U.S. city when most of these anecdotes took place.

I will complicate this story in subsequent chapters as I delve into how these mindsets, and the sexualization that arises from them, intersect with other forms of marginalization. Specifically, I will attempt to explain how different marginalized groups have come to be stereotyped as "promiscuous," "predatory," "deviant," "deceivers," "undesirable," and/or "fetish objects."

On a parallel track, starting in Chapter 6, I will propose a new framework for conceptualizing sexualization—one centered on stigma rather than attraction or objectification. This framework better explains women's diverse experiences with the phenomenon and accommodates the various ways in which sexualization is wielded against other marginalized groups.

In Chapters 9 and 10, in addition to analyzing the obstacles that sexualization imposes upon marginalized groups, I will consider how these various sexual double standards may nudge us toward different sexual interests and trajectories.

Finally, after having spent most of the book discussing "How Society Sexualizes Us," in Chapters 10 and 11, I will offer my suggestions for "How We Can Fight Back." Specifically, in addition to working to transcend the mindsets I've described, I will forward strategies that should foster sexual equity without sacrificing sexual diversity in the process.

As I mentioned at the outset, I will not be able to tackle every sex-related issue or answer every sex-related question. But I do hope to offer a unique perspective on these matters, and to provide an important missing piece of the puzzle for those interested in more thoroughly understanding human sexuality in all its diversity.

Before we begin, there are two potential misconceptions that some readers may have about this book. So in the rest of this Introduction, I want to preemptively address such concerns.

Sexologist Leonore Tiefer once made the following observation: While almost all textbooks on human sexuality begin with one or more chapters about human anatomy and physiology, music textbooks rarely delve into the relevant biological processes—auditory systems, neural processing, muscle coordination, and so on—that allow us to listen to, interpret, and perform music.[1]

In other words, while all human endeavors necessarily involve biology and bodies, when it comes to sex and sexuality, we tend to have an especially biology-centric view. Given this tendency, some readers might be disappointed to find that there will be very little discussion about biology in this book (with the exception of the next eight paragraphs, which can be skipped if you're uninterested in such particulars). I can imagine some people thinking, "How can you possibly write a book about human sexuality without discussing biology?" to which I retort, "How can you possibly write a book about this subject without considering how we perceive and interpret sex and sexuality?"

In any case, this lack of biological content might lead some people to presume that I must be in denial about the role that biology plays, when in fact nothing could be further from the truth. I happen to have a PhD in biochemistry and molecular biophysics from Columbia University and spent seventeen years as a researcher at the University of California at Berkeley in the fields of genetics, evolution, and developmental biology. In addition to that academic and professional experience, as a trans woman who has hormonally transitioned, I can attest firsthand that biology has very real tangible effects on our bodies and desires, although not always in the ways or to the extent that some people might expect.[2]

While I am hardly in denial about the importance of biology, I am highly critical of the way that biology is often portrayed in popular media, wherein genes, hormones, and various brain regions are often depicted as though they are binary switches that simply "turn on" certain behaviors or desires in some people while keeping them "turned off" in others. Throughout much of the twentieth century, such simplistic models were popular among biologists themselves. However, our understanding has evolved over the decades, and it is now widely recognized that almost all human traits are *complex traits*—that is, determined through the intricate interaction of countless different factors, some biological, others environmental, with a certain amount of randomness thrown in for good measure. As a result, instead of producing discrete outcomes—such as on versus off, or presence versus absence—human traits tend to fall along spectrums, often taking the form of bell curves, with many people being clustered close to the average but many outliers existing as well.

To illustrate how complex traits work, let's use the familiar example of height. While most people tend to fall within the average range, there are nevertheless plenty of exceptions to this—for instance, it would not be unusual for us to come across someone who is 4'10" or 6'7" over the course of our day. While height clearly has a genetic component (if your parents are tall, then you will likely be tall yourself), there is no such thing as a "height gene" that singularly determines this. In fact, hundreds of genes have been identified that influence height to some degree, with each making a relatively small contribution on its own.[3] Height is also greatly influenced by environmental and cultural factors, such as access to food, regional diet, and other factors such as accidents or illness. Finally, part of the reason why I chose height as an example is that it also happens to be a *sexually dimorphic trait*—the scientific term for a trait that shows differences between sexes. Specifically, if you undergo a typical male puberty, then you will turn out to be taller than if you undergo a typical female puberty. That said, we all know plenty of tall women and short men. Indeed, if you compare the bell curves for height of women and men, you will find considerable overlap between the two. This is true for all sexually dimorphic traits, although the amount of overlap may vary significantly from trait to trait.[4]

Sexually dimorphic traits are often described as falling into two categories. There are the so-called *primary sex characteristics*, which refer to genetic (XX or XY chromosomes) and anatomical (genitals, gonads, and other reproductive organs) differences that are typically present at birth. Then there are *secondary sex characteristics*, which arise later in life—generally during puberty—in response to sex hormones (estrogens and androgens). Secondary sex characteristics include differences in height, muscle and fat distribution, breast development in females, deepening of the voice and increased facial and body hair in males, and so on. These sex attributes are the ones that we tend to rely on most when we classify adults as women and men in everyday circumstances. While many people presume that sex hormone levels, sex chromosomes, genitals, and other reproductive organs are entirely discrete, showing no overlap between female and male individuals, somewhere around 1 percent of the human population are *intersex*—that is, one or more of their sex characteristics fall outside what is considered "standard" for female or male.[5]

Another class of sexually dimorphic traits to consider are those that are more psychological or behavioral in nature. These tend to be more disputed than their overtly physical counterparts, in part because they are not readily accessible or measured: We might all agree that a particular individual is 5'6", but it is difficult to objectively assess their internal feelings, desires, or tendencies. There is also a long-standing debate over where such traits originate. Given our partiality for biology-centric explanations, it is not surprising that most people assume that any real or perceived behavioral differences between the sexes must arise directly from underlying physical attributes, particularly in the brain. However, we also live in a culture where, from the earliest of ages, girls and boys are socialized very differently: encouraged to act in "opposite" ways and to cultivate disparate mannerisms, interests, and social roles. If you believe that early interventions in a child's life may facilitate their growing up to be more intelligent, extroverted, musical, multilingual, etc., then it should be relatively easy to accept the fact that the constant gender socialization that children are subjected to likely plays at least *some* role in facilitating or shaping differences between the sexes.

There was a time—particularly from the 1960s through the 1980s—when many psychologists, sociologists, and feminists proposed a strict *sex/gender distinction*, where the term "sex" was reserved for explicitly biological traits (such as the aforementioned primary and secondary sex characteristics), while the term "gender" referred to more psychological or behavioral ones—such as an individual's *gender identity* (whether they identify as a girl/woman, boy/man, or other) and *gender expression* (whether they are feminine and/or masculine in their mannerisms, presentation, and interests). Those who subscribed to this sex/gender distinction often presumed that traits associated with gender arose exclusively as a result of gender socialization and social norms, with no input from biology. Because of this belief, if a genetically male infant was born without a penis or else lost it in an accident, doctors of that time often encouraged parents to raise the child as a girl under the assumption that gender was entirely learned and that these children would lead more normal lives that way. However, follow-up studies demonstrated that despite having female-typical socializations, most of these children grew up to be stereotypically masculine in their behaviors, attracted to women rather than men, and many spontaneously announced that they identified as boys/men rather than girls/women, often despite being unaware of their early-childhood sex reassignment.[6] Such findings indicate that these traits are at least partially determined by underlying biology. I provide additional arguments against strict sex-versus-gender and nature-versus-nurture frameworks elsewhere.[7]

While a few people still adhere to the sex/gender distinction, it has been largely supplanted by our current understanding that gender and sexuality are complex traits arising from the intricate interplay of numerous biological, social, and environmental factors—indeed, this view is supported by all the available evidence. For instance, each of these traits yields a spectrum of outcomes with many outliers and overlap between the sexes, as seen in the case of sexual orientation (homosexual, bisexual, and asexual people), gender identity (transgender people), and gender expression (feminine men, masculine women, and other gender nonconforming people). Much like the previously described sex characteristics, gender identity, gender expression, and sexual orientation all appear to be somewhat separable in that these traits may not all align with one another within any given person.[8] Despite many decades of research investigating why people turn out to be gay, or transgender, or gender nonconforming, and so on, no singular cause has ever been found, which is precisely what we'd expect from a complex trait. Furthermore, much like the existence of tall women and short men, individuals who differ in these respects can be found across all cultures and throughout history, suggesting that they arise as a result of natural variation rather than due to something specific about any given society or time period.[9]

Here and now—in the United States in the early 2020s—people who fall outside gender and sexual norms are often described via acronyms such as *LGBTQIA+* or umbrella terms such as *queer* or *gender and sexual minorities*.[10] In other eras and cultures, these same individuals might have gravitated toward somewhat different identities, social roles, sexual practices, and self-understandings—in other words, social factors also play a crucial role in shaping our impressions and expressions of gender and sexuality. In recent years, the sentiment that LGBTQIA+ people are simply "born that way" has become increasingly popular. While that phrase does convey the fact that, for many of us, our exceptional genders and sexualities emerge unconsciously and inexplicably (rather than being deliberately chosen), I believe that it is more accurate to view such traits as likely involving natural predispositions or propensities, although the ways that we express and make sense of those feelings and desires are most certainly dependent on the language, concepts, and social possibilities available to us.

In summary, while biology plays a critical role in human sexuality and shapes many of the trends we see, it also produces considerable diversity, and it may be constrained, exaggerated, or otherwise influenced by social forces. While some authors are more interested in writing about the roles that anatomy, hormones, genes, etc. potentially play, I am more fascinated by how we perceive and interpret this biological variation, and the ramifications of those mental and social processes.

A second misconception about this book that I anticipate is that, because I am writing from the perspective of a bisexual trans woman, some may assume that the account I'm sharing must therefore be "anomalous" or "biased" in some way. While I admit that many of the personal experiences that I share here are atypical, that by no means renders them invalid. In fact, some of the most informative scientific experiments involve observing how seemingly ordinary systems function under unusual or extreme conditions. I argue that my transition, and the different ways I've been perceived and interpreted because of it, is precisely the type of extraordinary circumstance from which we can garner crucial insights. Furthermore, while my views have certainly been influenced by my personal experiences, the same holds true for every person who expresses opinions on these matters. We all have varied personal experiences with sex, gender, and sexuality, so there is no purely objective "view from nowhere."

Given our current political climate, rife with anti-transgender backlash, I'm sure that some people will immediately accuse me and this book of promoting some kind of "agenda." Of course, people who hurl the word "agenda" at those with whom they disagree are usually promoting an agenda of their own. While I've written more activist-themed books in the past—particularly my books *Whipping Girl* and *Excluded*—I am approaching this book more as a researcher than as an activist. Rather than trying to convince readers that they should accept me as a bisexual trans woman, what I am trying to communicate with this book is "Here are some of the things that I experienced during and after my transition, and here is some research from other groups (sexologists, psychologists, sociologists, historians, philosophers) that sheds light on my observations. After contemplating it all over the course of two decades, here are some conclusions I have reached."

Readers will likely vary in their knowledge of gender and sexual minorities, and those who are less familiar may find themselves having questions about these aspects of my person, especially the fact that I am transgender. Some of these questions may be of a more personal nature ("When did you first realize you were transgender?" "Why did you decide to transition?"), while others may involve trans-related issues that have recently appeared in the news.

While a few of these questions may be answered in these pages, most will not, as that is not the purpose of this book. I encourage those who are curious (or skeptical) about transgender people and issues to read my first book, *Whipping Girl,* or check out my many online writings that delve more deeply into those topics.[11] Importantly, understanding or relating to my identity as a bisexual trans woman is not a prerequisite for appreciating this book. I am perfectly fine with readers viewing me more as someone who has explored largely uncharted aspects of gender and sexuality, who is now reporting back on what I have witnessed and learned from those encounters.

Like all books, this one was written at a particular place and time. I live in the United States (specifically, in Oakland, California), and while what I say here may resonate with other Americans and people from other "Western" countries, it may have less import for those living in other regions, as cultural norms and beliefs about gender and sexuality can vary considerably.

I started writing this book in 2019. When I began this project, the cultural touchstone that I assumed would most shape its reception was the Me Too movement, which started in 2017 and resulted in society-wide discussions and debates about sexual harassment and assault. I will be addressing such issues throughout this book and will contextualize the Me Too movement itself in the final chapter.

But then, early in the writing process, the COVID-19 pandemic hit. Given that I am writing this while still in "lockdown," I will not venture to guess how COVID-19 may or may not impact the sexual landscape in the years to come. But I can say that some of the racist and xenophobic backlash to the pandemic here in the United States reminded me of the virulently homophobic reactions to the AIDS epidemic that I witnessed as a teenager and young adult during the 1980s. And perhaps the ever-present specter of "illness" and "infectiousness," and my rearranging my entire life in attempt to remain "free" of SARS-CoV-2, led me to increasingly think about sexualization in terms of social stigma—a concept that is often associated with the imagined properties of "contamination" and "contagion."

A couple more incidental notes about what follows: First, this book is very broadly about human sexuality, and I will often use the word "sexual" in an umbrella fashion to refer to some combination of attraction to other people, physiological arousal, erotic thoughts and fantasies, the act of sex, plus flirting, courting, dating, and romance that may or may not lead up to said sexual acts. These facets are often interconnected (hence the umbrella term), but it's important to note that they can also exist in isolation from one another for some people or in certain situations.

Second, the term "sexualization" has been used in different ways over the years. Some authors have used it rather narrowly, such as only in reference to women or objectification, while others have used it so broadly as to include simply imagining or appreciating someone sexually. For reasons that will become clear over the course of this book, I will be using the following working definition: Sexualization occurs when a person is nonconsensually reduced to their real or imagined sexual attributes (their body, behaviors, or desires) to the exclusion of other characteristics. Finally, this book will delve into heavy topics, particularly marginalization and sexualization, with sexual assault being discussed at various points throughout. I've endeavored to handle these subjects in a thoughtful and nonsensationalistic manner, but readers should be aware of this content before moving forward.

Before we can address the problem of sexualization, we first need to understand how sexual double standards work more generally. Such double standards rely on our tendency or ability to distinguish between seemingly different "types" of people, some of whom we project certain sexual (or sexualizing) meanings and assumptions onto, while others remain free of such assessments. In other words, in order to fully understand sexualization, we must first consider how and why we lump people into different gender and sexual categories in the first place. That will be the focus of the first chapter.

1 THE TWO FILING CABINETS IN OUR MINDS

If I were to ask you to define the word "sex," two potential answers would likely spring to mind. Sex can refer to whether a person's physical traits are female, male, or intersex (as previously discussed). Then there is the act of sex—some may immediately think of intercourse here, although the term may include a broad range of sexually arousing activities.

However, there is a third definition of "sex" that receives considerably less attention: to determine an individual's sex, or to assign them to a particular sex category. Typically, this verb form of the word is reserved for discussions of nonhuman animals. In graduate school, upon joining a lab that researched fruit fly development, the first thing I was taught was how to sex the flies: to distinguish males from females, based largely on the presence or absence of male genitals and certain abdominal pigmentation differences. Years later, when I began working in a lab that studied a particular crustacean species, I was taught how to sex individuals based upon claw size or by the occasional presence of eggs in adult females. In both cases, learning how to sex these species was a bit challenging at first, but over time, it became rote—instead of seeing a bunch of flies or crustaceans, I would automatically see females and males.

We pretty much do the same thing with human beings: As soon as we come across another person, or a group of people, we immediately sex them. And we do it constantly. Relentlessly.

Some readers might object to my framing this as an active process. They might instead argue that people simply *are* either female or male, and we just passively observe these traits in others. If you are inclined to think this way, then I encourage you to take a moment the next time you are in a setting where people congregate—perhaps a city street, shopping center, park, or college campus—and take note of how quickly you assign a sex to each and every person you see. Some of these individuals may be too far away for us to make out their faces or other physical attributes, yet we will still come to some kind of determination, perhaps based upon the cut or color of their clothing, or the way they comport themselves. Indeed, it may be more accurate to refer to this process as "gendering" (rather than "sexing"), given that we often rely on social cues rather than, or in addition to, physical ones. For most of us, gendering is primarily a snap visual assessment, although there are some cases—such as talking to a stranger on the phone—where we may rely more on other senses, and where the act of trying to figure out the person's gender becomes more self-evident.[1]

A main reason why we don't think of gendering other people as an active process is because we do it at an unconscious level, akin to how walking or comprehending language does not require any conscious effort for most of us—we just do these things automatically. Not coincidentally, these are all tasks that we learn to do very early in life, so as adults, we typically have no memory of having learned them in the first place. But they are all learned behaviors. We are not born with the innate ability to categorize people according to gender. Rather, it is a process that takes many years to develop. There is a large body of research examining how children learn to recognize and come to understand gender that I will be drawing from here.[2]

While there is evidence that infants pick up on gender differences to some degree, it is not until sometime around the ages of one or two years old that children realize that some people are "girls" and others "boys," and that they themselves belong to one of these two categories. Historically, this has been called the "gender identity" stage since many early researchers presumed that it was when children fully internalized adults' accounts of them (everyone calls me a "boy," so I must be a boy). We now know that in the case of transgender children, a different understanding may develop (everyone calls me a "boy," but I know that I am a girl). Indeed, it is upon reaching this stage that some trans children begin to explicitly assert their gender identities.

Even after reaching this stage, children's understanding of gender differs considerably from that of most adults. One major difference is that young children don't necessarily view gender as being stable over time. For instance, if you were to show preschool children a picture of a boy, and then another picture of the same boy wearing a dress, they will often conclude that the boy has now become a girl.[3] Or a child might mention in passing that when they grow up, they will be another gender (this is very different from such claims from trans children, who tend to be insistent, consistent, and persistent with regards to them). But as children grow older, they tend to relinquish this gender-flexible view in favor of "gender constancy"—the belief that if you are born a boy, then you will always be a boy, and if you are born a girl, then you will always be a girl.

The researchers who first described gender constancy (back in the 1960s and ensuing decades) seemed to view it as the most advanced of these early childhood stages, although in retrospect, it appears to be little more than an overgeneralization, if not an outright false assumption. More recent studies of transgender children and their cisgender siblings have shown that while these children do ultimately come to view gender as fairly stable, their perspective also accommodates the fact that, for a small percentage of the population, it may change over time.[4]

The other main way in which children's conceptualization of gender differs from that of adults involves the cues that they use to categorize people. Preschool-aged children tend to rely more heavily on what adults might consider to be "superficial" signs of gender, such as clothing—this helps to explain why they might assume that a boy who puts on a dress suddenly becomes a girl. Similarly, one of the more common mistakes that preschool children make is to presume that someone with long hair must be a girl or that someone with short hair must be a boy. I remember years back, a friend shared a story about how her preschool son exclaimed, "Mommy, I figured out the difference between boys and girls!" My friend braced herself for a conversation about genitals, but was relieved when her child's insight turned out to be that girls wear lipstick and boys do not. To her credit, my friend replied that the "girls wear lipstick" rule is true a lot of the time, but not always—advice that pretty much holds true for all gender-related cues.

It is noteworthy that my friend assumed that her child was going to raise the subject of genitals. While many adults view genitals as the ultimate determinant of gender (it is how we sex newborn babies, after all), many preschool children don't consider genitals to be all that important.[5] This makes sense given that we rarely see other people's genitals, so these children (who are still actively learning how to distinguish people by gender) might favor traits that are most visible to them (hair length, clothing). In contrast, adults seem to pay more attention to physical differences, especially secondary sex characteristics such as breasts or facial hair—traits that young children rarely cite when distinguishing between genders.[6] It has been proposed that gender constancy may be playing a role here: If you believe that a person's gender cannot change over time (as many adults do), then you may come to prioritize physical cues (which tend to be more permanent) over social ones (which are more amenable to change).

A recurring problem with research into how we gender people is that it relies heavily on retrospective accounts. For instance, by the age of three, children are almost as good as adults at labeling people according to gender, but if you ask them *why* they came to those conclusions, they often provide illogical or unrealistic explanations, perhaps because they are unable to put their thought processes into words.[7] Even for adults, it's often impossible to provide a definitive answer regarding why we perceive people the way we do.

Let's go back to that hypothetical place where people congregate, where I suggested that we try to consciously observe our own tendencies in gendering other people. I've done this countless times, and for the life of me, I cannot explain how my brain does it. Sure, we can provide plenty of post hoc explanations, such as "Well, he clearly walks like a man" or "Her hairstyle is a dead giveaway." But then again, if a woman walked that way, or a man had that exact same hairstyle, we wouldn't necessarily read them the same way. In those cases, other cues might seem more relevant ("She walked very butch, but I could tell she had breasts," or "Despite having long hair, I could see his five o'clock shadow").

Two book-length investigations into how we perceive gender—*Gender: An Ethnomethodological Approach* by Suzanne Kessler and Wendy McKenna and *Blind to Sameness: Sexpectations and the Social Construction of Male and Female Bodies* by Asia Friedman—took somewhat different approaches to this problem, but both reached a similar set of conclusions.[8] First, when we categorize people according to gender, we do not rely on any singular cue. Rather, our assessment is based on our overall impression of the person—or, as some of my statistics-inclined friends might say, gender perception is "in the aggregate."

Second, while any given person may display numerous possible (and sometimes conflicting) gender-related cues, we tend to weigh some cues more heavily than others. For instance, a person's genitals (if we were to see them) might influence us more than other traits, although the salience of any given trait may vary among individual observers and between cultures. Interestingly, using a series of drawings of people exhibiting a mix of female and male traits, Kessler and McKenna found that their subjects often weighed male cues (especially a penis) more heavily than female cues—they believed this was largely due to "male" being seen as the "default status" in our culture.[9]

Third, all gender cues are contextual, both with regards to perceiving an individual in isolation and assessing a large group of people. For example, at a prom (where all the women are wearing gowns and the men tuxedos), clothing becomes a highly relevant gender marker. But this would not be particularly true at a goth concert, where most people, regardless of gender, are dressed in black with elaborate hairstyles and makeup; there, we might rely more heavily on other cues.

Finally, both books detail how, by necessity, gendering people involves ignoring similarities between the sexes and filtering out any gender-ambiguous or conflicting information—I will be returning to this "filtering out" process in a moment.

That is a brief overview of how most of us learn to see gender and to sex other people. And while we spend much of our early childhoods trying to get a handle on gender, we tend not to think about any of this as adults. Instead, we simply glance at a person and spontaneously come to a conclusion without ever consciously analyzing all their various attributes. And we generally feel quite confident about our assessments, despite their subjective and speculative nature. For most people, this confidence probably stems in part from their own experiences with being correctly gendered by other people on a regular basis. After all, if you identify as a man, and everyone you come across correctly presumes that you are a man, then that might leave you with the impression that gender categorization is a straightforward and foolproof process.

Furthermore, while we all make mistakes in gendering people from time to time, these errors are rarely brought to our attention. In most cases, they involve strangers whom we see (and immediately gender) but never interact with, so our conclusions are never challenged. And even if we do interact with them, the subject of their gender might never come up, or if it does (if we use the wrong pronoun or honorific), they might choose to let it slide rather than correct us.

In contrast, those of us who happen to be transgender or gender nonconforming often have very different experiences—being perceived as both female and male at different points in our lives or, in some cases, within the same minute—that may shed light on how we (all of us!) see gender. To this end, I will spend the rest of this chapter sharing firsthand experiences from my own transition, especially the roughly six-month period when I went from being perceived as male to being perceived as female in the eyes of the world. These anecdotes will highlight the crucial role that context and conjecture play in how we gender others. My purpose here is not to simply demonstrate the fallible nature of gender perception. Rather, some of my experiences reveal unforeseen ramifications of gender categorization that impact all of us (not just transgender people), which I will further explore throughout the rest of the book.

Before sharing these anecdotes, it is important to stress that these are my personal experiences, and they may vary considerably from those of other trans people for a variety of reasons. For instance, factors that may seem on the surface to be independent of gender (such as race and age) may nevertheless influence how our genders are interpreted by other people; I happen to be white and was a relatively young adult (early thirties) at the time of my transition. Also, prior to transitioning, I struck most people as fairly gender atypical: I was significantly shorter than the average male (5'3"), had long hair, and did not have a particularly deep voice. While I typically wore unisex clothing (T-shirts, jeans, sneakers, hoodies) in my day-to-day life, I was somewhat feminine in my mannerisms and speech patterns—not in an extreme way, but enough that when I moved to the San Francisco Bay Area in the mid-1990s, I found that many people presumed that I was a gay man. Occasionally, a stranger would gender me as female, but in the vast majority of cases, people reliably lumped me into the male category.

I should also mention that my transition began in 2001, during a time when there was little to no mainstream awareness about transgender people. In fact, in cases where I had to explain my situation (upon coming out or when changing my legal name), I would tell people that I was transgender, or transsexual (an older term for people who transition that was more common back then), but I was often met with blank stares, as if they had absolutely no idea what I was talking about. Or perhaps they were confused because I didn't resemble the "man in a dress" pop-culture caricature. Given the sharp increase in trans visibility and awareness since then, onlookers today might be more likely to read an individual as transgender or pick up on signs that they may be transitioning, but that didn't seem to happen during my transition.

The manner in which I went about my transition is also relevant to some of the anecdotes I will share. While people may go about it in different ways, I chose to transition in "boy mode" (that's what we called it back then): Basically, I began hormone therapy (estrogen plus an anti-androgen) while continuing to go by my old male name and wearing my aforementioned unisex wardrobe. The idea was that you just keep going about your life until the hormonal changes are significant enough that strangers begin perceiving you as female, at which point it is easier to begin publicly presenting as female. Most people in my life were unaware of the fact that I was transgender until I came out to them when I reached that endpoint and was ready to go "full-time." There were a few people who did know that I was transitioning, most notably my partner at the time (whom I refer to as Dani in some of my previous writings) and my bandmates, Leslie and Steve. My bandmates and I performed together as a noise-pop trio called Bitesize—I was the guitarist and one of the vocalists.[10] At the time, we regularly played shows in the Bay Area and were very active in the local indie rock/pop music scene. This was the center of my social life back then, which explains why many of the anecdotes I will share take place at music clubs and events. More importantly, the fact that my transition was semipublic, as I was a musician and performer, led to a few situations that I might not have experienced otherwise. (Note: the names of other friends and acquaintances in this chapter have been changed, as I have since lost touch with many of them.)

Despite having thoroughly researched the subject beforehand, I wasn't quite sure what to expect from my transition other than the fact that it would likely reduce my gender dissonance.[11] Like most people in our culture, I had been socialized to view female and male as mutually exclusive categories, so I couldn't help but imagine that there was a giant chasm separating those two states of being. Thus, I assumed that traversing that chasm would entail having to spend a significant period of time in a kind of "gender limbo" where people would not be able to figure out what sex I was. And sure, this did happen on a few occasions. I remember one time walking in a residential neighborhood when a man standing on the other side of the street yelled at me, "Are you a guy or a girl?" To which I replied, "Yes!"—that answer didn't seem to satisfy him. A similar, albeit even more crass, encounter occurred in Portland when my band was on tour there. While we were playing a show, a guy came right up to the front of the stage and stared at me for almost a minute before returning to his seat. When the song was over, he shouted from the back, "I think you're a dude, because you don't have any boobs!" On the spot, I somehow managed the rather drag queen–esque comeback: "Just because you find me attractive doesn't necessarily mean that I'm a guy." The rest of the audience laughed, and that seemed to defuse the situation.

While there were a few moments like that—where people clearly had trouble figuring out my gender—they were actually quite rare. Rather, as I entered the "in-between" phase of my transition, I found that people almost always read me as either a man or a woman; it was just that I never knew which category they would assign me to. This phenomenon was most evident in stores and restaurants, where employees are expected to formally refer to customers as "sir" or "ma'am." Not only could I not predict how I would be perceived, but I also found that different individuals in the same setting often came to disparate conclusions. It was not uncommon for me to be greeted by one service person asking, "Can I help you with anything, sir?" only to have their coworker ask me a moment later, "Is there anything I can do for you, ma'am?"

While such instances were disconcerting, they hinted at an even more precarious underlying reality: If it was pretty much a coin flip whether a store clerk would "ma'am" or "sir" me, that likely meant that virtually every person I came across was doing the exact same thing—perceiving me as either a woman or man— but I had no way of telling what assessment they had made unless they explicitly stated it. There aren't words to describe how unsettling this period was for me. Many of us feel constrained and frustrated when other people expect us to conform to certain gender stereotypes—I have felt this both before and after my transition. That said, I found it exponentially more difficult to interact with strangers when it was entirely unclear which set of gender expectations they might be projecting onto me.

As I began working on this chapter, I reread the diary that I kept from my transition and found that I often used water analogies to refer to this period in my life: I was caught in the currents of a raging river, or surfing a wave of other people's expectations, or adrift out at sea without an anchor—basically, I felt untethered and not at all in control in such situations. So I relied heavily on improvisation: trying not to make any assumptions about how strangers might be gendering me while remaining alert for any signs that they had categorized me one way or another. Once it became clear that they were reading me a particular way, I'd just go with that—that would be my gender for that particular encounter. That seemed like the simplest and safest strategy. The problem is that many of our interactions with people are not one on one, but rather group engagements or conversations. And I would sometimes find myself in situations where some people in the group presumed that I was female, while others presumed that I was male.

Here is but one example: I was at a punk rock show, and the music booker (let's call him Evan), whom I had known for years, introduced me to the guitarist from another band. While Evan mentioned my name (which was an unmistakably male name), I don't think the guitarist heard it (perhaps because of the live music in the background), as he gave me a soft handshake, rather than the more firm handshake men usually give to other men. As the three of us talked, it became obvious to me that the guitarist was smiling at me a lot, and I was pretty sure that he was flirting with me. So I had to manage that dynamic while simultaneously interacting with Evan, who seemed completely oblivious to it all—it was as if he couldn't see the smiling and flirting because he interpreted us as two men.

When incidents like these first began to occur—where some people were reading me as female despite others still perceiving me as male—I wondered whether those in the former group were simply making some kind of tentative assessment. Perhaps they actually saw me as an androgynous person whose gender was unclear to them, so they just went with their best guess (woman). If this were true, one might expect them to be quite open to the possibility that I was "really a man" if they were subsequently presented with counterevidence. But it turned out that this wasn't the case at all. On every occasion when someone initially indicated that they saw me as female, but then learned my male name or overheard someone else refer to me as "he" or "him," they were invariably shocked, and would often say things like "That can't possibly be true." As the news sank in, they would inevitably give me "the look": They'd spend a second or two staring at me, often scanning me up and down, as if they were reassessing my body, searching for previously unseen—or, perhaps more accurately, "filtered-out"—clues regarding my gender.[12] Afterward, they'd usually apologize: "I'm so sorry; I thought you were a woman."

This happened to me enough times that I developed a stock response: "No worries; I take it as a compliment!" Admittedly, this statement may have confused them even more.

Another striking example of "the look" I'd often receive occurred when I went to vote that November. I showed up at the polling place in my usual unisex garb and handed the volunteer my driver's license, which not only sported my old name but listed my sex as "M." She scoured the list of registered voters but said she couldn't find me anywhere. I could see my name on the list, so I pointed it out to her, emphasizing that it matched the name on my license. The volunteer had to do a couple of double takes—examining my license, then staring at me for a few seconds, then reexamining the license, then giving me another look-over—before she finally accepted that I wasn't pulling a fast one on her. The last thing she said to me before letting me vote was "You're too pretty to be a boy."

If these accounts strike you as surprising, don't worry, you're in good company, as I could hardly believe them myself at the time. From my own vantage point, I had hardly changed. I hadn't altered my manner of dress or behaviors, and I wasn't actively doing anything to encourage others to read me as female. While hormones can, over time, lead to considerable changes in muscle/fat distribution, breast development, and so on, none of that was really obvious by this point. The only changes that were noticeable were that my complexion had softened somewhat and the distribution of facial fat, particularly around my cheeks, had become a bit more feminine. The hormones had also slowed down the growth of my facial hair, plus I was undergoing electrolysis, which together meant that I no longer had obvious beard shadow. That was the extent of the physical changes up to that point. However, in the context of some of my other features—being relatively small, having long hair, and being somewhat feminine in my mannerisms—those small changes were just enough to shift many people's overall impression of me in the female direction. And once they came to that unconscious conclusion, any potential masculine traits I exhibited were either ignored or reinterpreted—for example, people tended to view me as a tomboy or would assume that I was a lesbian, in much the same way that people used to read my feminine qualities as a sign that I was a gay man. Apparently, people see me as queer no matter what my gender is.

If a few subtle changes in my face were enough to "tip the scales" when I was dressed in a unisex manner, then I pretty much knocked the balance right off the table on the one day during my transition that I dressed overtly femininely. It was a Halloween-themed show that my band played at, which provided a convenient excuse. I didn't wear anything over the top—just a blouse, skirt, tights, and women's flats, sans makeup. By this point, I had become very adept at picking up on cues of how people were gendering me, and it was obvious as soon as I walked in the door that most people in the venue saw me as female—it was evident in how they acted around me, greeted me, and spoke to me. Given everything I had been through, I was not especially surprised by this—honestly, I found it quite a relief to finally, for the first time in months, not have to play the "what gender are they reading me as" guessing game when interacting with new people. But what really blew my mind were the reactions from friends and acquaintances who already knew me. They all seemed to recognize me immediately, perhaps in part because my band was performing that night, so they were expecting to see me there. I received a ton of compliments on how amazing my "costume" was, even though it wasn't really a costume—it was just me wearing a blouse and skirt. Many of their remarks hinted that they were on some level picking up on the changes in my appearance, but they couldn't quite process them. One friend said, "It's *scary* how much you look like my sister" (emphasis mine). Another male friend said, "If I didn't know better, I might be attracted to you."

That may have been the most surreal part of my whole transition: gradually having strangers come to the consensus that I was a woman, while the people who knew me best and saw me most often couldn't even tell that any of this was even happening. When I wasn't spending my time at music shows, I was usually at work in the lab, and there were always strangers stopping by: students looking for someone they knew, delivery people dropping off packages, people from other labs asking for advice, and so on. At the height of my "in-between" phase, I learned to avoid these people like the plague because they would often vocalize their presumptions about my gender to my coworkers, saying things like "The woman over there told me that I should speak with you." One time this happened right in front of me: A salesperson from a laboratory supply company was talking with my coworker and pointed directly at me and referred to me as "she." And my coworker gave me a side-eye glance as if to say, "What's up with this person? They can't even tell what gender you are!"

While none of my colleagues or friends seemed able to detect the changes in my gender, a few noticed that there was *something* different about me, although they couldn't quite put their finger on it. On numerous occasions during this period, friends sincerely asked me, "You've lost weight, haven't you?" To which I would truthfully respond "No" while holding back the urge to add, "Actually, I've turned into a girl and you didn't even notice!"

Eventually, it became impossible, both logistically and psychologically, for me to keep up the facade that I was male. So I began the arduous process of coming out to everyone in my life as transgender, and letting them know that I would now be going by the name Julia. It was at this point that I began incorporating female-typical clothing into my daily wardrobe. Granted, I was still wearing shirts and jeans most days, although they might be more feminine in cut or style. My breasts, which began developing when I started hormones, were still small but increasingly noticeable. While I already had long hair, I got my first feminine haircut, in that it was layered and sported bangs. With these additional changes in place, I was finally free of "gender limbo," and pretty much every stranger saw me as unambiguously female.

But of course, not everyone in my life received a coming-out email from me. And while some people had heard about my transition through the grapevine, others (fans of our band, other acquaintances from the music scene) were completely unaware of it until they happened to bump into me. That was what happened to Larry, who was a musician from another band who had sort of disappeared for a few months. I was at a show talking to a bunch of mutual friends the day he returned. We all said our hellos, and I noticed that he called me by my old name. We caught up for a bit, and then, when everyone else stepped away, I gave him my "Just so you know, I'm transgender and going by the name Julia now" spiel. He was completely taken aback. He even gave me "the look"—the one people used to give me upon learning that I was "really" male, but in his case, he was suddenly picking up on all the changes in my clothing, hairstyle, face, and so on that he had initially filtered out. It was as if he could not see these aspects of me because they didn't fit in with his preconceived beliefs about my gender.

I had a few other encounters like that, where people I knew seemed to ignore the recent feminine changes in my appearance because when they looked at me, they saw their male friend. But as more time passed, this occurred less and less often, and instead, the reciprocal scenario became far more common: Friends who had originally known me as male would initially gender me as female, and upon doing so, they were unable to recognize me as someone they knew.

I first began noticing this happening at a big annual benefit show that included lots of musicians from local bands, and I knew a ton of people there. On a couple of occasions, when I approached people I knew to say hello, they acted as if they had no idea who I was. The most bizarre of such incidents involved my friend Doug, who had heard that I had transitioned but hadn't seen me yet. He was chatting with my partner, Dani, and Steve, the drummer of my band. I walked up and joined them. As soon as there was a pause in the conversation, Doug turned toward me and introduced himself as if we had never met before. I responded, "Yeah, hi, Doug, it's me, Julia." He was horribly embarrassed—a common reaction once people realized they hadn't initially recognized me, just as it had been back when people realized they had misgendered me. Even in the context of talking to two of the people closest to me, Doug was unable to place me, all because he initially perceived me as female.

Over the next few years, this dynamic occurred so regularly that it became my working presumption whenever I randomly came across someone that I used to know pre-transition. It is quite strange to be in an elevator with someone you worked with for two years, or to have an old friend serve you at a restaurant or walk right past you on the street, without a trace of recognition in their eyes. And yet, whenever I *purposely* met up with old friends who hadn't seen me since my transition (but were aware of it), they would instantly pick me out of a crowd. And after catching up for a bit, they'd almost always remark about how surprised they were by how little I had changed; I seemed like the exact same person to them.

That is my personal experience of navigating other people's gender perceptions during my transition. After much contemplation, here's how I've come to make sense of all this: It's as if, when we look upon the world, we don't see people per se, but rather we see men and women, and we unwittingly regard them as completely different entities. Every time we meet someone new, we immediately gender them, and subsequently store all of our impressions about them into one of two gender-specific "filing cabinets" in our brains. During my transition, people who had already "filed" me into the "male" category were unable to perceive or comprehend the feminine changes in my appearance because they seemed incompatible with their interpretation of me as "male." Alternatively, if they gendered me as female before recognizing me, then I would seem like a complete stranger to them, because all of their information about me as a person was stored in a different "filing cabinet" that they never considered searching in. For the record, I am not suggesting that these are literal "filing cabinets"—as in different physical locations in our brains. Rather, this metaphor is simply intended to convey that we store information about people according to their (real or presumed) gender, such that we can no longer readily access or process that information if the person in question's gender seemingly changes.

This Two Filing Cabinets mindset can account for many of the seemingly strange circumstances that I experienced during my transition. It explains why, even at my most "in between," people almost always read me as either female or male, as these are the only two ways in which they were accustomed to processing information about other people's genders. It also explains why "the look"—the double take I'd often experience upon telling people that I was not the gender they initially presumed—seemed to take a few seconds, as the perceiver was not only visually reassessing me, but also potentially "re-writing" or "re-organizing" the mental "file" they had on me. Another transition-related reaction that trans people commonly report is having close friends and family members go through a "grieving period" in which they mourn us, as if we had died. This reaction often strikes trans people as non-sensical, given that we are very much alive, not to mention happier and healthier having transitioned. But this grieving response does make some sense if we imagine our loved ones having to "destroy" our original "file" before creating a brand new one for us in the other "cabinet." Consistent with this, friends who I first met after my transition generally have no problems reliably using she/her pronouns for me even though they know that I am transgender, whereas people who knew me beforehand may vary in this regard. Some old friends never slip up my pronouns, suggesting they have successfully "re-filed" me into the "female cabinet." Others accidentally call me "he/him" fairly frequently, which may be a sign that, in their minds, I still reside in their "male cabinet," and that occasions where they do correctly refer to me as "she/her" are likely due to conscious self-editing on their part.

The Two Filing Cabinets mindset also helps to explain why the few people I encountered who couldn't tell what gender I was, such as the heckler from Portland, acted so aggressively and intrusively toward me. Rather than seeing me as a human being who was just going about my business, they seemed to view me as a piece of aberrant information that did not fit neatly into their mental gender paradigm, thus causing them consternation. Relatedly, while our culture has made some strides toward accepting trans people who identify within the gender binary—who are often imagined as being "born" one sex, then "becoming" the other—there still remains significant reluctance toward nonbinary people, who identify as neither woman or man, and often wish to be addressed with gender-neutral pronouns such as they/them. Much of this uneasiness likely stems from us being socialized to mentally accommodate only two genders, and as a result, individuals who fall outside this binary may seem to pose a "filing problem" for people who are unfamiliar with them, at least initially.

To be clear, I am not claiming that these are the only meta-phorical "filing cabinets" in our brains, or that they exist entirely independent of other categories (because they do not, as will be addressed later in this book). Nor am I suggesting that these "filing cabinets" are innate or a permanent fixture in our minds. As with gender perception more generally, they are undoubtedly learned, and they can be unlearned to varying degrees. Many cultures have alternate gender systems that accommodate "third" or "fourth" genders—perhaps people raised in these cultures have additional "filing cabinets," or maybe they conceptualize other people in ways that are less gender-dependent. Here in the United States, many young people are now growing up in a world where they may personally know transgender and nonbinary family members or peers, so it wouldn't be a surprise if they came to understand gender categories in a more flexible or multifaceted way than those of us raised in previous eras.

At this point, I can imagine some readers thinking: "This is all very interesting, Julia, but transgender people make up less than 1 percent of the population. And most people identify with the gender that they are routinely perceived to be. So what's the big deal if we happen to correctly file these people into different gender categories within our brains?" The answer to this depends upon what purpose these categories serve. If gender categories merely provided an organizational scheme akin to alphabetiza-tion—where names that begin with the letter "A" are not viewed as fundamentally different from those that begin with "J" or "R" or "Z"—then this wouldn't be a problem. However, the two gender "filing cabinets" in our brain don't merely contain information about individual people; they are also full of all sorts of expecta-tions, assumptions, meanings, stereotypes, and value judgments. And all these additional ideas and unconscious presumptions in-evitably permeate our perception, shaping the way in which we see, interpret, and treat individual people. I caught a glimpse of this phenomenon firsthand during my transition, as friends and colleagues who knew me as male were literally unable to see the feminine changes in my face—changes that were so readily apparent to others that they led most people to categorize me as female. And as I will detail next chapter, in the wake of my transition, I continued to encounter such disparities. Specifically, I found that actions and aspects of my person that had long gone unnoticed or uncommented upon back when people saw me as male were suddenly interpreted very differently, or elicited very different reactions, once I was perceived female.

2   OPPOSITES

I played guitar in front of live audiences many times prior to my transition. But at that Halloween-themed show that I described earlier—the first show I ever played where the audience by and large perceived me as female—I received a comment that I had never experienced before. A man approached me about buying one of our albums. He said he'd never seen us before and really enjoyed our set. Then he enthusiastically added, "You're a really good guitarist!"

Now, I'd like to think that I'm a decent enough guitarist, although by no means amazing, but nobody had ever felt the need to tell me that before. But in the following years, I would receive numerous iterations of this compliment. I suppose it could be that estrogen somehow greatly improved my musical abilities! But the far more likely explanation is that people tend to view guitar playing as a masculine endeavor, so it seemed unusual or notable to them that a woman could play guitar competently.

Around this same time of my life, my postdoc fellowship was nearing its end, so I was applying for jobs. This started before my transition, and I went to a few interviews while I was still perceived as male. Upon resuming my job search post-transition, I applied for a teaching position at a local college. While visiting the school, I had a conversation with a woman from the department that I was applying to, and she gave me a bit of a sales pitch, which included a detailed list of all their family-related benefits (day care, family leave, etc.). And it suddenly struck me that in all of my previous pre-transition interviews, none of my potential employers had ever mentioned any of their family-related benefits to me. In subsequent years, I would receive countless other remarks or inquiries that presupposed that I either had children, wanted children, or was generally interested in children and family matters. Such comments rarely occurred when people saw me as male.

Trans people who transition mid-life often have scores of anecdotes like this—moments when people interpret your actions and/or treat you differently than they used to back when you were perceived to be a different gender. Granted, it's not as if everything changes—if I was forced to put an arbitrary number to it, I'd say that about 97 percent of my day-to-day life was not noticeably different. But the 3 or so percent that did change as a result of people now viewing me as female was quite dramatic, with some specific instances being downright surprising or disturbing. Rather than starting off with those more extreme cases, I want to use the relatively innocuous "guitar" and "family" comments that I opened this chapter with as a jumping-off point to explore sex- and gender-based double standards.

I am using the term "double standards" here to generically refer to instances where two groups (in this case, women and men) are perceived, interpreted, and/or treated differently in some manner. Some double standards may be subtle or minor, while others may be flagrant or severe. While some double standards may be justified—there are obvious reasons why we don't allow young children to drive cars, drink alcohol, or do other things that adults often do—others may be poorly justified or outright unjust. Furthermore, people may disagree about why a particular double standard exists or what impact it might have. Given the latter point, I will provide a brief review of previously existing frameworks for explaining double standards related to sex and gender. This necessary background information—which may be familiar to some readers but new to others—will help set the stage for me to introduce a few new ideas and frameworks of my own.

Perhaps the most popular lay theory to explain (or explain away) sex/gender-based double standards is to dismiss them as merely *generalizations*. The argument goes something like this: It is simply a fact that men are better guitarists than women, or that women are more interested in children and family than men; therefore, the people who made the aforementioned guitar and family comments were simply making informed generalizations about my likely capabilities and interests. Now, admittedly, we all make *some* generalizations over the course of our day: We may presume that other drivers will obey the traffic rules, or that other people will speak the dominant language of our country. While we could be wrong on these counts in a particular instance, these generalizations will likely be correct far more often than not. In stark contrast, the guitar and family comments are *really bad* generalizations. After all, lots of women play guitar, and some are actually quite famous for it. And plenty of men have children and families that they care deeply about.

I argue instead that these sorts of double standards function more as *expectations* than generalizations. Countless women have critiqued the commonplace assumption that they must want to have children and raise families, and the corollary expectations that often follow from it, such as the presumption that childcare and household duties should automatically fall to women for this reason, or that women will be less invested in their careers as a result. As someone who was socialized male, I can certainly tell you that the reverse expectation is also true: I distinctly remember upon becoming a young adult that people would give me strange or suspicious looks if I interacted with children who were not obviously related to me. Such reactions immediately disappeared once people began perceiving me as female. Still to this day, there is a fair amount of stigma associated with men who choose to be stay-at-home fathers or elementary school teachers—a sign that many people consider it to be "wrong" or "weird" for men to find life paths centered on family or children to be interesting or rewarding.

The claim that these double standards are merely generalizations also ignores the very real *value judgments* that often accompany them. For instance, the guitar comments seem to be steeped in the belief that men are inherently more skilled at guitar than women; other experiences I've had at guitar shops have brought this presumption into sharp relief. Back when I was perceived as male, as soon as I walked into such stores and started perusing the guitars, a salesperson would usually approach me and ask what I was looking for. They'd typically show me lots of options or suggest guitars they thought I might like, all the while barraging me with technical details about the instruments. But after I transitioned, it was a very different story: The salespeople often wouldn't even bother approaching me, or if I asked them a question, they wouldn't take me very seriously. I recall one occasion when I was potentially interested in two guitars, both Fender Telecasters, but one cost about a hundred dollars more than the other. I sought out a salesperson to ask him what the difference between them was, and he literally said, "The one that's more expensive is better." That was it. He offered no technical details or further explanation, and it was clear (given all my past experiences in guitar shops) that he presumed that, as a woman, I wouldn't be capable of comprehending any information beyond that.

If we reject the premise that these sorts of double standards are merely generalizations, then an alternative framework for viewing them is in terms of *sexism*. People sometimes define "sexism" in wildly different ways, so I want to take a few paragraphs to walk readers through my understanding of the concept.

Many people associate sexism with deliberate acts, such as when a person expresses blatant hatred or disdain toward women, or asserts that women should not have the same rights or opportunities as men. While such acts clearly constitute sexism, it is not particularly useful to limit the definition in this way. Indeed, part of the reason why I chose to use the guitar and family comments as examples throughout this chapter is precisely because the people who applied these double standards to me did not seem to do so purposely, and there was absolutely no indication that they were trying to demean or undermine me in the process. In fact, most sex/gender-related double standards occur outside our conscious awareness or intention. Many of them might be described as *systemic*—they are built into our language, customs, societal norms, policies, and laws in such a way that we may not even realize that we are participating in them. Examples of systemic double standards might include the prevalence of the "universal he" (the tendency to use male pronouns or labels when referring generically to people) or the tradition of the wife taking the husband's last name (rather than vice versa or each party keeping their own), to name but two.

Feminist efforts to reduce sexism are often centered on fixing or phasing out these systemic double standards—for instance, by introducing new language; changing our traditions, policies, and laws; and so forth. While such remedies may prove fruitful, I do not believe that they are sufficient. From my vantage point, even if we were able to eliminate all of these systemic issues, there would still be plenty of sex/gender-related double standards, as many of them occur on an *unconscious* level and are practically built into the way that we perceive and interpret other people's bodies, genders, and sexualities.

Because sexism is generally considered to be a bad thing (as it involves treating people disparately and unfairly), such acts often face criticism, and there may be a tendency to portray individuals who commit them as malicious or immoral—as "sexists" through and through. While some individuals surely fit such descriptions, these negative characterizations become more strained when applied to people who unwittingly or unconsciously express sex/gender-related double standards, such as the people who made the guitar or family comments to me. While public critiques of sexist acts certainly have their place, throughout this book, I will be making a somewhat different argument: All of us have been socialized to perceive and interpret women and men differently, and to apply double standards to them accordingly. In other words, all of us are sexist to some degree, even if we aren't conscious of it. By pointing out all these double standards over the course of this book, my intention isn't to embarrass, chastise, or shame people who may have unknowingly partaken in them in the past. Rather, my goal is simply to make these previously obscured disparities visible, and to encourage readers to critically examine their own unconscious biases, and perhaps even work to transcend them over time.

Another common misconception about sexism is that it occurs unilaterally—that is, that men are the perpetrators of sexism and women its sole victims. There is a certain amount of historical truth to this narrative: Until rather recently, throughout many parts of the world, men have held virtually all positions of power, and women have been denied many of the rights and opportunities afforded to men. Even today, women still bear the brunt of sexism. That said, it simply does not follow that men are the only perpetrators of sexism. Many of the sex/gender-related double standards that I have personally faced have been enacted by women. Within certain strands of feminism, instances where a woman expresses sexism toward others are often dismissed as being due to "internalized oppression"—that is, she has internalized the "male oppressor's" perspective of herself and other women. While "internalized sexism" may occur to some degree, the concept is woefully inadequate to explain the full breadth of sex/gender-related double standards that exist, including the fact that men themselves are often the targets of sexism.

To be clear, when I say that men can be the targets of sexism, I am not talking about so-called reverse sexism—the specious notion that attempts to curb or mitigate the sexism experienced by women are tantamount to "discrimination" against men. Rather, I simply mean that many long-standing sex/gender-related double standards negatively impact men, or at least some of them. I have alluded to one such double standard already: If women are seen as innately well-suited to and competent at caring for children, it can lead people to stereotype men as inherently *not suited* to and *incompetent* at these same tasks. In other words, this double standard (like many sex/gender-related double standards) creates reciprocal pressures on women and men, both of which may lead to negative repercussions for certain individuals (women who resent the implication that they must care for children, and men who are shamed for caring for children).

Sex/gender-related double standards aren't always centered on which gender is supposedly better at which tasks, however. In my personal experience, many times they involve undue scrutiny of acts, interests, or desires that would be overlooked or taken for granted if expressed by a member of another gender. In an example that should surprise no one: Before my transition, if I got into an argument or felt the need to assert myself for some reason, people might have disagreed with what I had to say, but they never questioned the firmness with which I articulated my position. But as soon as people began perceiving me as female, if I argued or asserted myself in a similar manner, people were quick to call me a "bitch," and in a few instances, they even suggested that it must be my "time of the month." As with my guitar-playing abilities, I highly doubt that estrogen increased my assertiveness or argumentativeness. Rather, it was the public at large who began interpreting these identical behaviors differently, solely because they viewed them as coming from a woman rather than a man.

I experienced this same phenomenon in the other direction as well. For instance, I speak with my hands a lot—here in the United States, this is generally read as a feminine mannerism, and it was likely one of the reasons why people often presumed that I was a gay man pre-transition. Back then, when I was conversing with a stranger, it was not uncommon for their eyes to veer downward to stare at my moving hands—a sign that they found this tendency unsettling or disturbing. Nowadays, this never happens, even though I still talk with my hands just as frequently. It's as if people no longer even see it because they view me as female and these gestures as female-typical.

In my first book, *Whipping Girl*, I chronicled numerous other instances in which relatively mundane behaviors (color-coordinating my clothes; using words such as "cute," "adorable," or "pretty"; or the fact that I owned a bright red umbrella) received undue inquiry and negative attention because they are culturally coded as feminine, whereas I was perceived as male.[1]

I occasionally come across other feminists who are not particularly sympathetic to these sorts of anecdotes. Sometimes, they presume that I am using them to suggest a false equivalency between women's and men's experiences with sexism. As I already stated, and as will become clearer over the course of this book, women do experience the lion's share of sexism. That said, I also believe that any thorough consideration of sex/gender-related double standards must address the fact that some of them do have a negative impact on men. A few of the more incredulous responses to the above examples have suggested that these are trivial or nonserious endeavors that no right-thinking person would want to pursue in the first place. My rebuttal is twofold. First, I did not consciously "choose" to speak with my hands or to have red be my favorite color—these are aspects of my personality or style that arose inexplicably in me. Sure, I *could have repressed them*—and did for much of my early life—but why should I be compelled to do so simply because I was assigned male at birth rather than female? Second, such responses appear to forward an unspoken value judgment: Why is talking with one's hands seen as a "less serious" gesture than keeping one's hands still? Why is having a red umbrella viewed as more "frivolous" than having a black or blue umbrella? Are the latter colors somehow more "practical"? Do they help keep the rain off better?

The assumption that it is reasonable and admirable for women to pursue masculine interests, but that it's somehow "irrational" or "trivial" for men to pursue feminine interests, suggests that—in addition to women and men being pigeonholed into certain ways of being—behaviors and desires that are associated with women are often devalued in and of themselves. When I was writing *Whipping Girl*, I made sense of this by arguing that most sex/gender-related double standards fall into one of two camps: *oppositional sexism* and *traditional sexism*.[2] Oppositional sexism is rooted in the belief that male and female are discrete, mutually exclusive categories, each possessing a distinct set of attributes, abilities, and desires, and it leads us to view people who fail to conform to these ideals with suspicion or derision. In contrast, traditional sexism stems from the presumption that traits that are associated with women, or coded as feminine, are inferior or illegitimate relative to their male and masculine counterparts. The existence of these two different forms of sexism makes a certain amount of logistical sense: If you wanted to establish a gender-based hierarchy from scratch, you would not only want to depict one gender as superior to the other, but you would also want to deny the possibility that there is any overlap between the two genders.

The existence of these two forms of sexism helps to explain the double bind that feminists have long described, where if a woman behaves in ways that are coded as masculine (being assertive or aggressive) she will be depicted as an "aberration" (due to oppositional sexism). But if she instead acts in a stereotypically feminine manner, she will be deemed "appropriate," but others may not take her seriously (due to traditional sexism). The existence of these two interrelated forces also helps to explain the well-documented phenomenon of feminine boys garnering far more negative attention and concern from adults than masculine girls.[3] In other words, while both groups of children face oppositional sexism for being gender nonconforming, traditional sexism ensures that additional stigma and scrutiny are placed on children whose gender transgressions veer toward the female and/or feminine.

This idea—that oppositional and traditional sexism can impact or influence one another—leads us to consider another feminist concept: *intersectionality*. This term arose out of the work of feminists of color, and refers to the fact that different forms of marginalization (sexism, racism, classism, ableism, etc.) do not exist independently; rather, they often intersect with and exacerbate one another.[4] On a rudimentary level, most people can comprehend why facing two (or three, or four) different forms of discrimination is more detrimental than facing just one. But what is less apparent, especially if one has not personally experienced it, are the specifics of what the intersection of sexism and racism, or of sexism and classism (to name but two), looks like in everyday life. One potentially promising way to explain these phenomena is in terms of specific double standards.[5] For example, if women are stereotyped as being not competent at a particular skill or task, then women who belong to additional marginalized groups that face the same or a similar double standard are likely to be viewed as especially unqualified or incompetent in this regard. Alternatively, if women face a particular expectation (that they should be nurturing), then women who belong to additional marginalized groups that are stereotyped in a contradictory manner (as "insensitive" or "aggressive") may experience additional obstacles or complications as a result (they may be viewed as insufficiently "womanly"). In future chapters, I will more closely examine how sex/gender-related double standards intersect with other forms of marginalization, often exacerbating sexualization in the process.

Finally, because sexism often occurs systemically, some people describe it in terms of an overarching system—"the patriarchy," "compulsory heterosexuality," "the gender binary," to name a few iterations. While I understand the rationale behind these framings, they have numerous shortcomings.[6] One common problem is that they often enable individuals to imagine themselves as "righteous liberators" who seek to bring down that system, and to portray people who in their eyes seemingly participate in the system either as "evil oppressors" or as "dupes" who have been subjugated by the system and now serve to "reinforce" it. I personally do not endorse these sorts of caricatures, as all of us (to varying degrees) are immersed in double standards—both in how we perceive and interpret other people, and in how others perceive and interpret us. As stated earlier, while it's important to challenge systemic forms of discrimination, we must also address these more unconscious biases if we truly wish to end marginalization.

That is a brief rundown of a few previously existing frameworks for considering sex/gender-related double standards. Hopefully, the personal observations and experiences that I have shared along the way have illustrated the shortcomings of some of these approaches, and clarified why I have chosen to focus primarily on the roles that unconscious perception and interpretation play in creating these disparities. While this is certainly not the only valid approach to understanding sex, gender, and the many double standards associated with them, I believe that it is a crucial one that has received insufficient attention thus far.

Rather than forwarding one singular overarching theory, over the course of this book, I will describe a series of "mindsets" that we tend to harbor (by virtue of having been socialized in our culture), and which shape our considerations of sex, gender, and sexuality. These mindsets may arise from a combination of cognitive biases, habits, and social beliefs, and they occur without much (if any) conscious thought, often taking the form of snap judgments. In our day-to-day life, we are likely to encounter all sorts of people who are diverse in their appearances, who engage in different behaviors, and who interact in various ways with others. The mindsets I will describe exist to help us to make sense of this world around us—to attribute meanings and motives to these individuals and actions—although they are not always accurate or equitable. Our conclusions will sometimes differ from those of other observers, as well as those of the very individuals we are assessing. Because these assessments are often incorrect, unfair, and denigrating to others, we should strive to fully understand the mindsets that produce them so that we can recognize when we are employing them and how they may distort our impressions of people.

In the last chapter, I introduced the Two Filing Cabinets mindset, which leads us to conceptualize women and men as though they are entirely separate entities. I suggested that this distinction is what allows us to project very different expectations and meanings onto each group. With the rest of this chapter, I want to introduce a second mindset that helps to explain precisely which expectations and meanings ultimately become associated with which groups. I call this the Opposites mindset; it is consistent with ideas that have been proposed by other researchers and theorists,[7] and it can account for most of the sex/gender-based double standards that I have detailed throughout this chapter.

The Opposites mindset arises from our tendency to divvy up people, despite all their complexity, into dichotomies, and to subsequently view those two categories as "opposites," even when that isn't warranted. One common manifestation of this tendency is an "us" versus "them" type mentality. Researchers in the fields of social cognition and social psychology refer to such divisions as *ingroups* (the group we identify with or belong to) and *outgroups* (groups we don't identify with or belong to). Their work has demonstrated that people tend to favor ingroup members, and to perceive outgroup members as more negative, extreme, and stereotypical—this occurs even in circumstances where such groups are assigned arbitrarily.[8] Another type of dichotomy that repeatedly arises is between a dominant or majority group (sometimes referred to as the *center*, as their experiences and perspectives are generally centered in society) and less powerful or populous groups whose experiences and perspectives are relegated to the *margins* of society.[9] Relatedly, within any given culture, certain bodies, behaviors, and beliefs may be deemed "natural" or "normal"; this process automatically creates a secondary class of people who do not meet these standards, and are thus conceptualized as "unnatural," "abnormal," or "alien." Sociological concepts such as *othering, alterity,* and *markedness* have been developed to describe the asymmetry inherent in these dichotomies.

The fact that human beings exhibit sexual dimorphism readily lends itself to this kind of dichotomous thinking—indeed, we even casually label male and female as "opposite" sexes. And once two different social groups are conceptualized as one another's "opposites," they tend to attract a host of other opposite pairs (or "binary oppositions," as they are sometimes called). Over the years, I have collected a series of opposite pairs that are routinely associated with sex and gender. I have arranged some of the more pertinent ones in the following Table of Opposites, which I will refer to from time to time over the course of this book.

TABLE OF OPPOSITES

big	small
strong	weak
hard	soft
tough	fragile
independent	dependent
active	passive
assertive	receptive
rebellious	conventional
dangerous	vulnerable
mature	immature
rational	irrational
cerebral	emotional
insensitive	sensitive
aloof	affectionate
serious	frivolous
practical	impractical
functional	ornamental
natural	artificial
sincere	manipulative

I'm sure that most readers will have no problem identifying the left-hand column of adjectives as being commonly associated with maleness and masculinity, and the right-hand counterparts to those terms as being associated with femaleness and femininity. The fact that I don't need to explicitly label these columns according to which gender they seem to represent is a testament to the pervasiveness of these subliminal associations. I should stress that these words are not actual or accurate descriptions of maleness/masculinity and femaleness/femininity. Rather, they are simply meanings that are often evoked (as a result of the Opposites mindset) when we consider these categories. It's also worth noting that while being female and being feminine are different things—you can be one but not the other—the meanings and connotations that we associate with these states of being largely overlap; the same also holds true for maleness and masculinity.

A few of these adjectives may appear to have some semblance of truth. For instance, men on average tend to be bigger and stronger than women, largely due to hormone-related differences in height and muscle/fat distribution. Of course, these differences are not discrete, as some women *are* bigger and/or stronger than certain men. In other words, the Opposites mindset takes the overlapping bell curves that I discussed in the Introduction and warps them into an illogical conviction that women and men should be complete "opposites" in these regards. In doing so, it gives rise to many of the unconscious expectations that we project onto women and men, as I have chronicled throughout this chapter. For example, if we happen to come across a heterosexual couple in which the woman is taller than the man, it might reflexively strike us as "wrong" or "weird" since it violates our Opposites mindset. If, however, we were to take a moment to rationally contemplate this couple, then we would recognize that it isn't at all surprising, statistically speaking, that one or both of these individuals might fall on the outlying ends of these spectrums.

While the "big/small" and "strong/weak" oppositions may take their cues from actual biological differences, other opposite pairs listed in the table ("active/passive," "mature/immature," "practical/ impractical," "serious/frivolous") appear to be nothing more than sexist myths. Whether the traits in question are based somewhat in reality or completely fabricated, the important point is that the Opposites mindset *creates expectations*—including how we expect other people to be or behave. This mindset also pressures people to conform to the expectations that we project onto them. The "big/small" and "strong/weak" expectations might compel some men to take up weight lifting and some women to strive to become especially thin in order to better fit these stereotypes. It also likely contributes to heterosexual women's preferences for taller partners and men's for shorter ones.[10] In other words, even when there are underlying biological differences between women and men, the Opposites mindset creates an additional layer of *social exaggeration* on top of it.[11]

The expectations created by the Opposites mindset also help explain the prevalence of gender-specific pejoratives for people who strike us as outliers or exceptions. To return to a previous example: If a woman acts assertively, people might call her a "bitch." But there isn't a reciprocal term for an assertive man because the meaning "assertive" (which is listed in the left-hand column above) is already "built into" our notion of maleness and masculinity. Similarly, a man who is small or weak might be called "scrawny," a "wimp," or a "wuss." But analogous terms don't really exist for women because "small" and "weak" are "built into" our notions of femaleness and femininity. In addition to singling out people and traits that defy the Opposites mindset, these gender-specific terms are almost always derogatory in nature. Thus, these terms are not merely descriptive, but also serve the purpose of policing or punishing individuals who do not adequately conform to our oppositional view of gender.

Many of the words listed in the Table of Opposites have multiple meanings. For example, while "strong" may refer to physical strength (for which there is actual sexual dimorphism), the same word is also frequently applied to unrelated traits, such as mental tenacity and fortitude, or repressing one's emotions (neither of which has anything to do with muscle mass). Thus, it's not all that surprising that men who openly express their emotions are also derided as "wimps" and "wusses." On a related note, it is common for people in our culture to pit "thinking" against "feeling," as though these were mutually exclusive acts, when in reality, all of us engage in both of these activities, often simultaneously. As a result of this imagined opposition, people sometimes conflate being "emotional" (a trait that is coded as feminine) with being "irrational." Taken together, the opposite pairs "strong/weak" and "rational/irrational," which may appear unrelated, actually serve to reinforce one another in creating expectations regarding gender.

Another word with multiple meanings that bleed into our impressions of women and men is "dangerous," which sits in the male/masculine column in the Table of Opposites. Dangerous can mean "unsafe" or "threatening," which is a common male stereotype, one that was sometimes projected onto me prior to my transition. But if men are preconceived as "dangerous," then what does that make women? Well, one potential opposite pair is "safe" or "unthreatening," which is how people have largely treated me since transitioning—they presume that I am incapable of, or unlikely to, inflict physical harm on others. However, another potential opposite of "dangerous" is "vulnerable," which is another stereotype of women and has clearer negative connotations, as it reinforces the notions that we are "fragile" and "dependent" (both listed in the right-hand column of the table). While the word "dangerous" is viewed in a largely negative light, it also has a few positive connotations that are most readily observed in action movies, where the male protagonist breaks all the rules and may even engage in violence, but he comes across as "powerful," "independent," and "rebellious" rather than as a "threat." When contrasted with this notion of maleness/masculinity being "powerful" and "rebellious," those of us who are female or feminine might appear relatively "ineffectual" and "tame" by comparison.

In addition to creating all sorts of expectations, the Opposites mindset is responsible for many of the sex/gender-related value judgments that I described earlier under the label "traditional sexism." Specifically, with a few exceptions ("dangerous" being one of them), the terms that we associate with maleness/masculinity are generally valued more and have better connotations than those that we associate with femaleness/femininity. This disparity could arise in one of two ways. It could be that once a trait is associated with women, it subsequently becomes devalued in our society. As an example, while being "sensitive" and "affectionate" (both associated with being nurturing) are clearly viewed more positively than being "insensitive" and "aloof," the former traits are not particularly rewarded in our culture. Alternatively, it could be that in a culture where men are viewed as inherently superior to women, maleness/masculinity tends to attract more positive meanings (being independent, active, rational, or practical) and femaleness/femininity negative ones (being dependent, passive, irrational, or impractical), even though there is no material basis to support these associations.

Because these opposite pairs are simply meanings that we associate with sex and gender, rather than being intrinsic to them, they may differ from culture to culture and evolve over time, and we are capable of unlearning them. Indeed, for many of us, coming to understand that there is nothing wrong with women being assertive or men being sensitive is among our earliest steps in overcoming sexism. Having said that, it is one thing to consciously understand that these are merely double standards, but another thing entirely to move past the sneaking feeling that there is something "wrong" or "weird" about assertive women or sensitive men.

When I introduced the Opposites mindset earlier, I mentioned that it often comes into play when we are confronted with dichotomous groupings of people. While facets such as race, age, and sexuality all fall along spectrums, we often view them in a strictly binary fashion—white/of color, adult/child, straight/queer—much as we divvy up people according to gender. Researchers in the field of social cognition have investigated how we categorize people along all these varying axes, and their work has revealed that we rely not only on physical cues, but also on stereotypes that we associate with those categories.[12] In other words, to some degree, we see what we already believe to be true about the social world; this goes a long way toward explaining why people seemed to "filter out" any gender-contradictory cues when gendering me during my transition.

While all of these various categories of people differ in their associated stereotypes, there is often overlap. One particularly well-studied example involves the intersection of gender and racial stereotypes. Specifically, white U.S. subjects tend to stereotype Black individuals as having more "masculine" characteristics and Asian individuals as having more "feminine" ones relative to whites.[13] I will revisit these stereotypes in future chapters. There is also significant overlap between the stereotypes commonly associated with men and adults relative to those associated with women and children; the latter are stereotyped as "weak," "fragile," "dependent," "immature," "irrational," "impractical," and "frivolous." The presumption that women are more "childlike" than men is a recurring theme in both subtle and blatant expressions of sexism. And the premise that men are, or should be, more "mature" than women can also be found in the gender-specific slang term "cougar," which is applied to women who seek out relationships with younger men, whereas men who prefer to date younger women remain unnamed and are deemed relatively normal.

Of course, the stereotypes that we associate with women and men don't always align well with other social categories. For example, if I were to create a list of meanings that people often unconsciously associate with transgender people, I would probably borrow a bit from both the left-hand ("active," "rebellious," "dangerous") and right-hand ("irrational," "impractical," "frivolous") columns of the Table of Opposites. That said, the last two opposite pairs in the table—"natural/artificial" and "sincere/manipulative"—always seem to break the same way, as marginalized groups are invariably depicted as less "natural" and more "manipulative" than the more dominant or centered group. The reason for this will become clear in the following chapter.

3 UNWANTED ATTENTION

While the Opposites mindset that I described in the previous chapter accounts for many of the sex/gender-related double standards that I have encountered, it does not explain the most dramatic disparity that I experienced upon transitioning: As soon as the world began perceiving me as female, I began receiving an exorbitant amount of unwanted attention.

Much of this unwanted attention took the form of what is often called "street remarks" or "street harassment." While street harassment may come in different varieties, I want to first focus on how strange men hurl random comments or provocations at women in public settings, often under the veneer of sexual attraction or appreciation. I say "veneer" here because these incidents may superficially seem like expressions of sexual interest—and many men claim that this is their sole purpose—but research into this phenomenon, as well as my own personal experiences, indicates that there is far more going on than that.

I was well aware, from both female friends and feminist writings, that I would inevitably face street harassment once I transitioned. And having been in male-only spaces as a teenager and young adult, I was familiar with the sorts of lewd and objectifying comments that some men make about women. So I (in retrospect, naively) felt like I knew what to expect. But I quickly learned that it's another thing entirely to be the direct target of such remarks rather than merely overhearing them. I cannot begin to describe the intense visceral combination of annoyance, frustration, anger, and fear that street remarks often evoked in me, all while I was simply going about my day. If you are a young woman (as I was at the time), street remarks can be rampant, often occurring multiple times during a single outing.

It is impossible to truly understand street harassment without first recognizing that it violates two well-established societal norms. First, there are well-accepted customs and settings for how, when, and where to express romantic or sexual interest in other people. Such expressions typically occur in particular social spaces (dating websites or apps, or certain bars, clubs, parties, or events) where people purposely congregate in the hopes of meeting new people and potential partners. Upon meeting someone new, there is usually some kind of "getting to know one another" phase during which two individuals attempt to gauge (from body language, enthusiasm, etc.) whether there may be mutual interest, at which point one of them might proposition the other. The very fact that such settings and etiquette exist implies that it is inappropriate to sexually proposition people in other spaces and situations. So when a strange man makes a sexually explicit comment or proposition to a woman who is walking down the street, both parties understand (or should understand) that such remarks are inappropriate, if not completely out of order.

The second violation, which sociologist Carol Brooks Gardner has chronicled in her research into street harassment,[1] is that it is generally considered a breach of social protocol to disturb or impose upon people with whom we are not acquainted. This is why, if we ask a stranger for directions, or even alert someone that they've accidentally dropped something, we usually begin with an apology: "Excuse me, sorry to bother you, but . . ." As children, we are generally taught not to talk to strangers or to stare at other people. And I know that most people are capable of following these norms because that is what I personally experienced as an adult before my transition. When I moved through the world as male, it was extremely rare for anyone to attempt to speak to me or try to attract my attention. But upon being perceived as female, I felt bombarded by such interruptions.

Perhaps because street harassers recognize that their actions defy these social norms, they often justify (or perhaps "rationalize" is more accurate) their remarks as being either innocent compliments or sincere expressions of sexual interest.[2] If this were indeed true, then one might expect such comments to be wholly positive or flattering, but that hasn't been my experience at all. The street remarks I have received run a gamut that might be described as "the good, the bad, and the ugly." The "good" refers to remarks that on the surface appeared to be complimentary, although they were often highly specific evaluations of my body or appearance that veered into the realm of invasiveness. The "bad" refers to remarks that also evaluated my body or appearance, albeit negatively ("You should smile more"; "You'd be prettier with makeup"). The "ugly" refers to outright sexually explicit comments, often involving graphic descriptions of what the harasser wanted to do to my body. It is impossible to view the latter comments as anything but "rapey," and on a few occasions, they were accompanied by attempts to touch or grope me. I can imagine that some readers might feel that it is unfair of me to lump the supposedly "good" comments in with the "bad and ugly" ones, but in my experience, the moment you acknowledge "good" street remarks, those individuals often quickly follow up with either a "bad" or an "ugly" comment.[3]

Finally, if the supposedly "good" street remarks were sincere compliments or expressions of sexual attraction, then you might expect that they would be reserved for the most conventionally attractive women. But this does not appear to be the case either. I don't think anyone would have ever described me as a "head turner," yet I received street remarks and harassment relentlessly back then. In fact, in going through the diary that I kept from my transition, I found one passage from a day when I was less than two months into hormone therapy and still dressed in "boy mode," yet I was "hey baby"-ed three different times within a span of eight city blocks. This was well before I developed a "feminine figure," so I highly doubt that this street harassment had anything to do with these men finding me attractive. Rather, it—and, I'd argue, most of my other experiences with street harassment—seemed to be predicated primarily, if not solely, on the fact that I was simply a young woman out in public.

Feminist theorizing of street harassment has tended to frame the matter in one of two non–mutually exclusive ways. One explanation is that historically, a woman's place was in the home, whereas the public sphere was considered the realm of men. Therefore, street harassment of women could be interpreted in terms of men signaling to women that they are not in their "proper place." While I wouldn't be surprised if this notion drove some men to engage in street remarks, especially in past eras, I have never gotten a "women belong in the home" vibe from most of the harassment I've received.

A second way to make sense of street remarks is through the feminist concept of *sexual objectification*—that is, these men viewed me as little more than an object for them to sexually evaluate, appreciate, and potentially use. I definitely believe that sexual objectification played a role in many of these instances, but not all of them. For example, street remarks sometimes took the form of the man making a crude joke, making some generic comment about sex, or even discussing his own body rather than focusing on my own. The latter instances felt more like "trolling" than anything else: Knowing that it's considered inappropriate to raise the subject of sex with a woman they are not acquainted with, these harassers purposely broke this taboo in order to get a rise out of me. Indeed, many of the street remarks I encountered made me feel as though I was merely a specimen that they were prodding with a proverbial stick in the hopes of getting any type of reaction out of me, whether it be embarrassment, offense, or other.

It was precisely these sorts of non–sexually motivated encounters with strange men that confused me the most upon transitioning, as I had no framework for understanding them. For example, there was the time that I was standing at an empty table at my local post office organizing packages (compact discs of my band's new album to be mailed out to college radio stations) when, out of nowhere, a middle-aged man came up beside me, said, "Don't work yourself too hard, sweetie," and then walked away.

Or the time that I bought tickets to a tour while on vacation, and the thirty-something guy behind the cash register briefly acted as though I hadn't paid him already: "What tickets?" he said with an obnoxious smile, as if he was playing some variation of the childhood game "I've got your nose" with an adult woman.

Or (in a completely unrelated postal anecdote) the time I was dropping a letter into a mailbox when a young male passerby remarked, "That mailbox is almost as big as you!" while laughing.

That last comment particularly stuck with me because I used to be on the receiving end of short jokes all the time while growing up male, but I am well within the average height range for a woman. Nor was this mailbox especially large. In other words, there was absolutely nothing "remarkable" about this incident, yet this guy felt the need to remark upon it.

In fact, during all of these incidents, I was treated as though I was "fuckable"—not in a "people want to have sex with me" way, but rather in that these people felt that it was totally okay to "fuck with" me—to interrupt or interrogate me, or otherwise intervene or interfere in my day-to-day life.

Perhaps the most infuriating aspect of all this was that even though all the aforementioned incidents clearly violated widely accepted social rules (not disturbing or imposing upon people we don't know, not expressing sexual interest in inappropriate settings or ways), my harassers expected me to simply accommodate these intrusions, preferably with a smile or some other form of acknowledgment. If, however, I were to protest, challenge, or even ignore these intrusions, my harassers would usually act as though I was the one whose behavior was "out of order."

For instance, if I pretended not to hear their remarks, they would often call me "rude," "cold," or a "snob." If I became angry, they would complain that I was "overreacting" to what they would insist was merely an innocent comment or playful interaction. When I first experienced these sorts of responses, I honestly thought that they were also part of the ruse. Surely these men knew that they were misbehaving, and they were likely feigning offense to further mess with me. But after numerous confrontations and sometimes even discussions—yes, I am that nerd who occasionally performed impromptu ethnomethodological analyses on my street harassers—I came to the conclusion that they generally did not view their own behavior as out of order in any way, and they sincerely did believe that I was the "bad actor" in the situation.

Here's how I have come to make sense of this reversal of standard social rules: My harassers acted as though I had invited their attention, when in fact I had done nothing of the sort. I'll refer to these as *phantom invitations*, as they existed solely in the minds of the people who perceived me. Normally, if someone invades your personal space, asks you intrusive questions, or insults you to your face, most people would agree that they have behaved inappropriately, and that you are warranted in calling them out on their bad behavior. But because I was perceived as "inviting" these men's attention (due to the fact that I was a woman out in public), my harassers' intrusions were suddenly deemed warranted, and it was my protests against those intrusions that were now deemed inappropriate.

Here is a particularly illustrative example of such phantom invitations: During the year leading up to my transition, I had a routine on Fridays where, after my late-afternoon therapy, I would go to a particular bar that I liked. This bar had good inexpensive beers, plus it was mostly empty at that time of day, so I found it a productive place to write. I always sat in a booth by myself, and nobody ever once bothered me. But shortly after I began transitioning—in fact, this was the same day that I was "hey baby"-ed three times—an older man approached me and asked if I was a "biker girl," presumably because there were motorcycles parked out front. I said "No," and he then said that he wanted to tell me a story. So I gestured at my notebook and told him that I was busy writing. He then started yelling at me for not being interested in his story and eventually stormed off. It was baffling to me at the time because I was very clearly busy writing. And if I were a man—as I had been (inasmuch as possible) on all of my previous visits to this bar—anyone watching this scene would have agreed that his interruption was "out of order." Yet this guy acted as though I had "invited" his interruption. And because he felt "invited," from his perspective, it was my refusal to participate that seemed "out of order."

While sexual objectification, and sometimes flat-out misogyny, often accompany the street harassment that women face, there seems to be more to it than that. Given the range of my own personal experiences, I want to suggest an alternative and non–mutually exclusive framework for understanding this phenomenon: Male street harassers seem to view and treat women as though we are *public spectacles*. The word "spectacle" implies some kind of "display," "show," or "performance" that is put on for the benefit of others.[4] This explains why these men (mis)perceive us as "inviting" their attention and remarks. Spectacles can take many forms: an awesome display of fireworks, a gruesome car accident, a confusing message spray-painted on the sidewalk, and so on.

Regardless of whether they are viewed positively, negatively, or neutrally, spectacles strike people as conspicuous, and perhaps even unexpected, so they attract attention and commentary. If you happen to be deemed a public spectacle yourself, then all of this scrutiny (strangers staring or making candid remarks about you) will seem like obvious breaches of standard social protocol. In contrast, these observers and harassers cannot fathom that they are doing anything wrong because from their standpoint *the public spectacle has demanded their attention.*

I believe this framing helps to explain the wide breadth of experiences that women often have with unwanted attention, whether sexual in nature or not. It also helps to explain why the men who make street remarks don't view themselves as misbehaving, and why people more generally tend to downplay the seriousness of street harassment, as we've all been socialized to unconsciously view women as "attracting" and "inviting" the attention they receive. But this phenomenon doesn't end here. In actuality, many different subgroups of people are treated as though they are public spectacles for reasons other than, or in addition to, being female. In fact, my understanding of unwanted attention has been strongly informed by two other aspects of my person that are often treated analogously.

Sublebrity

The word "celebrity" typically refers to people who are famous—literally "celebrated"—for one reason or another. Celebrity is often associated with certain privileges (wealth, power, influence), but it also evokes negative connotations. For instance, celebrities are often stereotyped as superficial, vain, frivolous, fake, and insincere—interestingly, many of these adjectives are also associated with women and femininity, and some of them even appear in the Table of Opposites.

More to the point, we (non-celebrities) tend to treat celebrities like they are public spectacles that (much like young women) seem to "invite" our attention. If a slew of photographers showed up outside your front door and followed you around wherever you went, and if media outlets published stories divulging intimate details of your personal life, you would likely call that stalking and an invasion of your privacy. Yet when people do these things to celebrities, we don't think much of it. In fact, we may be inclined to view these celebrities as "attracting" and "inviting" all that attention themselves.

If you were simply walking down the street and a stranger started hollering at you, you would likely consider that rude. If you were sitting in the booth of some bar or restaurant, just minding your own business, and someone came right up to you and attempted to initiate a conversation, you would likely consider that intrusive. Yet if you happened to see a movie star walking down the street, or sitting alone in a bar or restaurant, you might find yourself shouting out their name, or approaching them for an autograph. In other words, you might feel (phantomly) "invited" to interact with them, and assume that they will welcome your intrusion. And if they were to rebuff you, you might interpret their behavior as "rude" or "cold," and deem them to be the "bad actor" in the situation (no pun intended).

Years ago, a friend told me a story about their visit to New York City. While there, they walked into a random sparsely populated bar—perhaps not unlike the one I would enjoy writing in years later—and saw a famous comedian sitting by himself at the bar, just having a drink. My friend described the comedian as obviously "desperate" and "starved for attention." After all, why else would this comedian go to a bar alone, if not to attract the recognition and admiration of others? At the time, I totally bought my friend's account; it seemed perfectly reasonable to me. But over the years, I've come to question it. I mean, a lot of comedians live in New York City, so maybe it was simply this guy's local bar. Perhaps he was just getting a drink, much as I was doing in the earlier anecdote. Maybe the comedian, like me, actually wanted privacy, which was why he chose to go to a quiet bar with few people in it. Yet because my friend viewed this comedian as a public spectacle (rather than a "normal person"), they projected a whole series of ulterior motives onto him: The comedian must have been "desperate," "starved for attention," and "craving admiration"—all of which, noncoincidentally, are routine justifications for street remarks and harassment targeting women.

I am not, by any means, a celebrity. But a friend once called me a "sub"-lebrity, by which she meant someone who is famous within a smaller subculture. Specifically, while my first book *Whipping Girl* never made any best-seller lists, and you won't find it in any airport book displays, it did garner notoriety within LGBTQIA+ and feminist circles. So while the overwhelming majority of people have no clue who I am, in these spaces, my name often precedes me, which can lead people to perceive and treat me as a celebrity of sorts. I want to share a few of my experiences with "sublebrity" here, not to complain (as I am very grateful for the recognition my writings have received) but rather because I have found them fruitful for making sense of public spectacles, phantom invitations, and the reversal of social protocols that often accompanies them.

On occasions when I am going about my everyday life—out with friends or attending an event—it is not uncommon for people who recognize me to approach and share their thoughts with me. Let's call these "sublebrity remarks" (akin to "street remarks"). They too run a gamut that I will call "the good, the bad, and the neutral," as even the worst of these remarks is nowhere near the graphic "ugly" comments that I've received for being a woman. As you might imagine, the bulk of these are compliments or thank-yous from people who appreciate my work—these are the "good" remarks. On other occasions, I have had strangers walk right up to me and say, "I didn't like *Whipping Girl*," or "I am known for my critiques of your work," or similarly negative assessments. As a longtime author, I am very used to criticism, and people are obviously free to openly express their views about me and my work. But it is rather jarring to have people, in real life and out of the blue, interrupt my conversation with friends to levy such critiques.

Perhaps the most telling are the "neutral" remarks, so called because they are from people who do not have strong opinions about me or my work, but nevertheless approach me, likely because they feel phantomly "invited." Sometimes after saying "You're Julia Serano, aren't you?," they have nothing to add. Sometimes they will apologize for not having read my books; I always assure them that this is perfectly okay, as they are not "required reading" for talking to me. Other times, after confirming my identity, they will ask, "Why are you here?" I try to resist the temptation to flip this around and ask, "Well, why are *you* here?" Instead, I'll often say something banal, such as "I am at this queer karaoke event because I am a queer person who enjoys karaoke!" Anyway, the only way that the latter interventions make any sense is if, rather than viewing me as a "normal person" for whom standard social protocols apply, these individuals saw me as a public spectacle that they could inquire about or comment upon, even if they didn't have much to say.

Many people who approach me with sublebrity remarks recognize that I am a human being with my own life and concerns, and thus will make a point of opening with "excuse me" or "sorry to interrupt," as we typically do with strangers. Sometimes, however, this fact seems to elude the people who approach me, and they instead abruptly interrupt me as I'm in the middle of doing something. After exchanging a few words, if I politely mention that I need to get back to what I was doing, these people will sometimes act annoyed or upset, as though I had wronged them or denied them an experience that they felt entitled to.

One time at a conference, I was catching up with a friend whom I hadn't seen in a long while, and someone came up to us and hovered for a bit. Normally, I would have said hello and invited them into our conversation (as one does at conferences), but my friend was in the middle of telling me a story, so I didn't want to interrupt her. When she finally finished her story, this stranger pointedly said to my friend, "You're monopolizing all her time," as though I was merely a shared public resource with no autonomy of my own. While the remark was disconcerting in the moment, I've come to understand it and similar comments in terms of phantom invitations. Because they saw me as a public spectacle, these individuals felt entitled to interact with me, so if I or my friend seemingly denied them that opportunity, they interpreted that denial as unfair and out of order.

This last point dovetails with a final sublebrity experience that I believe sheds light on this phenomenon. Occasionally I will meet someone new, such as a friend of a friend, and we will strike up a conversation. At some point, after talking for a while, they will become aware that I am someone they consider a "sublebrity." Oftentimes, they simply express mild surprise, but occasionally they will become upset with me, or with their friend who introduced us, for not having let them know precisely who I was sooner. Basically, they feel as though they have been "tricked" or "deceived." I remember one person angrily insisting that I should have been "up front" with them from the beginning. Of course, if I had gone out of my way to introduce myself as "Julia Serano," they might have viewed me as a narcissistic sublebrity who must be "starving for attention" or "craving admiration," much as my friend presumed about the famous comedian. In other words, there seems to be a double bind at work here, where if I embrace being a public spectacle, I'm viewed as "inviting" any and all attention that I receive, but if I play it down or fail to acknowledge it, I may be accused of "deceiving" or "denying" people who feel that they have a right to treat me as a spectacle.

I haven't had an analogous experience to this as a woman, as nobody views me as "hiding" or "withholding" the fact that I am female from them. However, I most certainly have experienced accusations of "tricking" or "deceiving" people regarding my gender, albeit in a slightly different context, which brings us to a third aspect of my person that is often treated as a public spectacle.

Transgender

As with being a woman or a sublebrity/celebrity, when you are transgender, many people will treat you like a public spectacle, and act as though your mere presence has "invited" their remarks, intrusions, questions, and/or critiques. I previously described a few incidents of street harassment that I faced when people couldn't make out my gender, such as shouting at me from across the street or gawking at my body. My experiences with trans-related street harassment were even more common before my transition, during my early efforts at presenting as a woman in public, albeit without the benefit of hormones. As a result, people sometimes read me as a proverbial "man in a dress," which led to all sorts of nasty remarks, ridicule, sexual innuendos, staring, and so on. Since my transition, people almost always presume that I'm a cisgender woman now, so I experience very little trans-related street harassment. This changes, of course, if or when people discover that I am trans—which is quite often, given that I'm very publicly "out." Some of the scariest interactions that I've ever faced have occurred when someone who initially presumed that I was a cisgender woman subsequently learned that I'm transgender; the anger expressed in those situations was premised on the misconception that I had "tricked" or "deceived" them.

I won't delve into the various types of remarks that I've been subjected to as a trans woman, as I've chronicled many of them elsewhere.[5] But I do want to talk about all the questions I've received—so many questions! Over the years, I've had strangers ask me questions about anything and everything potentially related to my being transgender, including my childhood, family dynamics, gender history, sexual orientation, medical procedures I may have undergone, and their potential "side effects." That last question is very common, as people really seem to want or expect there to be negative consequences to transitioning.

Back when I transitioned in the early 2000s, I assumed that all these questions arose from a lack of trans awareness and a sincere attempt to better understand me, so I patiently answered every single one of them. But over time, I noticed that some people—especially those who were uncomfortable with my transition or identity—would often ask me the *exact same questions* on multiple occasions, as if they had no interest in letting the answers sink in. Furthermore, some of the questions were strange and seemed entirely unnecessary; for example, a common one was "Did you play with dolls as a child?" I've never once been asked this when I've been presumed to be a cis woman, plus many cis girls don't even like playing with dolls, so there seems to be no obvious point in asking this question. Still other questions felt inappropriate and intrusive, such as asking me about my genitals, how I have sex, how I urinate, and so on; these questions evoked the same visceral reactions in me as the graphic "ugly" street remarks I've experienced as a woman. While less common nowadays, such barrages of questions still occur, despite vastly increased trans awareness and access to information. All this leads me to believe that the primary factor driving these questions is not curiosity per se but an unconscious tendency to frame trans people as inherently *questionable* (read: suspect, dubious).[6]

A lot of the questions I've fielded focus squarely on *why* I am transgender, which was something I've never encountered as a woman (as people presume that I was "born that way") or as a sublebrity (as becoming well-known is generally viewed in a positive light). As discussed in the Introduction, gender-diverse people are a pancultural and transhistorical phenomenon, and the inevitable result of sex and gender being complex traits with overlapping bell curves. However, the answer "Some people *simply are* transgender" doesn't seem to satisfy certain people, so they may feel compelled to seek out some kind of alternative explanation. Once again, this isn't the result of pure curiosity—after all, we don't actually understand why most people turn out to be cisgender, yet very few people ever inquire about that outcome! In other words, people tend not to ask "Why are you cisgender?" or "How do you know that you're really cisgender?" because being cisgender seems normal and natural to them. In contrast, it's the fact that people perceive being transgender as "abnormal" and "unnatural" (as a spectacle) that leads to us being constantly questioned.

Oftentimes, people don't simply ask "Why are you transgender?" Rather, they seek to answer that question for themselves. That is, they will *attribute an underlying cause or ulterior motive* to trans people.[7] These attributions fall all over the map; here's a sampling of some of the more common ones I've encountered over the years: People are transgender because they have some kind of mental deficit or disorder, or had a dominant mother, or are merely seeking out attention, or are trying to fulfill some kind of sexual fantasy, or want to obtain privileges associated with the other gender, and/or are really gay but transition in order to fit into the straight world.[8] The last of these attributions is particularly fascinating because, until very recently, homosexuality itself was routinely subjected to its own "Why are you gay?" interrogations (and still is to some degree).

I have been debunking these failed hypotheses as both a scientist and a trans activist for almost twenty years now, and I've been amazed by two things. First, it's virtually impossible to kill these zombie theories, no matter how much evidence you provide to the contrary. Second, brand-new attributions are constantly popping up; some of the more recently proposed causes include "transgender agendas," "peer pressure," and "social contagion."[9] Frankly, it's exhausting to have to continually counter these lay theories, but it seems inevitable that they will continually be invented and flourish, despite all the evidence to the contrary, so long as people view transgender identities and experiences as inherently questionable.

When confronted with misguided or deleterious beliefs, people often argue that "sunlight is the best disinfectant" and that in the "marketplace of ideas," the best arguments and evidence will ultimately prevail. Unfortunately, that's not always how things work out when dealing with unconscious mindsets. In this case, once people perceive certain individuals or groups as "public spectacles," they will pay them undue attention and scrutiny, and attribute all sorts of underlying causes and ulterior motives to them. In contrast, people who are preconceived as "normal" (read: not spectacles) largely escape reciprocal attention, scrutiny, and attributions. This double standard between how we treat "normal" people and how we treat "spectacles" seems to lie at the heart of all of the varied anecdotes I have shared over the course of this chapter.

Markedness

It would be entirely reasonable to analyze the street harassment I've experienced as a woman in terms of sexism and sexual objectification, or the interrogations I've faced as a trans person in terms of transphobia or cisnormativity. But I've also received unwanted attention as a sublebrity, and undue questioning about my bisexuality. These experiences, plus accounts I've read and heard from members of other marginalized communities describing analogous situations, seem to add up to something larger than specific discrimination against one particular marginalized group. I've become increasingly interested in the underlying connections between these phenomena. To borrow from the "elephant in a dark room" parable, I didn't want to merely describe the tusk or the tail—I wanted to understand the entire elephant.

When I came across sociologist Erving Goffman's book *Stigma: Notes on the Management of Spoiled Identity*, some of these connections became clearer.[10] In it, Goffman surveys the experiences of various groups who face stigmatization, including people with disabilities, people of color, gay people, and sex workers, and chronicled the similar obstacles they faced in their interactions with "normals," his term for people who do not face such stigmatization. While some of Goffman's language and framings are anachronistic—the book was published in 1963—many of the scenarios he describes continue to exist and have clear parallels with what I have described here.

Eventually, I found a framework that, in my opinion, best summarizes this underlying dynamic: the Unmarked/Marked mindset (often referred to simply as "markedness").[11] This concept grew out of the field of linguistics, and has since been applied to sociology and other fields in the humanities. In my 2013 essay "How Double Standards Work," I described this mindset in great detail, showing how it helps to explain many of the double standards and double binds faced by marginalized groups.[12] With the rest of this chapter, I will provide a brief overview of this mindset, connecting it to the notions of public spectacles and phantom invitations that I have outlined here.

Human beings are comprised of countless different traits—aspects of our physical bodies, personalities, histories, social roles, experiences, behaviors, interests, desires, tendencies, and so forth. Most of these traits are "unmarked" in our eyes, meaning that we view them as mundane, unsurprising, and not particularly noteworthy; they seem "normal" to us and thus are taken for granted. In contrast, other traits are "marked"—they strike us as "remarkable" for some reason or other. What makes a trait marked? Well, it depends entirely on the individual, their background, and other situational factors. If you've lived your entire life in a small town but then travel to New York City for the first time, everything about the city—its scenery, inhabitants, the way locals talk and act, etc.—might strike you as "remarkable." However, if you grew up in New York City, all that would simply be the backdrop of your life, and it would be unmarked. For me, having grown up in a straight suburban household during the 1970s and '80s, the first time that I went to a transgender event or a gay bar, everything about the experience seemed absolutely "remarkable," whereas nowadays, such people and settings seem normal and natural to me.

While we may each have a different sense of what is or isn't marked, the one thing that holds true is that once a person is marked in our eyes, we will unconsciously be driven to pay them extra attention and scrutinize them disproportionately. We will likely perceive them as conspicuous, fascinating, unnatural, abnormal, questionable, suspect, or some combination of these qualities. This explains why we treat certain people (those we mark) as though they are "public spectacles," and why we may feel as though they have "invited" us to interact with them or remark upon them. Because marked individuals seem "striking" to us, we may also want to know how they came to be, or why they do the things that they do, and this may lead us to *question* them (in both the "ask questions" and "view them as suspect" senses of the word), and to attribute underlying causes and ulterior motives to them.

There are two common types of ulterior motives that we project onto people we mark. The first of these presumed motives (discussed throughout this essay) is that the marked individual must be doing whatever they're doing in order to attract attention—this explains not only phantom invitations, but also our tendency to feel as though marked individuals "have it coming" or "brought it on themselves" whenever they receive unwanted attention. The second presumed motive is that the marked individual likely does whatever they do *because of the thing that marks them.* As I alluded to in the previous chapter, it's not uncommon for women to have their actions dismissed as likely being due to their imagined menstruation or their "overly emotional" female nature. As a trans person, I cannot tell you how many times I've had people dismiss my perspectives on a variety of subjects (politics, pop culture, science, philosophy) as having been unduly influenced by my being transgender. Indeed, marked individuals are routinely accused of being biased as a result of our marked traits, especially when the issue at hand appears in any way related to said traits. For instance, I wouldn't be surprised if a few critics dismissed this book as irredeemably "subjective" on account of my being a trans woman, whereas a cis male (read: unmarked) perspective on gender and sexuality may strike these same critics as wholly "objective," despite the fact that people of all genders and sexualities may be influenced by their backgrounds and personal experiences.[13]

Here is a useful way to conceptualize the Unmarked/Marked mindset: The marked individual is viewed as having "something" that an unmarked person does not. As a result, this "something" may seem to "taint" every aspect of the marked individual (their actions, opinions, etc.), whereas unmarked people appear free of any such contamination. Furthermore, this "something" that marked people have is also "sticky" in that all sorts of things will tend to glom onto them, such as questions, comments, critiques, assumptions, stereotypes, attributions, and so on. In contrast, their unmarked counterparts will remain relatively free of such presumptions and allegations.

In the previous chapter, I mentioned that when we divvy up people into sets of two via the Opposites mindset, there is often a built-in asymmetry to these groupings; the Unmarked/Marked mindset provides a likely explanation for such asymmetries. While different categories of people may be associated with different sets of stereotypes, one consistency is that the more marginalized group in the "opposite" pair is typically viewed as "artificial" and "manipulative," while the more centered counterpart is viewed as "natural" and "sincere" in comparison. These particular assumptions appear to be a by-product of the Unmarked/Marked mindset. After all, even when we are consciously aware that a marginalized group occurs naturally in the population, their marked traits may strike us as "unnatural" or "abnormal" to some degree, perhaps because of our tendency to scrutinize them. And because we disproportionately project attributions onto marked groups, we may imagine them as being driven by ulterior motives and hidden agendas, or we may presume that they are trying to "trick" or "deceive" us if their mark is not immediately apparent to us. This helps to explain the recurring accusations that marginalized populations are inherently "manipulative" in one way or another.

While all marginalized groups are culturally marked, the converse is not true: Not all marked people are marginalized. For instance, celebrities are definitely marked, but that's because they are viewed as more special than "normal" people rather than inferior to them. Alternatively, if you walked down the street dressed as a pirate, onlookers might gawk at you and ask you why you're dressed that way (you'd be marked in their eyes), but that hardly constitutes systemic oppression.

It's also worth stressing that being marked has nothing to do with how rare a particular type of person is in the population. There are greater numbers of transgender people in the United States than there are plumbers or people from Delaware, yet if you met someone from the latter two groups, I doubt that you would stare at them and bombard them with questions. Similarly, one in four U.S. adults have a disability, and more than half the population is female, yet these groups tend to be marked relative to their able-bodied and male counterparts, respectively. When it comes to marking people, what seems to matter most is that there is an implicit socially agreed-upon "standard" regarding bodies or behaviors that marked individuals seem to deviate from. While certain patterns of cognition may contribute to the

Unmarked/Marked mindset,[14] the specifics of who precisely is marked and who is not appear to be largely learned. As children, we may be taught in a general sense to treat people with respect and to not stare at strangers, but if we also routinely witness adults and peers jeering at transgender people, or ogling women as they walk down the street, then we may come to view these groups as deserving of the extra attention and scrutiny they receive. As with all forms of socialization, we are capable of unlearning these tendencies over time, but the first step in doing so is to recognize that they exist and may be deeply entrenched.

Understanding the Unmarked/Marked mindset has helped me to make sense of many of my personal experiences described throughout this chapter. But it has also enabled me to become more cognizant of how I may be unconsciously perceiving and interpreting other people, especially those who strike me as "different" in some way. Just as importantly, it has also helped me to better understand the experiences of other marginalized groups.

When I hear stories of people of color's experiences with racism, or people with disabilities' experiences with ableism, while the specific obstacles and stereotypes they face may be unfamiliar to me, I can often relate to how they are treated as though they are "remarkable," "questionable," "unnatural," or "abnormal" as a result of being marked in other people's eyes. Some readers may be familiar with "privilege checklists," which chronicle some of the unseen advantages afforded to those in the unmarked dominant group (white, male, straight, able-bodied, etc.). While the particulars may vary from list to list, many of these advantages revolve around *not* having to experience the unwanted attention or undue scrutiny that the marked group routinely faces. Furthermore, the Unmarked/Marked mindset provides yet another potential explanation for intersectionality. Namely, being a member of more than one marginalized group may lead others to view you as "doubly" or "triply" marked, and thus even more conspicuous or suspect in their eyes.

It would be a mistake to reduce all forms of marginalization to the Unmarked/Marked mindset, as each has its own history and specific stereotypes, is institutionalized in different ways, and so on. But I have found this mindset especially useful in communicating and challenging marginalization in a general sense, as I have discussed throughout some of my more social justice-themed writings. The focus of this book, however, is how we perceive and interpret sex and sexuality. The Unmarked/Marked mindset will come into play at various points, as it often shapes our thinking about aspects of human sexuality that fall outside what our culture deems "normal." But even within the rubric of "normal" sexuality, this mindset enables us to perceive sexual desires and acts in vastly different ways depending upon the sex/gender of the person expressing them. To fully appreciate this, we must come to grips with one more mindset that helps shape and distort our impressions of sex and sexuality—this will be the subject of the next chapter.

4   THE PREDATOR/PREY MINDSET

When it comes to sexual attraction, experiences, and relationships, perhaps no set of double standards is more foundational than the Predator/Prey mindset.[1] According to this mindset, men are presumed to be sexual initiators or aggressors ("predators"), whereas women are conceptualized as sexual objects of male desire ("prey"). While this mindset is not quite as universally accepted in our culture as it once was, it remains pervasive enough that some readers might initially assume that I am simply describing the way people *are*, rather than how we view them. However, over the course of this chapter, I will show how the Predator/Prey mindset functions primarily at the level of perception and results in a host of unwarranted assumptions about other people's desires and motives.

Predator/Prey Is Built into Our Customs and Language

The social norms that govern romantic and sexual relationships have changed dramatically over the last century: from formal courting to dating, to trends such as "free love" and "hookup culture," to the rise of dating websites and apps, and so on. Despite these shifts in dating customs, a Predator/Prey dynamic still implicitly guides most of these encounters. For instance, it is generally expected that the man will make the "first move": He may start up a conversation, ask the woman out, initiate the first kiss or intimate gesture, and so on. Women, on the other hand, are expected to subtly signal their interest and desires rather than directly assert them. In other words, he is expected to *act*, and she is expected to *react*. Dating advice for men is usually framed in terms of "how to win her over" or, on some less savory corners of the Internet, "how to get in her pants," whereas dating advice for women often takes a decidedly more defensive stance, encouraging her to "play hard to get," or to "save" herself for the right guy. While most people, regardless of gender, have the capacity to experience love and to enjoy sex—with many hoping to experience both with the same partner—we nevertheless pigeonhole women as "looking for love" and men as "looking for sex," as though these were mutually exclusive pursuits. More to the point, not only does Predator/Prey depict men (but not women) as "wanting" sex, but it positions women as "having" or "being" the sex that men are after.

The asymmetry of Predator/Prey logic is even more pronounced in the language that we colloquially use to describe sex. The man "takes" the woman, or he "does" her, whereas she "gives it up." In romance novel clichés, the man "sweeps her off her feet," and she "surrenders" to him. A sex education book might describe the act more technically as "penetration sex," referring to the man's penis "penetrating" the woman's vagina. However, this same act could instead be described in terms of the woman's vagina "consuming" the man's penis, but that would probably strike most people as off (too active a role for the woman, or too degrading a role for the man).

Sports metaphors for sex are particularly illustrative of the Predator/Prey mindset. If a man has sex with a woman, people will say that he "scored," evoking sports in which one team's offense attempts to get the ball past the other team's defenses. The notion that men are perpetually on offense and women on defense is also found in the baseball metaphor for sex: A man who fails to get anywhere with a woman "strikes out," but his successes are chronicled in terms of circling the bases, with kissing being "first base," touching breasts "second base," touching genitals "third base," and penile-vaginal intercourse a "home run" (there are other permutations, of course). This baseball metaphor also highlights another common presumption: The only thing that "counts" in the end is intercourse, with everything preceding it (the first three "bases") merely being "foreplay."

Given all this language, it is not surprising that sex is often viewed as a "win" or "conquest" for the man, and a "loss" or "violation" for the woman, even when said acts are consensual. Thus, he will be encouraged to lose his virginity, whereas she will be implored to protect hers. If word gets out about their sexual encounter, his reputation may be enhanced, whereas she is likely to "get a reputation." Embedded throughout this language is the notion that the woman (but not the man) is somehow "tainted," "soiled," or "ruined" by the act of sex, with women who've had "too much sex" in the eye of the beholder often being derided as "loose" or "used up."

Predator/Prey in the Media

Media depictions can be particularly helpful in elucidating otherwise unconscious mindsets. After all, it's impossible to tell any story without tapping into certain shared social meanings and beliefs that are readily comprehensible to audiences. At the same time, many of us who consume media with a critical eye understand that what we read on the page, or see on the screen, is partially or completely fabricated; as such, it is likely to reflect the biases of its creators, and/or purposely pander to audiences' desires, rather than accurately resemble real life.

The Predator/Prey dynamic shapes virtually all mainstream media depictions of romance and sex. For instance, I highly doubt that you've ever seen a mainstream TV show or movie where the man was looking for love and the woman for sex, or where she made all the first moves and he was the reactive or reluctant partner, or where she was celebrated for her "sexual prowess" but he garnered a "reputation" for having slept with her; in contrast, the reverse scenarios are all fairly common. Another thing lacking in mainstream media are genuine depictions of romance or sex involving LGBTQIA+ people. After all, the Predator/Prey mindset is fairly strict—one masculine man pursues one feminine woman; thus, relationships that fall outside this construct tend to strike people as confounding.

Many works of fiction primarily serve the purpose of escapism, and as such, they offer a glimpse into our cultural ideals regarding love interests and relationship trajectories. Almost invariably, these are firmly rooted in Predator/Prey dynamics. For instance, in a typical Hollywood blockbuster, the male protagonist is likely to be an independent and assertive man who is confident to the point of being cocky—the perfect "sexual aggressor" archetype. The actor who plays him may be conventionally attractive, but this is not a necessity, as he is the sexual subject, not the object of desire. The female love interest, on the other hand, will most certainly be conventionally attractive, if not downright stunning—the perfect "sexual object" archetype. At the start of the film, she is likely to be unobtainable to him for some reason (she's too attractive, of a different class, or distrusting of "womanizers" like him), and she will rebuff his initial overtures. But because he's "not the type of guy who takes 'no' for an answer," he will continue pursuing her over the course of the film. Ultimately, he will "win" her over because it's romantic when "the guy gets the girl" at the end.

Another Hollywood variant of the Predator/Prey dynamic goes something like this: The protagonist is an "average Joe" or "girl next door" type who falls in love with someone who is "above their station." But over the course of the story, this protagonist will undergo a dramatic transformation that finally makes an impression on this love interest. In the case of the male character, he will likely have an adventure that imbues him with confidence, and he will cast aside his formerly meek and mild ways, thus becoming a worthy "sexual aggressor." The female character will likely let her hair down and put on a sexy outfit in order to catch his attention, thus becoming a worthy "sexual object." While these stories draw heavily from the Predator/Prey mindset, they also illustrate that these archetypes are *not* how men and women really are. After all, if men were simply "biologically programmed" to be sexually aggressive and women were "naturally" objects of male desire, then these protagonists wouldn't need to undergo these dramatic transformations in the first place. Rather, these archetypes merely represent *expectations* that we are all encouraged to strive for if we wish to find love and sex.

Finally, since Hollywood is serving us supposed "perfect renditions" of Predator/Prey archetypes, it is worth noting who is typically cast (or not cast) to play these roles. First, these actors are almost universally cisgender and heterosexual, or at least presumed to be so; historically, being out as LGBTQIA+ pretty much assured that an actor would never be cast as a love interest in a mainstream movie. Hollywood love interests are also typically white, able-bodied, relatively young (especially in the case of female actors), and normatively sized (fit or thin, and of course, no woman-taller-than-the-man pairings). In upcoming chapters, we will explore these particular differences and biases. But for now, let's consider the impact that the Predator/Prey mindset more generically has on women (in this chapter) and men (in the next chapter), as I believe it will illuminate many largely unquestioned presumptions and misconceptions that we tend to harbor regarding human sexuality.

Predator/Prey as a (Really Bad) Sexual Script

In previous chapters, I introduced two other mindsets that seem to give rise to, or at least mutually reinforce, Predator/Prey thinking. For instance, Predator/Prey is steeped in the belief that men are independent, active, assertive, and functional, and that women are dependent, passive, receptive, and ornamental—all of these unconscious expectations are listed in the Table of Opposites. Predator/ Prey also draws heavily on the Unmarked/Marked mindset, with women being marked as sexual objects (a kind of "public spectacle") that men (who are unmarked sexual subjects) are free to admire or pursue. But in addition to functioning as a mindset that shapes our perceptions and interpretations of people, Predator/ Prey serves as a rough "script" for us to follow in any potential romantic or sexual situation. In fact, there is an entire subfield of sociology called *sexual script theory* devoted to analyzing these scripts and how they provide a shared understanding of what's supposed to happen, when it should happen, and what it all means.[2]

For example, if I'm at a bar and a man offers to buy me a drink, I *know* that he's not simply being generous; rather, he's signaling his interest in me and trying to initiate a "getting to know one another" exchange. If I am mutually interested in him, rather than flat-out announcing my interest, I *know* that I'm supposed to subtly communicate it via body language or enthusiasm, and wait for him to make the first move. If, however, I was in the "male role," I would *know* that it would be up to me to gauge the woman's interest (via her subtle signals) and to potentially make said first move myself. The fact that these are indeed "roles," and that both parties are following a rough "script," becomes especially apparent when one has personally been on both sides of such exchanges, as I have.

I italicized the word "know" throughout that example to pose a further question: *How do we "know" these things?* In my case, well, my school obviously never offered any classes in dating or flirting, nor did I read any "how-to" books on the topic. Honestly, when I started dating as a teenager, most of what I "knew" about this script came from TV and movies, which is yet another reason why analyzing media depictions can be informative. Some of what I learned about this script came from my teenaged peers, who knew little more than I did, and such information was often conveyed in the form of "dirty" jokes, stories, and of course sports metaphors. As I grew into early adulthood, I picked up more from observing other people flirting, from my own experiences dating, and so on. In other words, all of these things that I learned—the "beats" in the script, if you will—were not *actual facts* about how human sexuality works, but rather merely *shared assumptions* about what particular romantic or sexual gestures mean, and the roles that each party is supposed to play. Every person raised in our culture is likely to be at least somewhat familiar with this script, even if they do not personally endorse or practice it. And as with other shared social protocols, if an individual doesn't stick to this script, they will likely be viewed as behaving inappropriately or acting out of order.

Since the Predator/Prey script basically determines what should happen and when, it's worth considering what is *not included* in it. One thing that immediately jumps out is that there is no explicit

discussion about what may or may not happen; it is simply assumed that the man will likely press forward with successive
"moves," unless the woman does something to stop him or slow
things down. In other words, two people can wind up having sex
without anyone ever even uttering the word "sex" or its many
synonyms. Second, only a few sexual acts are built into the script
(the "bases" in the baseball metaphor), which means that virtually
everything else is "off the menu"—by which I mean you have to
explicitly ask for it. While there is nothing inherently wrong with
having to ask for something "off the menu"—indeed, I believe
that explicit discussion is a good thing—a large segment of the
population will likely view you as "sexually deviant" if you express
interest in acts that fall outside the script, even if said acts are safe
and not all that uncommon.

Third, since the script is centered on what the man supposedly
wants, as he is the sexual subject, women's desires and needs are
also essentially "off the menu"—hence the long-standing cliché of
the man who rolls over and falls asleep as soon as he orgasms, ignoring the needs of the unfulfilled woman. Over the last half century, thanks to the advocacy of many feminists and sex educators,
there has been increasing awareness that women are quite capable
of enjoying sex too, although unfortunately, this information is often filtered through a Predator/Prey lens. For instance, articles on
this topic geared toward heterosexual men rarely encourage him
to be the receptive partner who caters to her desires and whims.
Rather, he remains cast as the active party, and he is encouraged to
"pleasure" and "satisfy" her as part of his own agenda (to display
his "sexual prowess," or to "keep her coming back for more"). And
the advice offered in these articles is typically touted as things that
"all women want," thus enabling him to press ahead with these
additional steps without having to check with her. While this may
charitably be considered an improvement over past sentiments

(that she has no sexual needs or preferences aside from his), it is clear that the Predator/Prey script remains quite limited, especially with regards to its failure to acknowledge women as sexual subjects in their own right.

The Virgin/Whore Double Bind and Sexualization

Given that men are deemed the sole initiators of sex, and women are viewed as merely sexual objects for men to pursue or act upon, we should ask: What happens if a woman *does* act upon her own sexual desires, and initiates (rather than passively communicates) her interest in other people? Well, rather than viewing her as an autonomous sexual being or a legitimate "sexual aggressor," most people will instead view the woman in question as opening herself up to being sexually objectified by other people. They will likely describe her as "easy"—by which they mean that she makes it easy for *other people to get what they want from her*. And she may be called a host of pejorative terms that are never applied to overtly sexual men ("slut," "nympho," "tramp," "hussy," and "whore/ho," to name but a few).

In other words, the Predator/Prey mindset is responsible for what feminists sometimes call the *virgin/whore double bind*. Women, as "prey," are expected to play down or repress their sexuality; they are supposed to be "virgins," either literally or figuratively. In contrast, women who do not play down or repress their sexuality—who do not act like prey—are dismissed as "whores" (or, in today's vernacular, "sluts"). I refer to this as a double bind because women who fall into the "virgin" camp are generally viewed as socially respectable, but this respectability comes at the price of having to deny or hide their own sexual desires and experiences. In contrast, women who fall into the "whore" camp may be free to openly act upon their sexual desires and share their sexual experiences, but they will inevitably be sexualized by other people as a result.

I introduced the term *sexualization* in the Introduction, but it's worth fleshing out the concept a bit further here. Every human being is complex, consisting of countless attributes, interests, needs, personality traits, lived experiences, and so on. Sexualization is the act of reducing a person down to their real or imagined sexual body or behaviors, to the exclusion of all those other characteristics. Sexualization can manifest in a number of different ways. In the previous chapter, I discussed two common forms: *sexual objectification* (treating a person as little more than an object to be sexually evaluated, appreciated, or used) and *sexual harassment* (subjecting a person to unwanted sexual comments, questions, propositions, etc.). At the more extreme end of the sexualization spectrum is *sexual assault*, which includes unwanted sexual touching and rape. Sometimes the umbrella term *sexual violence* is used to describe both sexual assault and sexual coercion—the latter referring to nonphysical attempts to pressure someone into having unwanted sex. Whether relatively minor or severe, what all forms of sexualization share is that they are all nonconsensual, and as such, they deny the sexualized individual's autonomy and agency.

An additional form of sexualization that plays a role in policing the virgin/whore double bind is *slut-shaming*, which refers to the practice of disparaging individuals for their real or presumed sexual behaviors. Slut-shaming typically targets girls and women who are deemed by others to be "too sexual" (being open about their sexual desires, having too much sex or too many partners, or dressing and behaving in a sexually provocative manner). Similar tactics are sometimes wielded against other individuals or groups, as we will soon see.

Research has shown that girls and women who are denigrated as "sluts" not only face stigma and social isolation as a result, but are often subjected to additional forms of sexualization, including sexual objectification, harassment, and assault.[3] Basically, slut-shaming creates a vicious cycle: A woman who is deemed a "slut" is imagined to be opening herself up to being sexualized by others, which leads other people to feel justified or entitled to sexualize her even further. Some of this subsequent sexualization may involve men attempting to "get what they want" from her, given that she is supposedly "easy." However, the bulk of this sexualization will come from people more generally (including women), and will primarily serve as a form of reprimand or punishment for her real or imagined sexual conduct.

Given these consequences, it might seem as if the safe bet for women would be to simply avoid being labeled a "slut"—indeed, this is what girls and women are generally instructed to do. However, this is an inadequate solution to this double bind. For one thing, women are simultaneously encouraged to be as conventionally attractive as possible—that is, to be an ideal "sexual object"—which leads to its own forms of sexualization, including objectification and unwanted attention. And even if a woman does play down or repress her sexuality in order to adhere to the "virgin" archetype, she may nevertheless be labeled a "slut" for extraneous reasons, including (but not limited to) her perceived attractiveness, class, or race; because she physically developed earlier than her peers; because she is considered unpopular; and/or due to rumors that she has been sexually assaulted.[4]

This last point—that women who are victims of sexual assault are often presumed to be "sluts" a priori—helps propagate the vicious cycle of slut-shaming: Being sexualized can lead to slut-shaming, and slut-shaming can lead to even more sexualization. This example also raises the important issue of *victim-blaming*, in which the target of sexualization is deemed primarily responsible for any abuse they receive. While most people abstractly understand that blaming victims of crimes or injustices is generally misplaced, they often reflexively resort to it in their attempts to explain incidents involving sexualization.[5]

Over the next few sections, I will demonstrate how this victim-blaming tendency arises directly from our conceptualization of men as "sexual aggressors" and women as "sexual objects," and thus is a feature rather than a bug of Predator/Prey thinking.

Phantom Invitations and "Leading Men On"

Throughout this chapter, I've detailed how women are expected to signal their interest in potential partners via subtle and indirect cues so as not to come off as too assertive or "slutty." But as discussed in the last chapter, it's also true that women (being marked as "public spectacles") are routinely misread as "inviting" the attention of men, even when that's not their intention. Taken together, this creates a nightmarish scenario for women, as virtually anything that we do (or don't do) could potentially be misinterpreted by a man as a sign that we "want it," or as an "invitation" for him to make the "next move." And if he acts upon these phantom invitations (which exist solely in his mind), and we protest or correct him, we are likely to be accused of being a "tease" or "leading him on."

I have had men accuse me of "leading them on" on two occasions. The more innocuous of the two occurred at a music show. I was at the crowded bar waiting to be served when the man next to me struck up a conversation. As we talked, I was polite, but I purposely didn't smile and was careful not to do anything that might make him think I was interested—that is, I tacitly signaled "no" to him to the best of my abilities. When I was finally served my drink and about to walk away, he asked me for my phone number, and I respectfully declined his request. He then accused me of "leading him on," when in actuality, all we had done was have a short conversation.

The second time occurred as part of an attempted date rape—what follows is not especially graphic, but feel free to skip ahead to the next paragraph if you'd rather be spared the details. It was a personal ad date (for the record, he knew that I was trans, which may have influenced what happened). Upon meeting in person, we talked for quite a while, then eventually we kissed. After a few minutes of kissing, he grabbed my hand and placed it on his crotch; then he started unbuttoning his shirt. I said, "No," but he continued unabated. When I pulled my hand away, he grabbed it and placed it back there. I was finally able to pull away, and reasserted that I was absolutely not interested in having sex, after which he verbally berated me for about a minute, much of it involving accusations that I was a "tease" who had "led him on." As I said, the only things we had done up to that point were talk and kiss.

Mainstream conversations about date rape often frame it as likely being due to "miscommunication" between the two parties. But this view presumes that legitimate communication is even possible when most people are working from a Predator/Prey script that insists that a woman is only ever allowed to tacitly signal what she wants, leaving it up to the man to interpret her real or imagined unspoken signals any way he sees fit. In other words, Predator/Prey dynamics ensure that his expectations and interpretations always trump any attempts she may make to communicate her wishes. There's a reason why anti-rape campaigns in the 1980s and 1990s felt it necessary to use the slogan "No means no." After all, if everything a woman does is viewed solely in terms of tacit signaling, then "no" could potentially mean anything in the eyes of her male interpreter. He could, as many men have, interpret "no" as her "playing hard to get," or not wanting to come across as "easy."[6] And even if he does accept her "no" at face value, he may then point to any of her earlier remarks or actions—which he perceived as phantom invitations—and declare that she has acted out of order by sending him "mixed signals." Thus, the expectation of indirect communication that is foisted upon women leaves us open not only to misinterpretations, but to accusations that we are disingenuous or deceitful—hence the "tease" and "leading him on" charges.

There is an additional presumption that is often folded into the "leading on" charge: the myth that male sexual desire is uncontrollable, and that once it garners momentum, it's like a runaway train that's incapable of stopping. The man from the second anecdote above played this card as he was complaining about me being a "tease." To paraphrase him, I had gotten him aroused, so it was somehow wrong for me not to "follow through," or "finish the job." In retrospect, it was rather farcical for him to lecture me about this because he knew I was trans and that, unlike most women, I had experienced "male sexual desire" firsthand (for all intents and purposes). Given the pervasiveness of this "uncontrollable male desire" myth, I will address it in the following section.

"Boys Will Be Boys" and "She Should Have Known Better"

People love to pit "male sexuality" versus "female sexuality," portraying them as though they are discrete, complementary, or competing entities, or else obfuscating them as "confounding" or "mysterious" when they occur in a member of the "opposite sex." Once again, this is the Opposites mindset at work, distorting overlapping bell curves and erasing the countless individual differences that exist. There is no singular "male sexuality" or "female sexuality," despite much speculation and theorizing to the contrary. One of the few things that we can say for sure is that men, on average, tend to have higher sex drives than women (although there are exceptions to this), and these differences appear to be mediated to some degree by androgen levels.[7] Elsewhere, I have described trans people's experiences hormonally transitioning, and the profound effect it often has on libido, with trans men reporting significant increases and trans women significant decreases.[8] While my sex drive was certainly much higher before I transitioned, when I had male-typical androgen levels, it was never "uncontrollable" or "unstoppable"; the same clearly holds true for the many cisgender men who never stoop to sexual harassment or assault. Most of us, at one time or another, have been denied a sexual experience, or have had to halt a sexual experience mid-arousal—it may be a bit frustrating, but we all survive just fine.

Aside from hormone-related differences in libido, it seems to me that the other major difference between female and male sexualities is that we expect the former group to play down or not act upon their sexual desires, while the latter group is relatively free (and sometimes even encouraged) to act upon theirs.[9] This is clearly another example of *social exaggeration*, where social norms seem designed to create even greater disparities between the sexes than would exist via biology alone, thereby reinforcing the notion that they are "opposites." These social norms hurt women in two ways, the first of which I addressed in the above "virgin/whore double bind" section: Women are coerced into either repressing their sexuality or facing slut-shaming. Second, the expectation that men should freely express their sexual desires, in conjunction with the false notion that male sexual desire is "uncontrollable" and "unstoppable," creates an environment wherein men's sexualization of women is tolerated or condoned. This attitude is perhaps best encapsulated in the common phrase "boys will be boys."

"Boys will be boys" provides a ready-made excuse for whenever boys and men behave badly—whether getting into fights, driving recklessly, acting rowdily, and so on. Notably, there is no "girls will be girls" equivalent to excuse female bad behavior. The phrase has also been repeatedly used to justify everything from crude sexual remarks to outright sexual assault. Basically, "boys will be boys" suggests that boys and men cannot help themselves from doing these things, because it's simply "in their nature." And if they supposedly cannot stop themselves from being literal "predators," then the onus is placed on women (as "prey") to avoid men at all costs, or at least to take every possible precaution when in their presence. As a result, when incidents of sexual harassment or assault come to light, it's historically been the woman rather than the man who comes under interrogation. And her account will be undermined if it turns out that she willingly chose to be in men's company, and especially if she "lets her guard down" around them. We are all familiar with the types of responses she will likely encounter: "You shouldn't have met with him alone," "You shouldn't have gone to that party," "You shouldn't have been drinking alcohol," and so on. In other words, the perpetrator-excusing sentiment "boys will be boys" gives rise to the common victim-blaming sentiment "she should have known better."

The only situations in which women are *not* routinely viewed as being potentially responsible for their own rape are "stranger in the bushes" scenarios: when an unsuspecting woman is suddenly assaulted by a strange man, often in a public setting. Indeed, these scenarios are what immediately come to most people's minds when they think of rape, even though they represent a minority of cases, as 80 percent of male-on-female rape is perpetrated by someone the victim already knows.[10] The benefit of the doubt that a woman receives in a "stranger in the bushes" scenario likely stems from the fact that she was not able to predict that the man would be present, and thus "she should have known better" doesn't seem to apply. However, even this limited benefit of the doubt is not universal. For instance, if the woman has a "reputation" or is considered "disreputable" for some other reason, then people may view her as "getting what she deserves" even when the assault was unforeseeable. Or if people believe that the woman dressed in a "sexually provocative" manner, they may view that as the precipitating event that led to her sexual assault.

This last victim-blaming point—that sexual harassment and assault may be justified based upon how a woman is dressed—is so pervasive and egregious that I will spend the penultimate section of this chapter unpacking it.

"Clothes Don't Make the Man," but "She Was Asking for It"

Clothing in our culture is largely gender-specific, with certain items being deemed masculine (a suit and tie, men's dress shoes), feminine (a dress or skirt, women's flats or heels), or unisex (T-shirts, jeans, sneakers). People often presume that if a woman dresses femininely (rather than in a more unisex style), she must be doing so in order to attract attention—more specifically, male attention. This belief is so widespread, in fact, that some feminists have railed against feminine dress under the assumption that it exists solely for men's benefit and sexual enjoyment. I believe that these presumptions are incorrect, and elsewhere I've presented long-form arguments explaining why.[11] What follows here is a more concise several-paragraph summary of those arguments, drawing on the mindsets that we've previously discussed.

For starters, there are numerous reasons why any given woman might choose to dress femininely on any given day. Since women are judged based on their appearance more so than men, some women may "dress up" in an attempt to display status or respectability. Others may feel compelled to present femininely because their jobs or particular occasions require it. Still other women may enjoy dressing femininely for purely aesthetic reasons or out of a genuine interest in fashion. For some women, it may simply be about expressing their gender—this was admittedly an important factor early on for me as a trans woman who had had to keep that aspect of myself hidden for so many years. And yes, sometimes a woman might dress up in order to impress or attract somebody, although usually they have a specific person in mind (their partner or date), and said person may not necessarily be a man, as in the case of femme lesbians. Thus, the blanket presumption that women dress the way they do to attract or appease men is horribly misplaced. In fact, oftentimes the exact opposite happens: There have been plenty of days when I wanted to dress more femininely but decided against it precisely because I didn't want to have to deal with the extra street remarks and unwanted attention that I knew I'd face.

The fact that dressing femininely often leads to unwanted attention suggests that this phenomenon is best viewed in terms of the Unmarked/Marked mindset. As with women more generally, feminine apparel and accessories are marked in our culture, and thus seem to phantomly "invite" our attention. We often ascribe ulterior motives to women who dress femininely: They must be trying to attract male attention and sexual interest. Because of this presumed motive, whenever feminine individuals receive unwanted attention, onlookers cannot help but feel as though they have "brought it on themselves" for having dressed that way in the first place. This explains why many people consider street remarks and staring justified if the woman in question is dressed especially femininely, and why the "she was asking for it" charge is so often levied against women who are dressed in a "sexually provocative" manner.

While we imagine feminine individuals as actively working to attract and impress other people, it never occurs to us that masculine individuals may be doing the same. For instance, in preparation for a date, a man is likely to shower and shave, spend time inspecting himself in the mirror and fixing his hair, actively choose what clothes to wear, and so on. Yet all this considerable effort is rendered invisible because masculine dress is unmarked in our culture—it's viewed as normal, natural, mundane, and unquestionable. In other words, we assume that masculine individuals dress for themselves, and that feminine individuals dress for the benefit of others. Given this, it's no wonder that feminine gender expression so often strikes us as artificial—akin to a performance—leading us to describe women as getting "all dolled up" for their dates. In contrast, in the unlikely event that we even talk about men's date preparation, we will likely call it "grooming," as though it were a wholly natural endeavor, similar to what animals do in the wild.

Those feminists who have critiqued feminine dress tend to stress not only its supposed artificiality, but also the fact that it's impractical, ornamental, and frivolous, whereas its masculine counterparts are practical, functional, and serious. This sweeping generalization disregards many examples of practical and functional feminine clothing. More to the point, it ignores the fact that all clothing is artificial in that it is made by human beings—we are not born wearing it! Thus, any meanings an article of clothing may seem to have (such as impractical, ornamental, and frivolous, which all also appear in the Table of Opposites) are entirely socially derived rather than intrinsic to the clothing itself. Arguably, there is no article of clothing more purely ornamental than men's ties, or as impractical as a three-piece suit, but notably, these items do not strike us as "ornamental" or "impractical." Rather, in our culture, such clothing seems to signal "powerful" and "serious."

Despite the existence of an entire spectrum of colors, masculine clothing (especially three-piece suits) is generally restricted to blacks, blues, grays, and a few other muted tones. Randomly limiting color options in this way seems extremely impractical to me. Yet, in our culture, these are the clothing colors that convey "seriousness," whereas the reds, lavenders, yellows, and (god forbid!) pinks a woman might wear supposedly convey "frivolity"— even though these are all merely different frequencies of light that have no intrinsic meaning. Men often wear sports paraphernalia, with logos and designs that are arguably as trivial or frivolous as anything a woman might wear, although they are rarely characterized as such. In fact, while attending a football game, some men will put on face and body paint, yet nobody would ever say that they have gotten "all dolled up" in order to attract sexual attention.

All this is to say that the meanings that we assign to various items of clothing and accessories are completely arbitrary—they are not inherent to those items but rather exist entirely within our minds. So instead of denouncing feminine individuals as artificial, impractical, ornamental, and frivolous (which is not how they likely see themselves, nor what they are likely intending to signal), perhaps we should ask instead: What function do these arbitrary meanings serve? Don't they seem designed to undermine feminine people, the majority of whom are women, while leaving masculine people unencumbered and untarnished by said meanings?

Which brings us to the issue of "sexually provocative" dress.

The aforementioned feminists who believe that feminine clothing and presentation exist primarily for men's enjoyment and excitement will typically cite the fact that much of it seems unnecessarily "revealing": it exposes bare skin or is tight-fitting enough to show off a woman's figure. Indeed, the more "revealing" a woman's outfit is, the more likely that she will be subjected to slut-shaming and accused of "asking for it" if she is sexually assaulted. And yet, men's shorts often show off as much of his legs as a typical short skirt would hers, but we would never consider his choice of such dress to be "sexually provocative." And while a woman's low-cut top may strike us as too "suggestive" or "revealing," on a hot summer day a man can go completely topless, and the only assumption that people will make about him is that he is likely overheated. Indeed, there is virtually no article of masculine clothing, aside from relative rarities such as Speedos or leather chaps, that a man can wear that will lead onlookers to project sexual messages or motives onto him.

If, however, a man did put on an expressly feminine item of clothing—even a "modest" one, such as a sweater dress, pumps with one-inch heels, or a touch of lipstick—many people *would* start reading sexual motives and messages into that. And this is *not* because "crossdressing" per se is viewed as inherently sexual in nature, as women who don masculine clothing are typically viewed as simply "tomboys" or "butch" (that is, in terms of gender expression) rather than presumed to be doing it for sexual reasons.[12] Similarly, clothing that is deemed "unisex" (largely comprised of historically masculine items that women are now free to wear, rather than vice versa) is also generally considered to be devoid of sexual connotations. It's hard not to conclude from all this that *all feminine clothing* and *specifically feminine clothing*—regardless of whether it's a "respectable" blouse or a "sexually provocative" minidress—is viewed as signaling "sex" to some degree. This is because feminine clothing is representative of women. And women are conceptualized as "sexual objects" according to Predator/Prey thinking.

Women Are Sex, and Sex Is Bad

Most people, regardless of gender, have libidos and experience sexual attraction toward other people. And research on sexual orientation has shown that the percentage of the population who are attracted to men is roughly equivalent to those who are attracted to women. Yet, despite this proportionality, the Predator/Prey mindset compels us to view one gender (men) as "desiring" sex, and another gender (women) as either "having" or "being" the sex that the former group desires. As the feminist philosopher Monique Wittig put it, "For the category of sex is the category that sticks to women, for only they cannot be conceived of outside of it. Only *they* are sex, *the* sex, and sex they have been made in their minds, bodies, acts, gestures."[13]

When describing the Unmarked/Marked mindset in the last chapter, I said that marked groups are viewed as though they have "something" that the unmarked group does not, and this "something" seems to taint every aspect of marked individuals' existence: their bodies, actions, opinions—and, apparently, even their clothing in this case. In our culture, women are marked by sex. We are viewed as sexual spectacles that give off phantom sexual invitations. We are often accused of being sexually manipulative, and our accounts of sex and sexuality are routinely deemed questionable and suspect. Women are regularly and readily reduced to our sexual bodies and behaviors, whereas men—even those who are conventionally attractive and/or scantily clad—are generally viewed as people (not sexual objects) who have agency, and who are not tainted by sex in the way that their female counterparts are.[14]

In addition to portraying women as "having" or "being" sex, the Predator/Prey mindset routinely depicts "sex" as a bad thing: It is something that a woman is supposed to play down if she wants to be taken seriously or treated respectfully; it can be "taken" from her, or she may willingly "give it up," upon which she may be described as having been "used," "screwed," or "fucked." Whenever people say that someone has been "screwed" or "fucked" in a nonsexual context, it means that something bad has befallen them, or that someone else has done them wrong—the same connotations permeate popular impressions of the female sexual role. If heterosexual sex is a "dirty" act, then it is women who are primarily "soiled" by it.

Discussions about human sexuality have long been complicated by a sense of shame and stigma that typically surrounds the topic. Over the years, I have heard countless sex educators, sex researchers, and sexuality-related activists of various stripes place the blame for these negative attitudes largely on religious or conservative political forces. Their argument typically goes as follows: *If only we could transcend these right-wing sex-negative attitudes, then people could finally appreciate sex for the wholly natural and pleasurable act that it is.* While I too am in favor of open and honest discussions about sex, and opposed to right-wing beliefs and policies regarding it, I feel that this argument ignores the fact that "the calls are coming from inside the house," as they say. Specifically, shame and stigma are *built into* the Predator/Prey mindset and script through which most of us view and pursue sex. If we truly want to transcend the rampant sex-negativity that pervades our society, then the first step is for us to reject the Predator/Prey mindset as a way of making sense of the world.

5   CONFUSED SLUTS

Male socialization is a mess of mixed messages. Or at least it was for me. Growing up as a young child in the 1970s and a teenager in the 1980s, I was explicitly and repeatedly taught to respect girls and women. But then I'd see men in TV shows, movies, and sometimes real life unabashedly ogle or make sexualizing remarks about women, sometimes even going so far as to suggest that they were "only good for one thing." I was also routinely told that "women and men are equals" and "girls can do anything boys can do." But then, if a girl outdid me in a particular task or, even worse, was picked before me for teams in gym class, the other kids would all laugh. "You got beat by a girl," they'd tease. Nowhere was this sentiment more blatant than in the way that even the slightest perceived feminine mannerism or interest expressed by a boy would unleash a torrent of epithets, derision, and bullying.

If adolescent girls' expressions of gender and burgeoning sexualities are largely policed via the threat of slut-shaming, then the policing of boys' genders and sexualities is often centered on a different "s"-word: "sissy." I heard that word all the time in elementary school; it implied that the worst thing that a boy could be was "girlish" in any way. During my teen years, "sissy" was largely supplanted by other feminizing slurs that had more sexual overtones. The word "pussy" was often used to shame boys and men by comparing them to female genitals. Then there's "faggot," which people nowadays tend to view in strictly homophobic terms (it denigrates gay men), but when I was growing up, the brunt of this insult was its implication that you allowed other boys and men to dominate and "use" you sexually, much as a woman would.[1] Same goes for the pejorative "cocksucker." Indeed, the slurs "slut," "cocksucker," "faggot," and "pussy," in their own ways, all reinforce the idea that assuming the "female sexual role," and allowing yourself to be "fucked" by someone, is a wholly deplorable act. This is no doubt an underlying source of sexual shame and confusion for many teenagers. It was especially so for me, as someone who ostensibly grew up as a boy who wanted to be a girl.

Not all trans women have boyhoods. Many know that they are girls from a very early age, and these days some girls are able to openly live as such, thereby eschewing male socialization entirely. I, on the other hand, did have a "boyhood" of sorts. When I was growing up, everyone saw me as a boy, so I went along with that assessment, even though I had a sneaking suspicion that something wasn't quite right with it. While I wasn't especially masculine in gender expression, I wasn't overtly feminine either, so I wasn't sure what to make of the "girl thoughts" I often had. By the age of eleven, after having explored those thoughts more, it became clear to me that on a deep unconscious level I knew that I was supposed to be a girl, or should be a girl—language utterly fails here.[2] This realization mortified me. I had been taught that the worst thing a boy could be was "girlish," and here I was *literally wanting to be a girl*. So naturally, I kept it all to myself; it became my most closely guarded secret. This all happened long before the Internet or any kind of mainstream trans awareness, so I had no language or information to help me make sense of my situation. Given this lack of knowledge, I initially assumed that my wanting to be a girl meant that I was likely gay. But then my sexual orientation kicked in, and I found myself attracted to girls. So with no other obvious course of action, I decided to follow the path of least resistance: I kept the girl thoughts to myself and tried to fit in as a straight boy.

While I don't think that I was actually a "boy" per se, and would never claim to know what other boys were experiencing (just as I couldn't know what other girls were experiencing), I was certainly treated as one, so I feel that I can speak to some of the social pressures that adolescent boys typically face, especially with regards to making sense of sex and sexuality.

For me, one of the most stifling of these pressures stemmed from the presumption that being emotional, sensitive, and affectionate are all feminine qualities, and thus should be avoided like the plague for fear of facing the aforementioned feminizing slurs. So, like most teenage boys, I cultivated an outwardly aloof veneer, trying to come across as rational and dispassionate as possible. But at the same time that I was actively working to repress my emotions, I was dealing with the raw intensity of my first teenage crushes. While my female peers sometimes spoke freely about the feelings they had for certain boys, it felt entirely unsafe for me to do the same, so I once again kept it all to myself. My male peers also seemed cognizant of this potential for sissy-shaming, because whenever the subject of girls came up among boys, the conversation was typically restricted to sexually evaluative quips such as "I think she's hot," or "I'd do her." This type of comment allowed boys to maintain the position of dispassionate observer rather than revealing any emotional investment or interest they may have felt for the girl in question. To this day, I cannot help but wonder how much of adult men's sexualizing of women has its origins in this inability to speak openly or emotionally about girls during these formative teenage years.

Another formidable obstacle for me—in both explorations of my transness and my developing romantic and sexual interest in girls—was *enforced ignorance*.[3] Here's what I mean: Given that we live in a male-centric culture, girls and women are routinely exposed to and expected to understand male perspectives and experiences. Similarly, most LGBTQIA+ people are quite familiar with straight lives and relationships, as these predominate in our culture, in the media, and so forth. However, oftentimes members of dominant groups are actively discouraged from learning or knowing too much about the corresponding marginalized group. Hence, enforced ignorance.

For example, during my teenage and young adult years—a time when anti-LGBTQIA+ attitudes were rampant—if I was caught reading a gay- or trans-related book or magazine, or if I was knowledgeable enough about LGBTQIA+ people to debunk someone else's stereotypes, then I would likely face the accusation "What are you, some kind of queer?" In other words, I would be subjected to anti-LGBTQIA+ stigma for knowing too much about LGBTQIA+ people. Similarly, during the same period, if I had been discovered reading a female-themed book or magazine, or expressed knowledge or interest in subjects associated with girls or women, I would most certainly have faced feminizing slurs and sissy-shaming.

Of course, I would eventually become familiar with female perspectives in adulthood—through reading and consuming women-centered media and art, through intimate discussions with female friends, and ultimately via my own experiences of moving through the world as a woman (this last one is obviously not a viable option for most people who experience boyhoods). However, back when I was stuck in my enforced ignorance phase, I couldn't help but develop a *mystified* attitude toward girls: Since they were seemingly "unknowable" (as a result of said enforced ignorance), my female peers struck me as "exotic," "alien," and "fascinating" to a large degree. Such mystified attitudes are evident in the way that men sometimes describe women as "bewitching" or "enchanting" creatures who use their "feminine wiles" to "cast a spell" on them. In contrast, I don't think I've ever heard anyone use reciprocal metaphors of mystification to describe their attraction toward men. Similar mystified attitudes can be found with regards to genitals and sexual arousal, as many men act as though penises function in an obvious and straightforward manner, yet treat vulvas like some nebulous netherworld that cannot possibly be understood.

There's an old Steve Martin stand-up joke that goes "I believe you should place a woman on a pedestal, high enough so you can look up her dress." It's intended to be a paraprosdokian—a type of joke where the humor is derived from the second part (looking up a woman's dress) defying the expectations established in the first part (putting women on a pedestal). But in reconsidering this quote now, I am struck by how it encompasses the two most common outcomes of viewing women as "exotic" and "alien": Either you worship them as "divine" or "heavenly," or you reduce them to the status of a "thing" that exists for your enjoyment or entertainment. As someone who spent my teen years desperately wishing I was a girl, I unsurprisingly fell solidly into the first camp. But there are obviously boys and men who fall into the second camp, or who fluctuate between the two. Frankly, both attitudes are unhealthy, as they interfere with relating to girls and women, and seeing them first and foremost as human beings.

This enforced ignorance and mystification also lead many boys and men to view the sexual landscape as unfairly tilted in favor of girls and women. While this is clearly misguided in light of the many female-specific obstacles and pitfalls that I chronicled in the last chapter, it makes superficial sense when viewed strictly through a Predator/Prey lens. Since these misconceptions are pervasive (I even bought into some of them myself early on), I think it's worthwhile to consider them briefly here.

We've all been conditioned, via a never-ending stream of cultural and media messages, to view women as sexual objects that men pursue. As a result, regardless of our own gender and sexual orientation, we all have internalized assumptions about what makes women desirable in the eyes of heterosexual men. In contrast, because men are portrayed as sexual subjects, what makes men desirable in the eyes of heterosexual women is less well articulated in mainstream culture, especially with regards to seemingly average men who do not resemble male "sex symbol" ideals. Thus, in my case, there seemed to be a huge disparity between my female peers being visibly desirable, and me (as a not-very-masculine "boy") seeming sexually invisible in comparison. While they often received sexual attention, it felt disheartening that nobody was overtly expressing sexual interest in me. Of course, what I didn't understand back then was that the lion's share of the attention that my female peers received was unwanted, and likely caused them far more trouble than good. And while I may have *felt* sexually invisible, in reality, people considered me to be a sexual subject (not object), and as such, I didn't have to deal with the constant sexual evaluations and interruptions that my female peers faced. There is a very real freedom to being able to go about your daily life without ever having to deal with other people nonconsensually imposing their sexualities and desires upon you. I recognize this now, although at the time I simply took that freedom for granted.

Predator/Prey dynamics also forced my female peers into a "gatekeeper" role[4] with regards to sexual matters: They were expected to fend off any unwanted attention or advances that came their way, and to be extremely careful about engaging in any potential sexual situation due to the many negative consequences they might face. These negative consequences include slut-shaming and possibly getting a "reputation," accusations of "leading men on" or "asking for it," and being pressured into unwanted sex or outright sexual assault, not to mention health-related outcomes such as pregnancy or sexually transmitted diseases (STDs). Boys and men are largely free from most of these ramifications, especially the social ones; for them, sex appears to be something that one seeks out or does rather than an act that can potentially stigmatize, ostracize, or injure a person. Thus, from this naive male perspective, women may appear "lucky" because it seems as though all they have to do is sit back and wait for men to proposition them; if they want to have sex, they can simply say so, and many guys would readily take them up on the offer. In other words, the idea that women have an unfair advantage when it comes to sex stems directly from a failure to recognize that women are disproportionately burdened by its consequences.

Back when I was a teenager, I admittedly bought into this notion that women seemed to hold all the cards when it comes to sex, but I was disabused of it over time as I learned more about my female peers' significantly different experiences, and began to seriously contemplate what it might be like to be on the receiving end of the objectifying and predatory attitudes they often faced. (For the record, some of what I've since experienced firsthand turned out to be more horrifying than what I imagined back then.)

Unfortunately, some men choose to remain willfully ignorant about women's perspectives on these matters, even after they've been exposed to them. Nowadays on the Internet, some of these men have coalesced into various online groups that go by different names—Men's Rights Activists, Incels, Pickup Artists, Men Going

Their Own Way—but are often collectively referred to as the *manosphere*.[5] While manosphere beliefs may vary, they typically portray men as being unfairly denied their "right" to sex on account of women "withholding" or "monopolizing" it. In addition to the obvious sense of entitlement in treating women like a public resource that should be made available to men, manosphere writings and ideology are characterized by a palpable sense of resentment. As an eventual trans woman, I never fully bought into the sexist premise that men are superior to women. But for those who did internalize that message during boyhood, the seemingly contradictory belief that this supposedly inferior group holds some kind of mystifying "sexual power" over men, and is in a position to sexually reject them, may lead to feelings of humiliation or even victimization, regardless of the actual social power dynamics. As a result, many of these men feel justified in expressing vitriol toward women as "retribution" for these perceived slights.

Sometimes this vitriol takes the form of sexualization, but it may also be expressed via other forms of verbal, psychological, and/or physical abuse. Given this book's focus, I will primarily be discussing the former, but it's vital to recognize that sexualization—whether directed at women or other marginalized groups—is often inflicted in concert with these other forms of violence.

Through my early twenties, I did my best to get by as a seemingly straight boy. And frankly, the Predator/Prey mindset might have been all I would ever know about sex and sexuality were it not for my gender dissonance. Unable to continue to repress the sense that I should be female, which grew more intense with each passing year, I set out to explore this aspect of myself more.

In the early to mid-1990s, I began attending my first transgender social and support group. Shortly thereafter, I moved to

Berkeley, in part to begin my postdoctoral fellowship but also because of the San Francisco Bay Area's reputation as a queer-friendly and sexually progressive place to live. For the first time, I began placing personal ads where I was up front about the fact that I was a "crossdresser" (what I was calling myself at the time, for lack of a better word).[6] Given my fluctuating gender status, most of the women I dated during this period turned out to be bisexual, and they introduced me to queer culture and sex-positive feminism, both of which opened my eyes to new possibilities.

Sexual minority subcultures have long existed and are varied. Some pretty much follow the standard Predator/Prey framework, albeit with a few additional possibilities or practices added to the script. Others may deviate greatly from Predator/Prey presumptions. I cannot speak for all of them. But the ones that I'm most familiar with have grown out of queer women's communities, and where they overlap with other sexual minority subcultures. It is no coincidence that queer women have played a major role in challenging Predator/Prey norms. After all, if you are in a same-sex relationship, or if your or your partner's gender and/or sexual orientation are flexible or nontraditional in some way, then Predator/Prey's reliance on strictly defined male and female roles quickly becomes untenable. Furthermore, given how disempowering the standard female role is in Predator/Prey, it makes sense that queer women would want to create alternatives that allow all individuals to express their sexual desires openly and without shame while maintaining their bodily autonomy and safety in the process.

"Sex-positive" is often used as an umbrella term to describe such approaches to sex and sexuality that exist in stark contrast to the many "sex-negative" attitudes inherent in the Predator/Prey mindset. For example, sex-positivity works to upend the notions that sex is bad or dirty, that it has winners and losers, that certain sexual desires or roles are deviant or unnatural, that certain bodies or body parts are disgusting, and so on. It would be a mistake, however, to presume that "sex-positive" implies that sex itself is always or intrinsically positive. In fact, the sex-positive approaches forwarded by queer women clearly acknowledge that sex can inflict harm on people, and they include built-in safeguards intended to circumvent those negative outcomes. One such foundation of sex-positive approaches is direct and honest communication between the parties, rather than relying on presumed scripts or tacit signaling and their inevitable misinterpretations. In practice, this often involves discussing one another's desires, wishes, and boundaries up front; conferring about what may or may not take place in any given situation; and checking in with one another from time to time to make sure all parties are enjoying what is happening.

Another foundation of sex-positive approaches is refraining from judging or shaming other people's sexual desires and experiences, provided that they do not involve sexualization, and that all acts occur between consenting adults. It is useful to emphasize the distinction between sexuality (our own attractions, interests, and desires) and sexualization (something that we nonconsensually impose upon other people). If I simply appreciate how someone looks, fantasize about a sexual encounter with them, or even have consensual sex with them, those are all expressions of sexuality. If, however, I were to lecherously stare at a stranger, blurt out my sexual fantasy to them, or attempt to make that fantasy come true without regard to their willingness to participate, then I would be imposing my sexuality upon them, thereby engaging in sexualization. In other words, consent lies at the heart of the distinction between sexuality and sexualization.

I will have more to say about sex-positive approaches to sex and sexuality, including how they are sometimes misused, in later chapters. But for now, suffice it to say that these approaches were vital for me as a developing trans person to explore aspects of my gender and sexuality in relatively shame-free settings. And they remain important to me now as a bisexual woman in ensuring that any partners I have will take my autonomy, agency, and desires seriously. In fact, upon becoming accustomed to the openness and relative safety of sex-positive approaches, the Predator/Prey script—which I had accepted at face value when I was younger—suddenly seemed like a sexual Bizarro World by comparison.

I satirized these contrasting worldviews in my first novel, *99 Erics*.[7] The protagonist, Kat, is a bisexual woman and an absurdist short-fiction writer who embarks upon writing a book about her experiences dating ninety-nine different people named Eric. Kat identifies as sex-positive and occasionally refers to herself as an "ethical slut"—a reclaimed term proposed by Dossie Easton and Janet Hardy in their book of the same name to refer to a person of any gender who believes that "sex is nice and pleasure is good," and who advocates honesty, responsibility, and consensuality in their sexual relationships.[8] One of the Erics whom Kat dates embodies all of the sex-negative attitudes that the Predator/Prey mindset tends to instill in boys and men. Over the course of the chapter, despite expressing interest in having sex with Kat, this Eric also uses the word "pussy" as a slur (indicating that he harbors negative views toward women's bodies), insults someone as a "cocksucker" (suggesting that he disrespects people who have sex with men), and calls women who are open about their sexuality "sluts" (showing he believes that women should be shamed for their sexual experiences and desires). In response to these sentiments, Kat calls Eric a "confused slut": someone who on the one hand supposedly wants to have lots of sex, yet on the other hand promotes highly negative attitudes toward sex.

I have since found the phrase "confused slut" to be a useful intervention to get people thinking about how confounding and paradoxical these stereotypical male attitudes toward sex are. Basically, the Predator/Prey mindset encourages straight men to foster simultaneously appreciative and derogatory attitudes toward women. Any successful resolution to this contradiction must begin with men jettisoning those negative views—especially the presumptions that women "are" or "have" sex, and that men need to "take" or "win" it from them. They must also end the practice of degrading female bodies and sexualities, and using gendered and sexual slurs to denigrate others.

In addition to fostering highly negative attitudes toward women and sex, the Predator/Prey mindset complicates the lives of boys and men in at least three other ways.

First, just as women are expected to strive to be ideal "sexual objects," men are often expected to be ideal "sexual aggressors" if they wish to be perceived as attractive. As discussed in the last chapter, this archetype is characterized by assertiveness, confidence to the point of cockiness, always acting in control of the situation, and not taking "no" for an answer. While such behaviors are routinely glamorized in action movies and romance novels, in real life, the men who practice them are likely to come across as arrogant or entitled, if not downright sexually harassing.

In one of my early essays on the Predator/Prey mindset, I described how during my late teens and early twenties, I witnessed several male peers who had initially been mild mannered and respectful of others gradually transforming themselves into stereotypical "sexual aggressors."[9] They teased and spoke over women they were interested in, and acted in a sexually forward or pushy manner. In subsequent years, self-described Pickup Artists in the manosphere have encouraged one another to follow similarly aggressive strategies in their sexual "pursuit" of women.

While many women want nothing to do with these sorts of men, others do seem to find stereotypical "sexual aggressors" compelling. There are a number of potential explanations for why this may be, but here is my interpretation: In a culture where Predator/Prey dynamics relegate women to passive, receptive, or reactive sexual roles, there's bound to be some romanticization and eroticization of an imagined "right guy" who confidently makes "all the right moves"—moves a woman desires but is not supposed to initiate herself. Pickup Artists often describe what they do in terms of a "game"—I would argue that the system they are gaming is the Predator/Prey script and its insistence that sex cannot happen unless there is an assertive man to initiate it.

In the same essay, I noted how the romanticization of "sexual aggressors" often results in men who eschew those tendencies (those who treat women with respect and equity) being viewed as less attractive by comparison, akin to how women who refuse to become "sexual objects" are correspondingly deemed less attractive. My reason for raising the issue was to emphasize how the idolization of both the female "sexual object" and male "sexual aggressor" archetypes perpetuates the sexualization of women, although the latter archetype has received considerably less attention in feminist discourses to date.

Unfortunately, this same observation has been increasingly weaponized in the manosphere, with self-professed "nice guys" claiming that they "deserve" sex (due to the fact that they treat women better than sexually aggressive men do) but are unfairly "denied" due to women's supposedly misguided or selfish natures.[10] In addition to a sense of entitlement and resentment toward women, such men display a troubling transactional mentality regarding sex. The belief that a woman ought to "give him sex" in exchange for his having "treated her nicely" clearly implies that women need *not* be treated with respect, equity, or compassion in instances when the man is not seeking sex, or if the woman in question is not willing to "put out." While this manosphere-driven "nice guy" argument is relatively new, the underlying presumption of quid pro quo (if a man does something "nice" for a woman, then she supposedly "owes" him sexual favors) has a far longer history, and has played a recurring role in certain instances of workplace sexual harassment.

The second way that the Predator/Prey mindset complicates boys' and men's lives is far more pressing than whether "nice guys" are getting their "fair share" of sex. Specifically, because we are all conditioned to view men as "predators" and women as "prey," we often have difficulty imagining the possibility that women can be sexual perpetrators (which does occur to some degree[11]) and that men can be the victims of sexual violence. According to a 2015 National Intimate Partner and Sexual Violence Survey of over ten thousand people in the United States, 2.6 percent of men (compared to 21.3 percent of women) reported having been victims of attempted rape at least once in their lifetime; when this is expanded to all instances of sexual violence (including unwanted sexual touching, sexual coercion, and being made to penetrate someone), then 24.8 percent of men (compared to 43.6 percent of women) have been victims.[12] I remember that the first time I heard this "one in four men experience sexual violence" statistic, I was honestly taken aback. For a phenomenon that is not all that uncommon, we rarely talk about it, likely because we don't have the language, or the mindset, to properly contemplate it.

When the subject of sexual assault against men does come up, it's typically in one of two contexts. First, there are so-called prison rape jokes in which a man—typically someone who is detested or seemingly deserving of punishment—is imagined to be sexualized by a larger, more predatory man. As many people prior to me have pointed out, such jokes trivialize a very real and serious problem, as sexual assault in any form is not a laughing matter. But I must add that, as with the feminizing slurs that I opened this chapter with, the supposed humor in these jokes stems directly from the presumption that being someone else's "sexual object" and being forced to assume the "female sexual role" is inherently humiliating. In other words, even though men are usually the targets of prison rape jokes, the jokes themselves have unmistakably misogynistic overtones.

The other context in which sexual assault against males comes up is with regards to the sexual abuse of young boys. Such cases tend to be taken more seriously—probably because people can readily imagine the adult as a legitimate "predator" and the child as "prey"—albeit only up to a certain point. For instance, there have been numerous reported cases of statutory rape involving adult women and adolescent boys, and they too are often trivialized and mischaracterized as humorous, with some media pundits going so far as to call these boys "lucky."[13] Such reactions are reminiscent of jokes that I've heard men make about how they wouldn't mind being raped by a woman. In both cases, the supposed humor stems from the Predator/Prey mindset rendering female-on-male sexualization utterly inconceivable. This pervasive notion—that men cannot be sexually victimized under normal circumstances, and especially not at the hands of women—undoubtedly makes it difficult for men who have experienced sexual violence to openly discuss these matters, and may lead them (and others) to view such nonconsensual acts as mere anomalies rather than violations. The same attitudes can negatively impact women as well. After all, so long as most men conceptualize themselves as sexually invulnerable, they may have trouble relating to *any* victim of sexual violence or sexualization.

A third way in which men are negatively impacted by the Predator/Prey mindset is that they are sometimes presumed to be

literal "predators." I am not necessarily talking about false accusations of sexual assault here—while those do sometimes occur, they
are relatively rare (the consensus is somewhere between 2 percent
and 8 percent of allegations).[14] Rather, I'm talking about everyday
experiences in which men are treated with suspicion or trepidation due to fears that they may turn out to be sexual predators.

It is crucial to acknowledge the underlying Catch-22 at work
here: Some men *are* actual predators, and many people (including
me) have experienced repeated sexual harassment and sometimes
assault at the hands of men. Thus, it's completely understandable
that we might put our guard up or be apprehensive upon encoun-
tering men we do not know—in fact, it would be unwise for us
not to do such things. That said, it feels pretty sucky to be on the
other side of these situations—to be the person who is viewed
with fear or trepidation. Elsewhere, I have described how I had
to change the way I interacted with young children once people
began perceiving me as an adult man, and how women would
sometimes be suspicious of me if I just so happened to be walking
behind them, or upon making a genuinely innocent comment.[15]
While I understand these reactions, it didn't make them feel any
less uncomfortable. And I didn't have it nearly as bad as others.

Over the last couple of chapters, I have contrasted all the street
remarks and sexual harassment I've received as a woman against
my relatively harassment-free existence back when people perceived me as male. But these are hardly universal experiences. The
lack of attention and scrutiny that I received as male was the result
of my being viewed as unmarked in other ways—in particular, the
fact that I am white. Trans men of color tell a very different story:
Upon transitioning to male, instead of being largely left alone (as
I was when perceived as male), they often experience a sharp increase in negative attention and harassment stemming from the
pervasive presumption that they may be dangerous or criminal.[16]

Here in the United States, there is a long history of Black men being depicted as overly sexually aggressive and prone to committing acts of sexual violence, leading many white people to stereotype them en masse as sexual predators.[17] Such stereotypes constitute a form of sexualization, as these men routinely find themselves reduced to their imagined sexual behaviors, to the exclusion of other characteristics—not unlike how women who are stereotyped as "sluts" are reduced to their imagined sexual behaviors.

While I am not the first person to describe these "sexual predator" stereotypes in terms of sexualization, I can imagine some readers being hesitant to accept them as such. Much as we have difficulty contemplating the possibility of female perpetrators and male victims of sexual violence, Predator/Prey thinking compels us to view sexualization as something that specifically targets women or, more generally, people who are the "objects" of other people's sexual desires. However, I believe this view is unnecessarily limiting. But before further exploring these "sexual predator" stereotypes, it is useful to think through how and why women are sexualized, and how this might relate to the sexualization of other marginalized groups.

6 SEXUALIZATION, OBJECTIFICATION, AND STIGMA

Over the last several chapters, I've discussed numerous ways in which women are often sexualized in our culture. To date, the most popular overarching construct for explaining this rampant sexualization is the *rape culture* paradigm.[1] As suggested by its name, this model attempts to explain the pervasiveness of rape and other forms of sexual violence against women. Within this model, less severe forms of sexualization (street remarks and harassment, slut-shaming, sexual objectification and media depictions) are framed in terms of creating an environment in which rape is routinely excused, enabled, or even encouraged.

I most certainly agree that less severe forms of sexualization can increase the likelihood of sexual assault. I said as much when I described the vicious cycle of slut-shaming, and how sexualizing attributions such as "she led him on" and "she was asking for it" are routinely used to justify rape. That said, I take issue with rape culture's teleological presumption—namely, that these other forms of sexualization primarily serve the purpose of fostering or promoting rape. For starters, sexualizing depictions and harassment often target people for reasons other than, or in addition to, being female. Furthermore, there is a large body of research demonstrating that forms of sexualization that fall shy of sexual assault can nevertheless have very real negative consequences in and of themselves.

Much of this research involves cognitive and social psychological studies assessing people's implicit and explicit reactions to varied sexualized depictions of women. These studies consistently find that women who are portrayed in a sexually provocative manner are not only viewed with less empathy and presumed to be responsible for any unwanted sexual attention or assault they experience, but also regarded as less intelligent, competent, capable, warm, trustworthy, and moral than their nonsexualized counterparts.[2] These presumptions bring to mind the "dumb blonde" and "airhead bimbo" tropes routinely found in media, which equate sexual availability and attractiveness (especially in women) with cluelessness and vapidness.

Those familiar with the research literature might additionally recognize these findings—particularly the presumption that sexualized individuals lack competence, warmth, and morality— as hallmarks of *dehumanization*. The field of dehumanization is too vast to fully cover here, but in brief, acts of oppression and violence are often premised or justified on the basis that the targeted groups are not fully human. This often involves conceptualizing said groups as being either animal-like (typified by an imagined lack of rationality, morality, self-control, and culture) or object-like (typified by an imagined lack of warmth, emotion, agency, and individuality).[3] Thus, the aforementioned findings seem to indicate that sexualized women are dehumanized along both of these axes.

Research has also shown that, consistent with this dehumanization, sexualized women tend to be "cognitively objectified" by perceivers.[4] Such studies take advantage of the fact that we visually process human faces and bodies in a holistic manner in which the context and relations between all the constitutive parts are important for recognition. In contrast, we process inanimate objects in a more isolated and piecemeal fashion, thus making it easier for us to recognize them based on their individual parts, or when they are displayed upside down. Across numerous studies from different research groups, when subjects are shown sexualized images of women (dressed revealingly and/or posed in a suggestive manner), they tend to process them more like objects (that is, the subjects readily recognize inverted images as well as individual body parts), whereas sexualized images of men and nonsexualized images of women tend to be processed as human beings. These perceptual biases are exhibited by both female and male observers, indicating that they are not simply a by-product of sex differences or sexual orientation, but rather represent social messages about women and sexuality that we've all internalized to some degree.

One intriguing exception to these results is that in experiments where female subjects are encouraged to imagine themselves in a position of power, they will then exhibit a tendency to "cognitively objectify" sexualized images of men, suggesting that having power over others may also facilitate sexualization.[5]

As a result of growing up and living in an environment in which they are routinely objectified, many girls and women additionally experience "self-objectification"—they internalize the fact that others view them as sexual objects, which may lead to a host of potential cognitive, behavioral, emotional, and physical consequences.[6] Taken together, all of these lines of evidence demonstrate that sexualization can cause very real negative ramifications for targeted individuals, independent of whether they additionally experience sexual assault.

One drawback of the research I just described is that it focuses largely on one particular aspect of sexualization, namely, objectification. There has been a similar focus on objectification within feminist theory, often raising similar concerns about its potential dehumanizing effects.[7] Much of this theorizing relies on a particular narrative that I will refer to as the *attraction/ objectification model of sexualization*, which typically takes the following form: Most men are sexually attracted to women. Men have also historically occupied a dominant social position over women. Therefore, objectifying women serves the purpose of fulfilling men's sexual desires, for instance, by making it easier for them to visually and/or physically access women's bodies for their own sexual satisfaction. The dehumanizing effect of this objectification enables men to discount women's perspectives, concerns, and bodily autonomy, which is why many men feel entitled to sexually harass or assault women with impunity and without remorse. This model provides the logic behind the rape culture paradigm that I described at the onset of this chapter. And the fact that women who are deemed conventionally attractive also happen to be the ones who are most regularly sexually objectified in our culture illustrates the importance of sexual attraction to this model.

There certainly seems to be some truth to this narrative, and it is consistent with many of the Predator/Prey dynamics I described earlier. However, I do not believe that this model captures the full breadth of sexualization. Take, for instance, some of the street remarks and harassment I've experienced as a woman. I began receiving such remarks very early into my transition—back when some people were still reading me as male, and well before I developed a feminine figure—suggesting that I was being targeted, not because my harassers found me attractive, but simply because they perceived me to be female. On later occasions, sure, sometimes my harassers would make comments about my body almost as if they were remarking to themselves about an object they were appraising. But far more often than not, they seemed intent on provoking a reaction out of me, whether it be appreciation, embarrassment, or fear—this is not something one normally does with objects! After all, if a man refers to a woman as a "nice piece of ass" to her face, it's probably not because he literally sees her as an inanimate "piece of ass," but rather because he *wants her to know* that that's how he regards her.

Earlier, I argued that Predator/Prey thinking compels us to believe that *women are sex, and sex is bad.* If this is indeed how many of us unconsciously view women and sex, then many of the street remarks that I just described can be (more appropriately, I believe) interpreted as attempts to put me in my place, or to punish me for what I supposedly am ("sex"). This would explain why so many of these remarks were unapologetically mean-spirited and derisive rather than complimentary, as one might expect if these men were truly appreciating my body or imagining the two of us having sexy fun times together. When men made explicit comments about my sexual attributes, or described what they would like to do to me sexually, they were in effect reminding me of my supposed role, my station in life ("sex"). And the ugliest and most graphic of these remarks were thinly veiled threats of rape, imbued with barely disguised disgust—they felt far more like condemnation than lust.

While the standard attraction/objectification model of sexualization seems to explain certain cases, it appears woefully inadequate to account for these instances and others. To fill in this gap, I will spend the rest of this chapter proposing an alternative *stigma model of sexualization.*

I introduced stigma, and Erving Goffman's influential book by the same name, back when I was first describing the Unmarked/ Marked mindset. To relate these two concepts to one another: Stigmas are marked traits that are viewed extremely negatively, so much so, that they seem to "discredit" and "spoil" a person's entire identity. Not only are stigmas treated as if they "contaminate" every aspect of the person in question (their motives, opinions, disposition, trustworthiness), but they can also "spread from the stigmatized individual to his close connections"—a phenomenon Goffman called *courtesy stigma*.[8] Due to this spreading effect, people often feel social pressure to distance themselves from stigmatized individuals and groups, and to disregard or publicly denounce them. In other words, those who possess stigmas are not just looked down upon, but often face social isolation and exclusion. Given these harsh consequences, stigmatized individuals may feel the need to play down, cover up, or outright hide their stigmas in order to freely participate in society.

The notion that certain aspects of sex or sexuality may be stigmatized is nothing new. Psychologist Gregory Herek argues that what's commonly called "homophobia" is better conceptualized in terms of "sexual stigma" that is projected onto nonheterosexual identities and behaviors in our culture, leading to their ostracization throughout the twentieth century and still somewhat to this day.[9] In the last chapter, I discussed how back in the 1980s, if a person was found to be in possession of a gay- or trans-themed book or magazine, or if they publicly associated with LGBTQIA+ people, they would likely be accused of being queer themselves. I called this phenomenon "enforced ignorance" to highlight how it prevents us from understanding and relating to marginalized groups, but it can also be viewed in terms of courtesy stigma—that is, anti-queer stigma is capable of "contaminating" or "infecting" anyone who gets too close to LGBTQIA+ people. Herek and other researchers have also examined the stigma experienced by people who have HIV or other STDs.[10] Still other studies have analyzed how the stigma associated with sex work has wide-ranging negative effects on sex workers' lives, and even impacts service providers who interact with them.[11]

To understand how sex-related stigma functions in the afore-mentioned cases, it is useful to consider the distinction between *having sex* and being *marked by sex*. In "normal" situations (those deemed normal by society), a person can have sex with some-one, and when it's over, that moment doesn't follow them around wherever they go; it remains squarely in the past. But in situations that involve stigma, it's as if the individual in question becomes permanently "marked by sex" in the eyes of others. So even if they were to quit doing sex work, have their STD cured, or disavow their homosexuality, other people will nevertheless view them as forever "tainted" by those past events. And future potential lovers might balk upon learning about this "sordid" history for fear that it might ultimately "blemish" their own reputation as well.

Researchers who have studied slut-shaming, or what is some-times called "the sexual double standard" (that women are often disparaged for being sexually active, whereas men tend not to be), have also sometimes used stigma as a framework for understand-ing this phenomenon.[12] As one would expect of stigmas, girls and women who are deemed "sluts" by their peers (often irrespective of their actual sexual history) find it nearly impossible to shed the la-bel (as though they've been permanently marked by sex) and often experience profound social isolation as a result (as courtesy stigma makes others reluctant to associate with them).[13] There are at least two different ways to conceptualize this stigma. It could be that it manifests once the woman in question is believed to have broken some kind of social norm or taboo regarding sex (such as being "overly sexual"). Stigmas are often associated with transgressing norms or rules, so this explanation certainly makes sense. However, I want to raise a second possibility that may appear less intuitive at first but I believe has significantly more explanatory power. Namely, as a result of Predator/Prey thinking, women are viewed as "sex," and sex itself is stigmatized. Or, as I put it earlier, *women are sex, and sex is bad.*

If what I'm suggesting is true—that sex-related stigma is constitutive for women—then the virgin/whore double bind that women face might be better understood in terms of stigma management: A woman who adequately hides or plays down her "sex" may be able to garner considerable respectability, akin to how a queer person who is "in the closet" or comes across as "straight-acting" may garner similar respectability. In both cases, said respectability is contingent on the individual being able to prevent their sexual stigma from "showing" or "surfacing" in any way. This explains why a woman need not be a literal virgin (as pre-marital sex is largely condoned these days, particularly within committed relationships), provided that her exploits do not become the subject of gossip, or that she's not the victim of revenge porn or sexual violence. It also accounts for why a woman who is a literal virgin but wears a low-cut top or short skirt might nevertheless be called a "slut" or similar slurs; such shaming targets not her sexual activity, but rather her "showing off" or "revealing" her sexual body for all to see. Similarly, a common story among women who were labeled "sluts" during adolescence—often despite never having had sex up to that point—is that they developed faster or were bigger-chested than other girls.[14] In other words, their sexual attributes "surfaced" prior to, or more so than, those of their peers. When considered from this perspective, slut-shaming is not all that different from the cultural stigma that surrounds menstruation, menopause, breast-feeding, and other reproductive functions associated with women.[15] So long as all these sex-related activities occur in private—out of sight, out of mind—the stigmatization a woman faces may be minimal. But once her "sex" is "exposed" in some way, the stigma associated with it is unveiled too.

While men are not necessarily immune to sex-related stigma, so long as they stick to the Predator/Prey script and distance themselves from any female/feminine signifiers (feminine-coded clothing, behaviors, and desires), they may largely avoid experiencing it. In fact, many aspects of the Predator/Prey mindset—especially the notion that men "pursue" or "take" sex from women rather than possessing it themselves—seem designed to keep the stigma associated with sex entirely on women and completely off men. Indeed, many of the "confused" male sexual attitudes that I discussed in the last chapter seem to be informed by an unconscious understanding that women are readily undermined by sex-related stigma, combined with an inability to relate to what it might be like to experience that stigma firsthand or to constantly have to manage it themselves.

When a male street harasser leers at a woman or makes comments about her sexual attributes, he does so knowing full well that there is nothing she can possibly say about his sexual attributes that would have the same effect or impact. And while his staring and remarks can certainly be described as "objectifying" her, it is also true that these acts may be intended to remind her of what she supposedly is ("sex") and to invoke the stigma associated with that. Nothing about the stigma model of sexualization that I have just described contradicts or refutes the attraction/objectification model I discussed earlier. In fact, in many instances (such as this example), both objectification and stigmatization may occur simultaneously to varying degrees, and they may have similar dehumanizing effects.[16]

While these two models are not mutually exclusive, I find the stigma model to be more accommodating of diverse experiences in two important ways. First, objectification-centric models appear to act in a one-size-fits-all manner: If a woman is objectified, it dehumanizes her, thereby potentially harming her, and perhaps all other women by proxy. Indeed, this is the rationale behind why some feminists have championed bans on pornography and/or curbs on other sexually objectifying representations of women, as they seem to be inherently dehumanizing. But there are some situations (such as dressing in lingerie for a partner) in which a woman might actually enjoy being viewed as an object of desire, and not feel dehumanized in the process. Such scenarios have generated considerable feminist debate, ranging from claims that these women must suffer from "false consciousness" or even "Stockholm syndrome" as a result of patriarchal oppression, to reimaginings of objectification that allow for pleasurable and non-harmful forms of the phenomenon to exist.[17]

In contrast, the stigma model of sexualization readily accommodates these sorts of scenarios, as it is understood that stigmas are simply social meanings that some people subscribe to while others do not. To use a different example, trans people are stigmatized in our society, albeit to varying extents: Social conservatives view us as abominations that are highly "contaminating"; the mainstream increasingly treats us as defective or inferior but not necessarily threatening; and in pro-LGBTQIA+ circles, we may even be viewed downright positively. Any given trans person may fall along a similar spectrum, from "self-hating" (buying into the idea that we are "spoiled" by our transness) to "out and proud" (disregarding that stigma altogether). These differing views may lead to all sorts of nuanced scenarios. For instance, when confronted by a transphobe, I may broadcast my transness loudly to let them know that I'm not at all ashamed of who I am. Or when among pro-trans friends, I might make a trans-related joke that I would never share with the general public, as the latter might misinterpret it as reaffirming anti-trans stigma, whereas the former will not.

Similarly, women will inevitably vary in our reactions to the sex-related stigma that is projected onto us. We may be made to feel ashamed of our bodies and desires, or we may shamelessly flaunt them, depending upon the audience or context. While phrases such as "You look hot tonight" or "I really want to get into your pants" may feel horribly invalidating when uttered by a street harasser who is intentionally attempting to stigmatize us, they may take on very different meanings when spoken by a lover who we know respects us and sees us as a whole person, and who may even be female herself.

Over the last half century, there have been recurring debates about whether feminism should move more in the anti-pornography direction or more toward sex-positive approaches. It seems to me that the major impasse in these debates stems from these two movements using very different frameworks to make sense of women's predicaments. Anti-pornography feminists seem to rely on the attraction/objectification model, in which objectification is viewed as wholly negative because it dehumanizes women more generally. In contrast, sex-positive feminists seem to be working primarily from the stigma model of sexualization (even if they do not explicitly call it by this name), which explains why they place so much emphasis on destigmatizing women's sexualities and desires provided that they occur consensually.

A second way in which the stigma model is more flexible than the attraction/objectification model is that it can also account for the many varied forms of sexualization that target people for reasons other than, or in addition to, being a woman. To draw on an example from the previous chapter, if a young man is disparaged by his male peers as a "pussy" or "cocksucker," he is most certainly

being sexualized—reduced to sexual body parts or behaviors—
but in a way that appears to have nothing to do with attraction
or objectification. Rather, this sexualization stems directly from
stigmatization—more specifically, from his being compared to, or
lumped into the same category as, women or queer men (both
groups who are marked by sex in our culture). Given the existence
of courtesy stigma, one does not need to be a member of a particular stigmatized population in order to experience that stigma to
some degree; all that's required is some kind of association with
that group, whether through resemblance or proximity. Indeed,
gender and sexual norms are regularly policed via threats of stigma
by association, and anyone who even slightly fails to conform can
be subjected to one of many all-too-familiar sexualizing taunts:
"fag," "dyke," "whore," "pervert," and so on.

For readers who are new to the concept of stigma, thinking
about sexualization in these terms may seem a bit abstract at first,
so allow me to illustrate this with a real-world example. Imagine
that you are an unscrupulous political operative, and you are given
the task of destroying your opponent by any means necessary. How
might you go about that? Well, you could go after their record and
stated positions, or paint them as a typical two-faced politician,
but these approaches would likely have limited impact. If they've
committed some kind of crime, that might raise some eyebrows,
depending on the charges. But what would probably excite you
the most—the thing that would likely do the most damage to your
opponent—would be if you could pin some kind of "sex scandal"
on them. What if they are an adulterer, or a "closeted homosexual," or have some kind of "fetish"? Maybe someone out there has
nude photos of them, or sexually explicitly texts they've sent, or
perhaps there's even a "pee tape"? Or what if you could brand their
entire political party as a cabal of pedophiles and child sex traf-
fickers? Notably, none of these things are illegal (except for the

final charge, which comes from the QAnon conspiracy theory), yet they would all likely garner far more negative attention than most financial crimes or political corruption scandals. The sex scandal would likely follow your opponent around wherever they went, "soiling" their entire person and reputation in many people's eyes. This is a testament to the power of sex-related stigma.

Of course, as a savvy political operative, you would also intuitively understand that simply uncovering or inventing a sex scandal is not necessarily enough. You also need the charges to "stick" to your opponent. If they are widely considered to be a normal, respectable, upstanding member of the community, then voters might have a hard time believing the accusation is true without a preponderance of evidence, and even then, they might not be convinced. In contrast, if your opponent was . . . I don't know, let's say *me*, then you might feel fairly confident that at least some voters would accept the sex scandal at face value, even if the evidence is rather flimsy. Why is that? Well, as we discussed with regards to the Unmarked/Marked mindset, accusations and attributions tend to "stick" better to people who are marked relative to their unmarked counterparts. Not only am I marked, but people are likely to view me as "marked by sex" in a number of different ways: for being female, bisexual, and/or transgender, not to mention the fact that I regularly write about sexuality, including sharing some of my own past sexual experiences—talk about letting my "sex" show!

Thus, while any person can theoretically be sexualized in a number of ways, in practice, some individuals are significantly more susceptible to sexualization than others. In particular, marked groups, especially those that are widely stigmatized, are especially prone to sexualization. Over the next several chapters, I will provide an overview of some of the ways in which this phenomenon plays out with regards to various marginalized groups.

7 INTERSECTIONALITY AND HYPERSEXUALIZATION

When I first introduced the Predator/Prey mindset, I described its male "sexual aggressor" and female "sexual object" roles as ideals that people are generally encouraged to strive for. Those who successfully achieve these standards are deemed attractive and widely admired, while those who fail to do so are deemed unappealing and socially devalued. However, it is also possible to overshoot these goals. After all, someone who over-enthusiastically embraces their status as a "sexual object" will likely face slut-shaming, and someone who appears overly sexually aggressive may be taken for a literal sexual predator. In other words, these individuals may be viewed as *hypersexual*—exhibiting an excessive amount of sex or sexuality—and will likely be stigmatized as a result.

In theory, any person may be deemed hypersexual if they behave in ways that strike others as "too sexual." In reality, however, people often face vastly different criteria for what counts as hypersexual: Some have quite a bit of latitude in their behaviors; for others, it's more of a tightrope where one small misstep may trigger this assessment; and still others are misconstrued as hypersexual no matter what they do. As a general rule, men tend to have more leeway than women for all the reasons I've previously described. But even within a given gender, there are significant disparities. Studies of slut-shaming within high school and college settings have found that the label tends to stick more to girls and women who differ from the norm in some way, often as a result of their class or ethnicity.[1] We've also touched on how Black men in the United States are often stereotyped as "sexual predators" on first sight, entirely independent of their behaviors, while on the other end of the spectrum are men such as Brock Turner—a white Stanford University student who many people refused to believe was a sexual predator even after he was caught in the act of raping an unconscious woman.[2] In writing about Turner, philosopher Kate Manne points out that such public sentiments of disbelief and sympathy toward perpetrators of sexual violence are typically reserved for "white, nondisabled, and otherwise privileged 'golden boys'" and stem from a "mistaken idea of what rapists must be like: creepy, uncanny, and wearing their lack of humanity on their sleeve."[3] To paraphrase, we often presume that marked individuals are likely dangerous or hypersexual but have difficulty imagining such qualities in those who remain unmarked in our eyes.

To understand this "hypersexualization" of marked and marginalized groups, it is necessary to revisit the concept of intersectionality. Given everything we've discussed so far, it appears that there are at least three different non–mutually exclusive pathways that may contribute to intersectional marginalization. Over the next three paragraphs, I will briefly outline them with an emphasis placed on how they might contribute to hypersexualization.

Earlier, when discussing the Opposites mindset, I suggested that intersectional marginalization can be partially explained via overlapping, or conflicting, sets of double standards. For example, because men are stereotyped as more aggressive and dangerous than women, and Black people are also stereotyped as more aggressive and dangerous than their white counterparts, this combination may render Black men especially susceptible to being misinterpreted as aggressive and dangerous—and thus potential "predators"—regardless of their actual behaviors.[4] Similarly, since Black women are also read as aggressive and dangerous relative to white women, onlookers may perceive them as "insufficiently feminine" or "overly masculine"—this is in fact a common stereotype.[5] And since "aggression" is built into our cultural conceptualization of sex and sexuality, onlookers may misperceive Black individuals as "overly sexually aggressive" or "asking for it" in contexts where, if the individual was white, these onlookers would not jump to the same conclusions.

A second way in which intersectional marginalization may occur is through the Unmarked/Marked mindset. Given that we tend to perceive marked individuals as conspicuous, artificial, and questionable, someone who possesses multiple marked traits may seem *extra* conspicuous, artificial, or questionable in our eyes. The fact that we tend to pay such individuals undue attention may lead us to unconsciously dwell upon aspects of their bodies or behaviors that would normally go unnoticed if they appeared in the corresponding unmarked group(s). Some of these traits that we dwell on may be sexual in nature, thus leading us to perceive the individual as "excessively sexual," even though they aren't fundamentally different from their unmarked counterparts in this regard. Or, since marked traits tend to be "sticky"—attracting all sorts of stereotypes, assumptions, and meanings—we may project sexual connotations onto them, even when they are not inherently sexual. Relatedly, since we tend to attribute ulterior motives to marked individuals, we may presume that even their most innocuous gestures or behaviors may be driven by sexual desires or hidden sexual agendas. These are but a few ways in which marked groups may be mistakenly interpreted as "hypersexual," and multiply marked individuals may face such misinterpretations to an even greater extent.

A third possible framework for understanding intersectional marginalization involves systemic practices and institutions. As but one example, here in the United States, there is a long history of racial bias within policing and the criminal justice system. As a result, when certain sexual activities or identities become criminalized—such as with sex workers today or queer people in the not-so-distant past—people of color tend to be disproportionately targeted and prosecuted for such crimes.[6] Relatedly, studies have shown that 75 percent of rape exonerees (people convicted of that crime but later proved innocent as a result of DNA evidence) are Black or Latino, even though these groups comprise a far smaller proportion of the overall U.S. population; this suggests significant racial bias in false accusations and/or prosecutions of sexual assault.[7] Of course, systems and institutions are comprised of individuals, some of whom may be influenced by previously mentioned unconscious mindsets. In other words, the three potential causes of intersectional marginalization that I just outlined often act synergistically and may contribute to varying degrees in any given instance of hypersexualization.

In order to better understand why and how marginalized groups tend to be misconstrued as hypersexual, it is useful to examine another system, namely, the field of sexology. While human sexuality has always been with us, a scientific discipline dedicated to studying it first emerged in the late 1800s, closely on the heels of the fields of biology and psychiatry as we now know them.[8] While scientists may strive to be objective in our accounts, we may nevertheless be unwittingly influenced (to one degree or another) by the ideologies and beliefs that are taken for granted in our culture. During this particular period, it was widely accepted within all these fields that men of Northern European heritage (who just so happened to be the people carrying out this theorizing and research) were superior to both women and people of other ethnicities. And much of this early research was geared toward "uncovering" these groups' imagined deficiencies and defects. Today, this body of work is often described as *scientific racism*, which is an apt label, although it must be said that many of the same researchers were also quite interested in examining (and affirming) other social hierarchies.

Based on now discredited methods (crude measurements of skeletons and skulls, brain volumes, and other superficial anatomical differences) and specious interpretations of Darwin's theory of evolution (which was still a relatively new concept at the time), sexologists and other scientists of this period converged on an overarching narrative,[9] which I will outline here. First, these researchers claimed that Europeans were more "highly evolved" than other ethnicities, not only because they were the most "civilized" (in their humble opinion) but also because they purportedly exhibited the highest levels of sex differentiation—physical differences between women and men—which they presumed was a sign of evolutionary progress. They also believed that the sex differentiation that existed among Europeans was likely the result of men having become "more evolved" than women,[10] as evidenced by the former's supposed superior intelligence and self-discipline. In contrast, the imagined lack of sex differentiation in non-white ethnicities was attributed to the fact that they were "bisexual"—this was not meant to denote sexual orientation, but rather that members of these groups supposedly expressed a combination of male and female characteristics.[11] A supposed lack of sex differentiation is also found in another concept invented around this same time, namely, "sexual inversion," which referred to people who were externally male but had "feminine souls" (or vice versa). Sexual inversion was the proposed cause of homosexuality—also a new term coined by sexologists during this period—although in retrospect, many individuals who were labeled "inverts" would today be described as falling elsewhere along the LGBTQIA+ spectrum.

So to sum up thus far, late-nineteenth-century researchers placed themselves atop their own imagined evolutionary hierarchy, and argued that everyone below them was 1) "less evolved" (often described as "childish," "savage," or "primitive" in their accounts), 2) comprised of a mixture of male and female sex characteristics (and thus excessively sexual), and 3) lacking in rationality, reason, and self-discipline.

There is one more piece to this narrative, namely, "degeneration," a once widely accepted (but now discarded) theory claiming that more "highly evolved" individuals can revert to a simpler, more primitive state over the course of their lifetime, and ultimately pass those inferior traits on to their offspring. During this period, degeneration was many scientists' go-to explanation for all sorts of behaviors that were deemed socially undesirable, including prostitution, criminality, poverty, mental disabilities, and, of course, sexual inversion/homosexuality.[12] Whenever people of European heritage exhibited any of these qualities, it was typically presumed that they had degenerated—due either to their own personal failings or those of their parents—to the point that they now resembled the "lower races," particularly in their lack of self-control and intelligence.[13]

And how, pray tell, did this degeneration "spread" throughout the population? Through sex, of course. These researchers routinely cited masturbation and promiscuity as causes and/or symptoms of degeneration. Even worse, in their minds, were sexual interactions with other degenerates (such as inverts and prostitutes) and with people of non-European ethnicities. Women were believed to be especially susceptible to being "corrupted" by these groups, given that they too purportedly lacked the rationality and willpower to restrain their passions and desires.[14] Calls from scientific authorities and politicians alike to protect white women and the supposedly superior Northern European bloodline from the perils of degeneration were used to justify systemic practices, such as the criminalization of sexual minorities and interracial relationships, and the eugenics movement, which advocated forced sterilization, exclusion, or outright elimination of individuals deemed "unfit" to reproduce.[15]

It is clear today that human beings do not "de-evolve," especially over the course of a lifetime or generation. In this light, these researchers' fears—of supposedly "pure" bloodlines becoming "contaminated," and individuals becoming forever "spoiled" via sexual intimacy with a queer person, sex worker, or person of color—seem to have been driven at least in part by race- and sex-related stigma.[16] Indeed, the fact that these varied groups were all socially stigmatized likely facilitated the homogenizing theories that these researchers penned about them, in which they were all, in one way or another, deemed excessively sexual and unable to control their sexual desires. In her book *Racism and Sexual Oppression in Anglo-America: A Genealogy*, philosopher Ladelle McWhorter traces how these scientists' concerns and constructs ultimately gave rise to "the weak-willed sexual predator in all his/her guises: the black rapist . . . the alluring syphilitic whore, the sex-crazed imbecile, the conniving female invert poised to recruit, and the homosexual child molester. Scientific racism, with its intense fear of genetic corruption, created this figure."[17]

Intersectionality teaches us to refrain from making the kinds of sweeping analogies that these nineteenth-century researchers relied upon, comparing women to people of color, people of color to queer people, etc. There are countless differences both within and between all these groups, and many people fall into more than one of these categories simultaneously. While these nineteenth-century theories are no longer taken seriously within sexology and related fields, some of the hypersexualized stereotypes they espoused remain with us to this day. And while most of us now reject the strict hierarchies that informed these theories, we may still harbor unconscious mindsets that enable similar patterns of thinking. Specifically, marked and marginalized groups are often perceived as less "mature" and "rational" than their unmarked counterparts. This combination of supposed immaturity, irrationality, and emotionality—which were constant themes in the historical narrative above—can lead people to presume that these groups are unable to control their own sexual urges and behaviors. When the "immature" individual in question is deemed otherwise "good" or "innocent" (straight white women and children immediately come to mind), these presumptions may evoke paternalistic attitudes of protection, such as measures to "save them from themselves" or shield them from potentially "corrupting" influences.[18] But for marginalized groups who are viewed as "other," these presumptions can lead to their being viewed as hypersexual in ways that are to be feared and/or exploited.

Perhaps no marginalized group has been more pervasively hypersexualized in Anglo-American and European settings than people of African descent.[19] One of the more infamous early expressions of this tendency centered on Saartjie Baartman, an African woman who, during the early nineteenth century, was exhibited barely clothed in "freak shows" in London and Paris under the moniker "Hottentot Venus." During the same period, Black people were often displayed in similarly dehumanizing ways at U.S. slave auctions. As numerous historians and theorists have pointed out, this juxtaposition of fully clothed white people gazing upon naked or near-naked Black people served to reinforce racist notions that the former were "civilized" and "pure," while the latter were supposedly "savage" and "sexually deviant." These same double standards also influenced conceptualizations of rape during this time. Despite facing widespread and largely condoned sexual violence at the hands of white men, enslaved Black women were excluded from rape laws, while Black men who were accused of sexually attacking white women were subjected to far more extreme punishments (such as castration and death) than their white counterparts.[20]

Even after slavery officially ended in the United States, the rampant sexualization of Black people continued throughout the Jim Crow segregation era and still persists in some capacities to this day. In her book *Black Feminist Thought*, sociologist Patricia Hill Collins describes how "long-standing ideas concerning the excessive sexual appetite of people of African descent conjured up in White imaginations generate gender-specific controlling images of the Black male rapist and the Black female jezebel."[21] The "Jezebel" stereotype depicts Black women as inherently lascivious and seductive, and has long been used to discount Black women's experiences of sexual assault under the premise that they presumably "brought it on themselves." Collins chronicles how this stereotype has given rise to the pervasive cultural associations between Black women and prostitution, and continues to inform sexually explicit Black-themed media depictions and pornography. Like all stereotypes, this one has had numerous real-world ramifications. Studies akin to those I described in the previous chapter have shown that people tend to objectify Black women more than white women, particularly in sexualized contexts.[22] It is not uncommon for Black women to be mistaken for (and sometimes even charged for being) sex workers simply because they are Black.[23] As a result of Black women being hypersexualized in all these various ways, numerous reports have shown that they experience higher levels of sexual violence than white women.[24]

In her 1981 book, *Women, Race and Class*, activist and scholar Angela Davis raised awareness about the "myth of the Black rapist."[25] There are several facets to this myth that require unpacking. First, there's the previously discussed stereotype that Black men are inherently sexually "aggressive" and "predatory," which persists to this day. While this stereotype is egregious in its own right, what especially concerned Davis was the way in which it has historically been wielded. Specifically, while the white majority has expressed little concern about Black women's experiences with sexual assault, which have frequently occurred at the hands of white men, this myth exaggerated fears about the far less common scenario of white women being sexually victimized by Black men. More to the point, the specter of the Black rapist was routinely invoked—often in cases where no sexual violence actually took place—as a justification or pretense for acts of violence and terrorism committed by whites against Black communities, often in the form of mob lynchings. Between the 1860s and the 1950s, approximately five thousand cases of Black individuals being lynched were documented in the United States, one of the more high-profile incidents being that of Emmett Till, a fourteen-year-old who was brutally murdered in 1955 for supposedly whistling at or flirting with a white woman.[26] To this day, while Black-on-white rape represents a small fraction of sexual assault cases, such incidents are considerably overrepresented in both prosecutions and exonerations.[27]

Despite having vastly different historical trajectories, there is noticeable overlap in stereotypes between Black and Hispanic/Latinx people in U.S. settings. Latino men are often racially profiled as "dangerous" or "criminal," and are prone to being falsely convicted of sexual assault.[28] Similar to the way the "Black rapist" trope has been weaponized to incite rage against Black communities, Donald Trump kicked off his explicitly anti-immigrant presidential campaign by equating Mexicans with "rapists."[29] Pop-culture images of Latina women often highlight "seductive clothing, curvaceous hips and breasts," thereby creating the impression that they are "oversexed" and "sexually available."[30] Relatedly, in a 2014 survey of six hundred popular films, both Latino men and Latina women were found to be the race/ethnicity most frequently depicted in "sexualized attire" and "showing exposed skin," with Latina actors being "shown partially or fully naked on screen" in 37.5 percent of the films they appeared in.[31] To be clear, Black and Latinx stereotypes differ in countless other ways, but they seem to share similar hypersexualized overtones.

While the "promiscuous" female and "predatory" male are common hypersexualized stereotypes, they are not the only ones that exist. In his book *The Erotic Margin*, Irvin C. Schick researched European colonialist literature and other texts spanning several centuries and numerous geographies, documenting the ways in which non-European people and cultures were depicted in a sexualized manner. While the accounts varied, Schick observed a recurring pattern: "Foreign women are alternatingly portrayed as sexually alluring or threatening, foreign men as effeminate weaklings or dangerous rapists."[32] One way to make sense of these tropes is that they arise at the intersection of racism and xenophobia on the one hand, and Predator/Prey gender stereotypes on the other. Specifically, if a particular population is imagined to possess masculine-coded traits (whether physical, dispositional, or cultural), then that population may be caricatured as "sexually aggressive," with women being construed as "licentious" and men as "predatory" (as we saw with the aforementioned Black and Latinx stereotypes). In contrast, groups that are imagined to possess feminine-coded traits may be caricatured as "sexually submissive," resulting in desexualized or emasculated male stereotypes, and passive and deferential female stereotypes (with the latter potentially being deemed "appealing" from a white heteronormative male standpoint).

For some marginalized groups, different combinations of these stereotypes may simultaneously be in play. One example can be found in late-nineteenth-century sexological depictions of Jewish men, who were characterized as "effeminate" with "a strong disposition toward homosexuality," while alternately being associated with more masculine-coded desires for "prostitution, pornography, and rape."[33] While these two depictions may seem contradictory on the surface, they both serve the same purpose: They paint this group as "excessively sexual," thereby facilitating their dehumanization and demonization.

All four of these racism/xenophobia-meets-Predator/Prey stereotypes can be found in white colonialist depictions of Native Americans.[34] In her essay "'Sexual Savages': Christian Stereotypes and Violence Against North America's Native Women," sociologist Alexandra Pierce shows how the presumption that white Christians were "virtuous" and "civilized," while Indigenous people were "depraved" and "savage," fueled hypersexualized beliefs and depictions of the latter. As supposed "savages," Native American men were sometimes portrayed as "sexual brutes" who posed a potential threat to white women, particularly in what have come to be known as "captivity narratives."[35] Alternatively, the fact that Native American cultures tended to be egalitarian and sometimes matrilineal (in contrast to their staunchly patriarchal European counterparts) led some colonialists to presume that Indigenous men were "undersexed" or unmanly. As Pierce puts it, "The stereotyping of Native women as sexual savages and Native men as sexually inadequate gave male colonists license to engage in forcible rape without incurring any legal, moral, or spiritual consequences."[36]

Native American women faced their own dichotomous sexualized stereotypes. Nowadays, people tend to be more familiar with the "Indian princess" archetype, as emblematized in the story of Pocahontas. The "Indian princess" is typically depicted as exotic and alluring yet compliant, and she invariably caters to the wishes or needs of white male colonizers. At the other extreme is the "squaw" archetype, who is portrayed as aggressive, ferocious, and of course sexually voracious. Rather than being romanticized like the "Indian princess," the "squaw" is dehumanized, viewed as both sexually available and disposable. Once again, these stereotypes have real-life consequences for those who are targeted by them. Pierce spends the last few sections of her essay delving into studies demonstrating that Native American women experience sexual violence at higher rates than any other U.S. ethnicity, including more stranger and interracial sexual victimization than any other group.[37]

Somewhat similar hypersexualized stereotypes are projected onto Asians (particularly East Asians). While there are occasional examples of Asian men being depicted as dangerous or predatory, they are more routinely depicted in an emasculated or desexualized manner, likely as a result of Asians more generally being stereotyped as "feminine" relative to other ethnicities.[38] In an article entitled "The Orientalization of Asian Women in America," Aki Uchida describes the recurring dichotomous Asian female stereotypes as "the docile doll/'Lotus Blossom' or the diabolic Dragon Lady."[39] Both are overtly sexualized, albeit in different ways: the former depicted as passive and subservient, the latter as aggressive and deceitful. Borrowing from Patricia Hill Collins, Uchida refers to these stereotypes as "controlling images" to emphasize the political and material impact that they have on Asian American women. Uchida demonstrates how these controlling images emerged from the long history of Asian women being sexually exploited in the United States, from primarily be- ing associated with prostitution starting in the late 1800s (which continued through the Korean and Vietnam War eras) to the "war bride" and "mail-order bride" phenomena of the 1900s.[40] Uchida goes on to show how these controlling images—which frame Asian women as exotic and sexually available—continue to shape Americans' perceptions and expectations: "Some people, both men and women, are surprised if the Asian woman does not behave accordingly, and the dissonance is attributed to her devi- ance, to the fact that there is something wrong with her instead of the image."[41]

That's a brief overview of some of the hypersexualized stereo- types that have plagued people of color. To reemphasize a point that I've alluded to throughout this chapter, these stereotypes ar- en't merely obstacles that people of color have had to deal with; rather, they directly inform how we conceptualize whiteness. Spe- cifically, the taken-for-granted assumption that white people's sex- ualities are "normal," "modest," or "respectful" is predicated on the presumption that other people's sexualities (in particular, those of people of color) are inherently "deviant," "excessive," and "savage." And propaganda painting men of color as supposed "sexual preda- tors" belies the reality that white men have historically committed the lion's share of sexual violence and exploitation, not the other way around. This asymmetry—wherein white people's sexualities always remain unmarked and untainted—is perhaps most obvious in the fact that if I were to engage in acts that others consider to be "excessively sexual," no one would ever attribute those acts to my ethnicity (as they would with people of color). Instead, they would likely view them as a personal failing, or perhaps the result of a faulty upbringing. Or, if I happen to be marginalized in some other way, then that *would* likely be cited as the cause of my "devi- ant" sexuality.

In addition to people of color, there are at least three other marginalized groups that are routinely subjected to hypersexualization. The first is poor and working-class people (as we saw in the nineteenth-century sexology narrative that I detailed earlier). Contemporary studies have shown that not only are economically disadvantaged women stereotyped as promiscuous and inordinately subjected to slut-shaming, but they are blamed for any sexual violence they experience more so than women from more privileged economic classes.[42] With regards to the stereotype of working-class men being prone to commit sexual violence, sociologist Alison Phipps points out that while there is "little or no evidence that rapists tend to come from any one social class . . . working-class defendants are more likely to be arrested, charged and convicted, and receive more severe sentences than middle-class offenders."[43] Given that people of color tend to be disproportionately economically disadvantaged, these class-related sexual stereotypes may intersect with, and further exacerbate, the previously described racialized stereotypes.

A second marginalized group that is routinely sexualized is people with disabilities. Disability theorists have articulated the dichotomous sexualized stereotypes they routinely face, frequently being depicted in a desexualized manner on the one hand while at other times being construed as "excessively sexual." In the anthology *Sex and Disability*, coeditor Anna Mollow writes about this "insistence that disabled sexuality is somehow both lack (innocence, incapacity, dysfunction) and excess (kinkiness, weirdness, perversion)."[44] One of the examples that Mollow offers to illustrate this dichotomy is how "cognitively disabled people are commonly depicted as childlike and asexual but are also often feared as uncontrollable sexual predators."[45] We saw the latter stereotype earlier with nineteenth-century sexologists' invention of the "sex-crazed imbecile," and it would later come to dominate twentieth-century thinking (in media, politics, and the legal system) in the form of the "sexual psychopath."[46] We now know that people with mental disabilities are not more likely to commit acts of sexual violence than the general population. In fact, study after study has shown that people with disabilities (whether mental or physical) are far more likely to be victims of sexual violence than their non-disabled counterparts.[47]

In their article "Reinforcing the Myth of the Crazed Rapist: A Feminist Critique of Recent Rape Legislation," legal scholars Christina E. Wells and Erin Elliott Motley critique this pervasive image of rapists as "psychopathic, violent, sexually-compulsive (usually black) strangers."[48] They point out that this stereotype is not only incorrect (and thereby unfairly maligns people with mental disabilities) but also provides cover for the overwhelming majority of actual rapists who will claim "innocence" on the basis that they do not resemble this stereotype. In other words, this ableist stereotype obscures the fact that most sexual assaults are perpetrated by seemingly "normal" acquaintances of the victim, not marginalized strangers. Thus, we should be suspicious of any attempt to mischaracterize an entire minority group (whether due to their race, class, ability, etc.) as being especially prone to, or disproportionately responsible for, sexual violence.

This brings us to a third group that is routinely subjected to hypersexualized stereotypes: queer people. While other marginalized groups tend to be envisioned as exaggerations or caricatures of the Predator/Prey "sexual aggressor" and "sexual object" archetypes, LGBTQIA+ people tend to be viewed somewhat differently, as anomalies or subversives who defy Predator/Prey presumptions. For this reason—plus the fact that queerness is my personal entry point for considering why and how people are sexualized—I will explore LGBTQIA+ people's experiences with sexualization in the following chapter.

8   QUEER AS A THREE-DOLLAR BILL

The Predator/Prey mindset and script rely heavily on assumptions. Their purpose, after all, is to allow romantic and sexual encounters to develop without anyone ever having to explicitly discuss their desires and what they would like to happen next. Perhaps the most central of these presumptions is that all people fall into two readily identifiable classes (masculine men and feminine women) that are naturally attracted to one another (heterosexual) and fulfill complementary sexual roles ("aggressors" and "objects"). Colloquially, people who adhere to all these presumptions are referred to as "straight," a word that has a host of other meanings, including *direct, frank, candid, honest, honorable, reliable, right or correct, unmodified or unaltered, without embellishments, not engaged in crime*, and *law-abiding*.[1] The implication is clear: straightness is deemed natural, normal, and in "proper order."

Of course, not everybody lives up to this straight standard. Some people are attracted to members of the same sex/gender (gay and lesbian), or more than one sex/gender (bisexual), or do not experience sexual attraction to anyone (asexual). And some people fall outside straight standards regarding gender identity and/or expression (transgender) and physical sex (intersex). About 5 percent of the U.S. population currently identifies as lesbian, gay, bisexual, or transgender; these studies did not survey intersex or asexual identities, which would presumably raise this number even more.[2] When survey questions focus on same-sex attraction and behaviors rather than identity, up to 10 percent of men and 20 percent of women are found to be not completely straight.[3] In a perfect world, all these individuals would be seen as simply part of natural variation, as I described in the Introduction. But we don't live in that world.

In fact, throughout much of the twentieth century, LGBTQIA+ people have been criminalized (via sodomy, indecency, and anti-crossdressing laws) and pathologized (via psychiatric diagnoses and, in the case of intersex children, nonconsensual surgeries). While gender and sexual minorities have experienced significant social and legal progress over the past two decades, 24 percent of the U.S. population still believes that same-sex relationships should be illegal, and 32 percent believes that society has gone too far in accepting transgender people.[4]

While our existence imposes no harm upon others, many people nevertheless view and treat LGBTQIA+ people as though we constitute a threat. What we threaten, in their minds, is the notion of perfect "opposite sexes" and the sanctity of the Predator/ Prey script. Such sentiments are especially evident in the word "queer"—a term that was historically used to disparage us before LGBTQIA+ people reclaimed it and began using it in a positive self-referential manner. Most of us are familiar with the fact that "queer" can also mean "strange" or "odd," but other definitions associated with the word include *of a questionable nature or character, suspicious, shady, to jeopardize,* and *to spoil or ruin.*[5] These meanings suggest that we purposely set out to undermine the "natural order" of things. Perhaps the most telling definition—the one enshrined in the idiom "queer as a three-dollar bill"—is "phony" or "counterfeit": "obviously false or fake; not genuine or authentic in the slightest."[6]

In this chapter, I will chronicle some of the ways in which gender and sexual minorities are perceived and sexualized. Some of this discussion will be akin to what I described in the last chapter regarding how marginalized groups are often portrayed as "hypersexual." But there are also instances in which LGBTQIA+ people are conceptualized as insufficiently sexual (not womanly or manly enough, or lacking the appropriate heterosexual desires). I believe that these varying, and sometimes contradictory, stereotypes start to make sense when we recognize that LGBTQIA+ identities and sexualities are routinely misinterpreted through a Predator/Prey lens. Our apparent failure to adhere to Predator/Prey rules and logic is what leads to our being routinely mischaracterized as "fake" and "deceptive"—notions that undergird much of the sexualization we face.

Straight Assumption and Queer "Fakeness"

In order to understand why people view gender and sexual minorities as "fake" or "deceptive," we must first address the phenomenon of *straight assumption*—the unconscious tendency to presume that every person we come across is straight by default.[7] This belief arises at the confluence of mindsets discussed in earlier chapters: the Two Filing Cabinets mindset leads us to view all people as falling neatly into one of two gender categories; "gender constancy" leads us to assume that those gender categories are immutable and unchanging over time; and the Opposites and Predator/Prey mindsets lead us to expect people to behave in accordance with the gender that we perceive them as, particularly with regards to their gender identity, gender expression, and sexual orientation. Together, these mindsets lead most people to perceive and interpret everyone they meet as straight unless they are provided with evidence to the contrary.

There are varying degrees of straight assumption. Back when I was a young child, I literally did not know that there were *any* exceptions to straightness, which is why it was so difficult for me to make sense of the "girl thoughts" I previously described. Over time, I learned about various exceptions, albeit in an incomplete and piecemeal fashion: First I learned about gay men, then trans people, then lesbians, and so on, although these were initially two-dimensional stereotypes that I picked up from watching TV and from queer-disparaging jokes. Notably, even upon learning about these exceptions, I still presumed that every person I encountered was straight, which seems ridiculous in retrospect given that I myself was a queer person who went undetected (in that people assumed I was straight). With increasing queer awareness, I eventually moved into what might be called the "gaydar" phase, where I felt that I had enough insider information to allow me to spot queer individuals by reading telltale signs. While I was correct on some occasions, it turned out that there were exceptions to this as well: people I assumed were queer who turned out not to be, and people who came out to me as queer whom I did not expect. Over time, I realized that "gaydar" was merely a variant of straight assumption, albeit with two categories rather than one for me to clumsily force all people into. After several decades of being immersed in queer communities, I've come to recognize the multiplicity of identities and the heterogeneity of bodies, personalities, and experiences that exist within it, making it impossible to predict where any given person will fall along those axes. Nowadays, I strive to not make any assumptions about people's genders or sexualities until they share that information with me, or when it comes from a reliable source (such as someone who knows them personally).

While many of us today take queer individuals at face value and view them as authentic, this has not historically been the case, and plenty of people still insist on viewing us as "phony," "counterfeit," and "fake." This presumed "fakeness" arises directly from straight assumption, and it comes in two general flavors. The first is *delusional fakeness*, which occurs when perceivers who are ignorant of, or in denial about, a particular LGBTQIA+ identity conceptualize the individual as an otherwise "normal" person (typically straight, although sometimes gay) who is pretending to be something they are not. Because the individual's identity, desires, and behaviors are presumed to be "fake," they are often imagined as engaging in purposeful artifice. For instance, perceivers may presume that the queer individual is merely "seeking out an alternative lifestyle," putting on an "affectation," or staging a contrived "performance." Alternatively, the perceiver may imagine the individual as a victim of "self-deception": They must be "confused" about their gender or sexuality, or merely going through a "phase."

Then there's *deceptive fakeness*, which often occurs in perceivers who are at least hypothetically aware that LGBTQIA+ people exist but nonetheless discount our potential presence. In such cases, the perceiver initially presumes that the individual in question is straight, as per straight assumption. But when they later learn that the individual is queer in some way, the perceiver will view this new information as a "surprise" or a dramatic "reveal," one that leads them to consciously reinterpret the individual's past presentation and actions as merely an "act" or "ruse" intended to "trick" or "deceive" the perceiver into thinking they were straight.

In all likelihood, the queer individual was not purposely hiding that information; rather, their queerness was simply erased by the perceiver's straight assumption. But you would never know this from the language we tend to use in such situations, in which queer people are often described as "passing," "closeted," or "straight-acting." These phrases give the impression that the queer individual is the sole active party who is single-handedly engaged in purposeful deception, while simultaneously discounting the perceiver's own active (if unconscious) processes of categorization and straight assumption. Of course, if "deception" is supposedly involved, then there must be some kind of underlying motive. Often the motives attributed to queer people in these cases are fairly banal ("Julia was pretending to be straight in order to avoid discrimination"), but sometimes they can be quite nefarious, as we will soon see.

The two types of queer "fakeness" that I have just described are not mutually exclusive—for instance, one can believe that a "deceptive" queer person is also "delusional" about their identity. Furthermore, the rationales that people propose to explain our supposed "delusions," and the motives attributed to our supposed "deceptions," are often illogical and may even contradict one another. After all, their purpose is not to reflect reality but rather to reaffirm that straightness is "natural" and "real." Indeed, queer "fakeness" and straight "realness" are intrinsically linked: Straight individuals are presumed to be "natural" and "authentic" by default, but as soon as anyone begins to question their desires, or colors outside traditional Predator/Prey roles, onlookers will begin to label them as "queer" and perceive them as "fake."

Throughout the rest of this chapter, I will show how these tropes of "fakeness" and "deception" play recurring roles in the ways that queer people are sexualized in our culture. But before doing so, there is one more matter to consider. Specifically, because queer people uncouple gender identity, gender expression, sexual orientation, and/or physical sex from one another, a question arises as to which of these traits should take priority when people claim that we are "really X" but "pretending to be Y." For reasons discussed earlier, physical sex—and especially birth-assigned sex—tends to take precedence in most adults' minds. And if an individual's physical sex traits are deemed ambiguous or seem to send mixed signals, most adults will ultimately rely upon whether the person possesses a penis; notably, vulvas do not have a similar effect.[8] Therefore, we must make a brief excursion to consider why the penis is supposedly so important.

It's Not the Size of the Wand but the "Magic" That It Does

Penises are often glorified in our culture as symbols of power and domination. Other times, they are demonized as tools of rape and oppression. They are sometimes even anthropomorphized, described as having "a mind of their own." In any case, people tend to have extremely intense and absolute feelings about penises. As someone who once possessed such an organ, but has since parted ways with it (or, more accurately, had it reconfigured), my feelings are far more ambivalent.[9] The reality is that penises are made of flesh and blood, just like the rest of our bodies. If anything, they are far more *sensitive* and *vulnerable* than most body parts due to all those nerve endings—though I'll be the first to admit that these are probably not the first adjectives that come to most people's minds, given that they fall on the female/feminine side of the Table of Opposites. If we take a step back from all the symbolism, what we can say with certainty is that some people have penises and/or appreciate penises, while others do not—the same can be said about virtually any other human trait. So there is really no need to attribute special powers to them that they do not actually possess. That is my two cents on the matter.

But I appear to be in the minority on this. Even though having a penis is most certainly *not* a prerequisite for participating in sex, many people seem to harbor penis-centric views of the act. Numerous surveys asking college students what "counts" as sex have found virtually unanimous agreement that penile-vaginal intercourse constitutes sex, with about 80 percent saying the same about penile-anal intercourse, and roughly 40 percent about oral sex; all other intimate acts lag far behind.[10] So while people may differ in their definitions of sex, most seem to believe that it involves a penis penetrating another person and that a vagina need not be involved.

To put this in the context of our previous discussions about the Predator/Prey mindset, if women (or whoever is cast in the "sexual object" role) *have* or *are* "sex," then it seems as though the penis is the thing that *takes* that "sex" from them. Consistent with this, it's always the person who accepts or accommodates the penis (rather than the person who possesses it) who is viewed as having been degraded by the act, as is evident in the sentiment that women (but not men) are "used" or "dirtied" by heterosexual sex, and the widespread use of the slur "cocksucker" (whereas no analogous universally demeaning term exists for those who receive fellatio or engage in cunnilingus). And if a person intentionally hurts or humiliates another person, we often call them a "dick." While penises, and those who are attached to them, are not stigmatized themselves, they do seem to possess the ability to impart sexual stigma upon others.

In her writings on the differing social meanings attributed to nakedness in our culture, philosopher Talia Bettcher points out how "it is generally considered a privacy violation for a male to view a female's naked body, while it is a decency violation for a male to show his body to a female."[11] I interpret this asymmetry as follows: When an individual exposes their penis, onlookers do not view them as opening themselves up to being sexualized (as is the case for women who expose themselves); rather, they are interpreted as attempting or threatening to "take sex" from (and thereby disgrace) other people. This is why, if a man "whips it out," it is widely understood as an aggressive move—it basically means "fuck you," either literally or figuratively.

To be clear, I do not believe that penises actually possess the power to "take sex" from other people, or to magically bestow sexual stigma upon anyone they touch. Nevertheless, these symbolic meanings remain quite pervasive in our culture. And, as we will see, they often influence common misperceptions of gender and sexual minorities.

Sexualized Stereotypes of LGBTQIA+ People

Because queer people confound Predator/Prey roles and rules, we are "marked by sex" in many people's eyes. When I was growing up, people who fancied themselves tolerant would often say, "I don't care what you do in your own bedroom; just don't flaunt it in front of me," in response to people who simply mentioned that they had a same-sex partner or who engaged in displays of affection such as hand-holding. These acts—which would have gone unnoticed or un–commented upon if they occurred in the straight majority—were treated as if they were *sexual acts* that needed to be kept private. Even today, chaste kissing between queer couples is sometimes viewed as indecent, and books that include LGBTQIA+ characters are among those most targeted for censorship, even if they are bereft of any explicit sexual content.[12] In other words, we are seen as *sexual beings* through and through. And because many people view us as "fakes," they routinely invent ulterior sexual motivations to explain who we are and what we do. Here are a few of the more common sexualizing stereotypes and attributions that we are subjected to.

One way in which people rationalize queer individuals and relationships is by presuming that we merely mimic our straight counterparts. For instance, when confronted with a same-sex couple, people will often ask questions or make assumptions about which partner is the butch/"boy" and which is the femme/"girl," even though many queer relationships do not break down along clear masculine/feminine or top/bottom lines. Another example of how we are imagined to be inferior copies of straightness is *implicit inversion*—the presumption that queer men are inherently more feminine in appearance, mannerisms, and behaviors than straight men, and queer women reciprocally more masculine than straight women.[13] While we can all think of examples of people who seem to fit such descriptions—as is true of any stereotype— multiple lines of evidence have shown that queer people are far more diverse in our personalities and behaviors than this, and that perceivers cannot accurately deduce a person's sexual orientation based solely on appearance.[14]

Furthermore, studies have shown that perceivers who are told that a man is gay will rate him as less masculine/more feminine than perceivers who are not given this information, thus illustrating that implicit inversion is a function of perceiver bias.[15] While the belief that queer people must be either "womanly" men or "manly" women directly contradicts the previous presumption (that same-sex couples must fall into "boy"/"girl" pairings), both these stereotypes make superficial sense as attempts to preserve Predator/Prey logic.

In addition to supposedly striving to imitate the "opposite sex," queer people are paradoxically portrayed as adhering to the Predator/Prey roles associated with our birth-assigned sex. For instance, gay male relationships are widely stereotyped as "hypersexual," in part because they seem to possess an excess of "sexual aggressors." But also, because gay male relationships seemingly lack a proper "sexual object," people often imagine gay male sex as being primarily about personal gratification rather than sexual attraction or interpersonal desire. Indeed, this likely informs the recurring stereotype of male homosexuality as "hedonistic" and "decadent."

Lesbian relationships pose a different problem. While two women being attracted to one another is not so far-fetched, as they are both deemed "sexual objects," people tend to view them as lacking a legitimate "sexual aggressor" to initiate sex. Indeed, in many people's minds, the lack of a penis renders lesbian sex either nonexistent or irrelevant.[16] This presumption—that two women cannot possibly have "real sex" (read: male-initiated and penis-centered) together—surely influences popular stereotypes of lesbian relationships as merely involving expressions of affection and commitment sans sex, as seen in the popular "lesbian bed death" and "U-Haul syndrome" memes. Perhaps the quintessential example of this presumption can be found in the "lesbian porn" created by and for straight men, wherein the supposed "lesbians" (usually played by straight-appearing female actors) engage in kissing and fondling ("foreplay") until a male actor enters the scene and says something like "Can I join you, ladies?," at which point the "real sex" begins.

The fact that many people don't consider woman-on-woman sex "real sex" can also be gleaned from how lesbians and asexual women face many of the same delusional fakeness tropes. Specifically, both groups are told that they will inevitably "turn straight" once they "meet the right man" or experience "one good fuck" (involving a penis), and both are sometimes threatened with or subjected to "corrective rape" (so named because perpetrators believe that the assault will either turn or scare the victim straight).[17]

In her book *The Invisible Orientation*, asexual activist Julie Sondra Decker lists (and refutes) common myths about why people are asexual, and it is striking how many of them are also used to explain (and undermine) homosexuality, despite these orientations being quite different. These "explanations" include having had bad past relationships or sexual experiences, having been sexually abused as a child, merely going through a phase, repressing sexual feelings, or being unattractive or insufficiently womanly/manly to attract a partner.[18] This suggests that both groups are viewed as similarly "lacking" the appropriate heterosexual desires.

Bisexuals, on the other hand, are not seen as lacking desires but rather as having an overabundance of them. Because bisexuals do not limit our dating pool to a single sex/gender, we tend to be viewed as impulsive and indiscriminate in our partner choices— hence the hypersexualized stereotypes of us being attracted to "anything that moves" and unable to commit to other people.[19] As we saw in the disparity between lesbian and gay stereotypes, there are notable gender differences in how bisexual women and men are viewed. While bisexual men are largely invisible and even presumed by some to not exist, bisexual women are often publicly sexualized and portrayed as "easy" or "asking for" sexual attention; the latter presumptions likely contribute to the fact that bisexual women experience rape at levels roughly three times higher than either our lesbian or heterosexual counterparts.[20]

Another gender difference that's been repeatedly observed is that perceivers who view bisexuality through a prism of delusional fakeness often presume that bisexual men are "really gay" and that bisexual women are "really heterosexual." The best explanation that I've seen to account for this discrepancy comes from an essay entitled "Phallocentrism and Bisexual Invisibility" by Miki R.[21] As the title suggests, the author makes the case that male- and penis-centric views of sex lead men to be labeled as "gay" as soon as they have a single sexual experience with another man, and forever afterward, regardless of any future sexual experiences with women.

In contrast, a bisexual woman's experiences with other women don't "count" in many people's eyes due to the lack of male initiators and penises, as discussed above for lesbians. But for these same reasons, her sexual experiences with men do "count"; thus, she's misconstrued as a heterosexual who merely "fools around" with other women.

In making this case, Miki R. uses the refrain "dick contaminates" to emphasize how our perceived (rather than actual) sexual orientations are largely determined by whether or not we've been "contaminated" by penises (and I would add, the sexual stigma they allegedly bestow). The essay also highlights the parallels that exist between sexual categories that are deemed "pure" (virgins, "real" men, "gold-star" lesbians) as a result of eschewing penises, and those that are considered "tainted" ("slut," "faggot") as a result of coming into contact with them.

A different gender disparity can be found in popular presumptions about transgender people. Despite the diversity of transgender life trajectories and experiences (some of us transition, while others do not; some identify as women or men, while others are nonbinary; some "pass" as cisgender, while others are visibly gender nonconforming), we tend to be perceived in one of two general ways depending upon the sex we were assigned at birth. People on the trans male/masculine spectrum (who were initially assigned female) are usually imagined to be "really lesbians" (even though many never have a lesbian history[22]) who are trying to escape homophobia and sexism, and perhaps even access the social advantages associated with men. In other words, despite being portrayed negatively for transgressing sex/gender roles, they are also conceptualized as striving for normalcy and social legitimacy. For those who harbor such presumptions, people like me on the trans female/feminine spectrum may seem perplexing given women's subordinate status in our culture. After all, why would anyone *want* or *choose* to be female or feminine? The way that people typically resolve this quandary is that they imagine that we must be seeking out the one type of "power" that women are envisioned to have in our society, namely, the ability to be sexual objects of heterosexual male desire.[23]

Interestingly, people didn't always think this way. Historian Joanne Meyerowitz chronicles the rise of the "eroticization" of trans women.[24] It began in the early 1960s—about a decade after the U.S. mainstream public became aware of trans people transitioning—when "tabloid newspapers and pulp publishers produced a stream of articles and cheap paperback books on [trans women] who had worked as female impersonators, strippers, or prostitutes." These articles and books were often accompanied by "photos that revealed breasts, legs, and buttocks."[25] Meyerowitz also notes that as the media's and public's interest in trans women became increasingly sexualized, their interest in trans men reciprocally declined.[26]

When I first began doing research on transgender media depictions spanning 1970–2005, I was struck by how many were of sex workers—invariably walk-on characters and usually the butt of jokes. These tropes contradicted other media messages about us at the time: that we were supposedly extremely rare, and that no one in their right mind would be attracted to us.[27] It is hard not to conclude that the cisgender media producers who created these characters were likely working from the now pervasive presumption that trans women transition because we wish to be sexualized.

In that analysis of trans media depictions, I described two recurring archetypes of trans female/feminine characters, which I labeled "deceiver" and "pathetic."[28] Independently, in an academic article about everyday people's reactions to trans women, Talia Bettcher described the same archetypes as "deceivers" and "pretenders."[29] These archetypes differ from one another primarily with regards to whether the trans woman in question "passes" as a cisgender woman. Those who do "pass" are imagined or portrayed as "really gay men" who transition in order to sexually attract (and thus "deceive") straight men. The "pathetic"/"pretender" archetype is applied to trans women who do not "pass" (and thus are incapable of "deceiving" anyone), and they are imagined or portrayed as "men" who transition in order to fulfill some kind of bizarre sexual fantasy.

In addition to dominating media depictions of trans people, these stereotypes pervade certain twentieth-century sexological theories about trans people, most notably psychologist Ray Blanchard's 1989 theory of "autogynephilia." While Blanchard's theory—which, like the media, dwelled on trans women's imagined "erotic anomalies" while completely ignoring trans men—has since been disproved, it still garners support among those who compulsively attribute sexual motives to trans women.[30]

I dissected these sexualized stereotypes of trans female/feminine people, and their various manifestations, throughout *Whipping Girl*. I did so in part because they are horribly sexist. After all, the notion that trans men transition because they *want to be men* but that trans women transition because we *want to be sexualized by men* is not only male-centered, but also implies that women as a whole have no worth beyond our ability to be sexualized. These messages—both about women generally and trans women specifically—were a constant obstacle that prevented me from accepting myself and making sense of my predicament in the years prior to my transition. And after my transition, they led to me being sexualized in ways that were often more hardcore than what I encountered when presumed to be a cisgender woman. Much of this hypersexualization that I experienced was driven by the "asking for it" trope: If people believe that you have become a woman because you want other people to sexualize you, then some will use that as an excuse to be exceedingly sexually explicit and forward, and any protests you raise will be dismissed via the usual "leading on" and "what did you expect" charges. But other times, the sexualization I faced as a trans woman was substantially unlike how straight women are typically sexualized, although it had parallels with other gender and sexual minorities' experiences with sexualization. I will explore these instances in the next section.

Sexual Deceivers and Queer "Contagiousness"

As we've just seen, the notion that transgender people (and particularly trans women) "sexually deceive" other people is built into popular stereotypes about us. Concerns about "sexual deception" can also be found in historical accounts of intersex people.[31] These tendencies seem to be rooted in *deceptive fakeness*, wherein people presume that LGBTQIA+ people must be actively trying to "pass" as straight in order to "deceive" other people. And perhaps the most sinister motive that people can attribute to this supposed "deception" is that we are "pretending to be something we're not" in order to "take sex" from other people. In other words, "sexual deceivers" are imagined to be a form of sexual predator. But unlike canonical "sexual aggressors" who wear their intentions on their sleeve (by being men who adhere to the traditional masculine Predator/Prey role), "sexual deceivers" purportedly "trick" or "trap" people by virtue of initially appearing "normal" or "safe"— we are proverbial wolves in sheep's clothing.

As with other mindsets, this "sexual deceiver" narrative exists in perceivers' minds rather than reflecting LGBTQIA+ people's intentions. Most people I've talked to about this have said that they are open about being trans or intersex with their sexual partners, but nevertheless have been accused of being "sexual deceivers" at one point or another, typically by perceivers who have just learned about this aspect of their person and immediately jumped to that conclusion. The fact that this is a mindset that does not accurately reflect reality can also be found in sociologists Kristen Schilt and Laurel Westbrook's analysis of over seven thousand U.S. news stories covering trans-related murders (overwhelmingly cis male perpetrators and trans female victims). They found that the "sexual deceiver" narrative dominated this news coverage, noting that "even in cases where there is evidence that the perpetrator knew the victim was transgender prior to the sexual act, many people involved in the case, including journalists and police officers, still use the deception frame."[32] The fact that we are imagined to be inherently "deceptive" and "predatory" also explains why Hollywood creators (who are overwhelmingly cisgender and largely trans-unaware) relentlessly churn out villains and killers who are ultimately "revealed" to be transgender, intersex, or sexually ambiguous or duplicitous in some way.[33]

There are at least two ways to make sense of people's reactions to imagined "sexual deceivers." The first stems from how seemingly "mismatched" sex/gender characteristics are interpreted via a Predator/Prey mindset. I refer to this interpretation as "the worst of both worlds." It's a play on the phrase "the best of both worlds," which is sometimes applied to transgender people (especially in the context of pornography) to euphemistically refer to the fact that some of us possess anatomical features associated with both women and men. In contrast, "the worst of both worlds" refers to how, when cast as "sexual deceivers," we become vulnerable to being simultaneously sexualized in ways associated with both men and women. Specifically, we are conceptualized as "predators" capable of violating and imparting sexual stigma upon others, but also as "prey" who attract and seduce others, often becoming violated ourselves in the process.[34]

This "worst of both worlds" phenomenon helps to explain why reactions to imagined "sexual deceivers" frequently involve inflicting sexual violence upon the individual. Perpetrators of such sexual violence likely view it as comeuppance or punishment for the imagined "deception" or gender transgression. But these acts are also enabled by the fact that the "deceiver" is understood to be female and/or feminine (at least to some extent) and thereby susceptible to such violations. In the case of trans male/masculine individuals, this sexual violence may be construed as "putting them back in their proper place" (as "women"); for trans female/feminine individuals, it's often rationalized as "if you want to be treated like a woman, then I'm going to treat you that way" (via sexual violation).

This use of sexual violence to punish gender transgression and supposed "deception" is evident in the high levels of sexual violence that trans people face.[35] Across numerous studies, the general consensus is that roughly 50 percent of trans people experience sexual violence, with many (in some studies, over half) reporting that they were targeted because they are transgender. Compared to cisgender experiences of sexual violence, transgender people's tend to start earlier in life (often in association with school bullying), are more likely to be perpetrated by a stranger, and are more likely to be accompanied by physical violence.

Two prominent examples of trans people being subjected to both sexual and physical violence can be found in the high-profile murders of trans man Brandon Teena in 1993, and trans woman Gwen Araujo in 2003.[36] Upon being discovered to be trans, both victims were sexually assaulted (Araujo had her genitals groped and exposed; Teena experienced the same and then was subjected to "corrective" rape) before being murdered. Factors that put trans people at increased risk of both sexual and physical violence include being visibly transgender, a person of color, poor, and/or a sex worker, with many victims falling into multiple (and sometimes all) of these categories.[37] In a study entitled "'Black Trans Bodies Are Under Attack': Gender Non-conforming Homicide Victims in the US, 1995–2014," Janae Teal found that Black trans people (and particularly trans women) not only make up the majority of victims (despite comprising a relatively small percentage of the trans community as a whole) but are also most likely to experience "overkill" (where "murder victims are destroyed or obliterated, rather than simply killed") and to be depicted as "deceivers" in subsequent media accounts.[38]

These incidents of physical and sexual violence obviously occur at the intersection of transphobia, racism, sexism, and other forms of marginalization, and thus don't fit neatly into any simplistic overarching narrative. But it seems clear from Teal's and other researchers' analyses that the "sexual deceiver" trope is invoked in many of them, either as a justification for said violence or in other people's post hoc interpretations.

While "the worst of both worlds" likely plays some role in contributing to these incidents, I believe that it offers an incomplete picture of "sexual deceiver" dynamics. After all, many cisgender people whose anatomies fall squarely into the "male" or "female" camps are also misconstrued as "sexual deceivers." Straight people often claim to feel "deceived" when a same-sex acquaintance whom they assumed was straight expresses romantic or sexual interest in them. In some cases, they may even respond with violence, much as they do with transgender "deceivers."[39] Furthermore, as with trans and intersex depictions, there is a long history of fictional bisexual, lesbian, and gay characters being depicted as "deceitful," "sexually driven" killers and villains.[40] Thus, it appears that any gender or sexual minority may be saddled with the "sexual deceiver" stereotype as a result of forgoing Predator/Prey roles and rules that others expect them to follow.

Given our earlier discussion of how lesbians tend to be viewed as incapable of initiating "real sex" due to a "lack of penis," it's worth considering the seemingly contradictory stereotype that they may nevertheless be "sexual deceivers" and thus "predators." Fears that lesbians sexually "prey" on women and children were pervasive throughout the twentieth century.[41] Writing in 1983, feminist Andrea Dworkin articulated how conservative women of the time often stereotyped lesbians as "rapists, certified committers of sexual assault against women and girls. . . . To them, the lesbian was inherently monstrous, experienced almost as a demonic sexual force hovering closer and closer."[42] More recently, sociologist Jane Ward wrote about how lesbians often face accusations of being a "sexual threat," including "being told to stay away from the children in one's extended family; keeping your distance in locker rooms and bathrooms and other places where straight women presume the absence of same-sex desire and panic when they realize it could present."[43]

While concerns about lesbians "sexually preying" on women and children appear inconsistent with the standard Predator/Prey mindset, there is another way to conceptualize them. Essentially, the "sexual deceiver" narrative establishes a secondary Predator/Prey dichotomy in which straight people imagine themselves to be potential "prey," and envision queer people as "predators" who (via deception) attempt to "take sex" from them. And just as men (and their penises) are imagined to impart stigma upon those whom they come into sexual contact with, queer individuals are similarly presumed to impart queer stigma upon those whom we sexually interact with. In accordance with this, if a queer person expresses sexual interest in a straight individual (or vice versa), the latter may feel as though they've been "dirtied" or "soiled" by the interaction.

There's a scene in the film *Ace Ventura: Pet Detective* that seems to visually symbolize this: When the protagonist realizes that a woman he kissed in an earlier scene is trans, he engages in what's intended to be a comical series of cleansing rituals—using an entire tube of toothpaste to brush his mouth out, burning the clothes he wore, and taking a shower while crying—as if he were trying to purge all the queer "contamination" away.[44]

This "queer stigma" model helps to explain two recurring reactions that are not adequately addressed by the "worst of both worlds." First, it explains why some straight people fear that they might be "turned queer" by such interactions, even if no actual sex or intimacy takes place. On an intellectual level, most of us understand that an individual's gender identity and sexual orientation will not magically change if a queer person unexpectedly propositions or interacts with them. (If this *were* true, there would inevitably be queer rogues running around propositioning people willy-nilly in an attempt to turn them all queer.) Yet, on a gut level, many straight people do react to these incidents as though their own gender and sexuality have been "brought into question" or "compromised." I'd argue that this is because people imagine that queer stigma is capable of "contaminating" others. Indeed, there is a long history of people presuming that queerness must be "contagious"—we saw an example of this last chapter in sexologists' claims that people can be "turned into inverts" via interactions with other "degenerates."[45]

A second recurring reaction (which we've already seen with regards to lesbians) is that queer people are often imagined to "prey" not only on straight adults but also on children. Research has demonstrated that queer people are no more likely to commit acts of child sexual abuse than straight people.[46] Thus, these "preying on children" claims are nothing more than a defamatory stereotype, one that has been weaponized against other marginalized groups as well. Historian Warren Blumenfeld writes at length about the parallels between how LGBTQIA+ and Jewish people have been depicted by the straight Christian majority, including how both groups have been accused "of acting as dangerous predators concentrated on ensnaring, torturing, and devouring primarily women and children of the dominant group."[47]

Historian Gillian Frank's work highlights the overlapping rhetoric employed by white social conservatives against Black and LGBTQIA+ people in the United States during the 1960s and 1970s.[48] This includes unsubstantiated charges that desegregation would ultimately lead to "child molestation" and "black sexual violence against white women and children." Similarly, Anita Bryant's 1977 "Save Our Children" campaign charged that gay people were "pedophiles" and "child molesters" who were out to "recruit children."

While the "gay child molester" stereotype has subsided in recent years, it has not completely disappeared. Sociologist Amy Stone analyzed religious right campaigns against LGBTQIA+ people spanning several decades and uncovered a precipitous shift starting in the early 2000s, in which the main targets switched from gay men to trans women. The later campaigns typically depict trans women as "'men in dresses' who are a danger to women and girls in the bathroom and locker room."[49] This claim is made despite the fact that numerous empirical studies have shown that trans women and trans-inclusive restroom policies pose no such threat.[50]

Elsewhere, I have chronicled countless other attempts by anti-trans campaigners to conflate trans people with "sexual predation" and "child molestation," typically via mischaracterizing completely nonsexual things—such as attempts to raise awareness about trans people, nondiscrimination policies, interactions with transgender adults, and attempts to accommodate trans students—as either "grooming" or "sexualizing" children.[51]

Child sexual abuse is a serious problem, but statistics show that the perpetrators are almost always family members or other close acquaintances of the child.[52] Therefore, it makes no logical sense to dwell on the unlikely possibility that a member of a minority outgroup might molest your child—unless, of course, your primary aim is to whip up a "moral panic" against them. Indeed, calls to "protect the children" are a staple of moral panics: They churn up negative emotions (anxiety, fear, anger) against these outgroups, plus they create a powerful false dichotomy in which being "pro–gay rights" or "pro-integration" can be twisted into charges that you must be "against the children."

Another regular feature of these moral panics is that efforts to "protect the children" are never extended to children of the outgroup. Instead, the dominant group tends to *adultify* these children—treating them as if they are just as dangerous and threatening as adult members of the group. Examples of such adultification include how social conservatives have portrayed young trans girls as potential "sexual predators" who might "prey" on their female peers, and how white parent groups often argue or imply that Black girls' "excessive" sexualities will have a "corrupting" influence on white girls.[53] In other words, fears of contagiousness seem to be playing a role here. These child protectionist stances serve as thinly veiled rationales for secluding supposedly "pure" and "innocent" dominant children from the stigmatized outgroup. Thus, purveyors of moral panic are hypocrites twice over: They claim to be concerned about "the children," when in actuality they only care about a subset of them. And while they raise fears about children being inappropriately "sexualized," *they* are the ones who are adultifying marginalized children and projecting sexual meanings and motives onto them.

Since LGBTQIA+ people differ from the norm with regards to our sex, gender, and/or sexuality, our stigma is often viewed as inherently sexual in nature. Hence the ease with which social conservatives reappropriate language intended to describe actual sexual violence and deploy it against us, even in entirely nonsexual contexts. That said, I don't think that this is a queer-specific phenomenon. Since many people unconsciously conceptualize sex itself in terms of imagined transfers of stigma from one person to another, it's not that much of a stretch for perceivers to read sexual motives and meanings into nonsexual interactions with other stigmatized groups. This is especially the case for perceivers who are already apprehensive about sex and sexuality to begin with.

Perhaps this is why white segregationists were so quick to connect the issue of school integration to seemingly unrelated fears about "child molestation" and "miscegenation" (as Gillian Frank recounts). Of course, some agents of moral panic know exactly what they're doing: They have a clear racist (or homophobic, or transphobic, etc.) agenda, and they purposely make baseless claims about "sexual predation" in order to smear that group. But the success of these campaigns—the reason why they resonate with the masses—likely stems from our tendency to unconsciously view stigma as both contagious and deeply intertwined with sexual violation.

Sexualization-Centric Approaches to Queer Activism

In response to the preceding section, some might suggest that things are nevertheless slowly getting better, and that trans people will eventually transcend these awful "deceiver" and "predator" stereotypes, just as lesbian and gay people largely have. But I don't believe it's that simple. The sharp increase in acceptance of same-sex relationships here in the United States may not be replicable for other gender and sexual minorities for two main reasons: *respectability politics* and *contagiousness politics*.

"Respectability politics" refers to attempts by marginalized groups to garner acceptance by convincing the dominant majority that they too are "normal" and therefore worthy of respect. We saw this happen with the mainstream gay rights movement over the last half century, as activists and organizations worked to shift the public discourse away from the "disreputable" topic of sexuality, and toward more "respectable" issues, such as marriage, adoption, and military service. This respectability strategy is perhaps best captured in the popular slogan "We're just like you, except for our sexual orientation." Notably, this slogan does not call for straight people to accept queerness per se, nor does it claim that all queer people deserve to be treated with respect. Rather, it implies that there are "respectable" people and "disreputable" ones, and that the "we" in "we're just like you" deserve to be in the former category.

Of course, in a society where many people are deemed "disreputable" because of their race, class, disability, or other traits, these appeals to respectability failed many multiply marginalized queer people. Furthermore, queer subpopulations who were viewed as particularly "disreputable" at the time—such as bisexual and transgender people—were often explicitly excluded from the movement over concerns that we might "hold back" the progress of gay and lesbian people. In other words, respectability politics always leaves behind the most marginalized, as well as the most sexualized, segments of any minority group. For these reasons, many contemporary queer activists are opposed to recycling this strategy.

"Contagiousness politics" is a term of my own making, and it refers to attempts to placate the dominant majority's fears that they might become "infected" or "contaminated" by a particular marginalized group. For LGBTQIA+ people, such fears have typically centered on the assumption that straight people can be "turned queer" via interacting with us. Perhaps the most effective contagiousness-politics slogan of the gay rights movement was "we're born that way." There have been extensive debates about this slogan, with some queer people expressing concerns that "born that way" suggests that we must suffer from some kind of "birth defect." Others are concerned that the phrase implies that no one would willingly choose to be queer, and/or that it erases some individuals' experiences with shifts in identity or gender/sexual fluidity. While I agree that the slogan fails to capture many intricacies regarding how queer people come to be, I believe its effectiveness lies largely in its ability to allay straight people's fears of contagiousness. After all, if people are "born queer," then that means that straight people can't "catch" it from us.

There is another gay rights–era message that has received considerably less attention but seems to have served a similar purpose. Namely, lesbians and gay men would often assure straight people that they were not sexually interested in them. They would point out that gay men are attracted to other gay men, and lesbians to other lesbians, and they meet one another in queer-specific settings, such as gay bars or m4m/f4f dating sites. These messages seemed designed to convince straight people that they need not "panic" about being "seduced" by a queer person.

While the notion that queer and straight people inhabit entirely separate dating pools may hold true for exclusively lesbian and gay people, it doesn't necessarily apply to other gender and sexual minorities. Bisexuals are attracted to people across multiple genders, trans and intersex people vary in our sexual orientations, and so on. In fact, this "separate dating pools" message insinuates that it *would* be a bad thing if a queer person were to take an interest in a straight person, or vice versa. Such flawed messaging helped to create the apparent paradox that we now find ourselves in, where the straight majority openly accepts people who are in same-sex relationships, while simultaneously harboring fears of "sexual deception" and being "contaminated" by queerness themselves.

I am not suggesting that the progress that has been made regarding same-sex marriage or issues such as adoption or military service is unimportant. But it's crucial that we recognize that these matters are downstream effects of prejudice. And the primary source of this anti-LGBTQIA+ prejudice is the fact that many people view us as "fakes" and "deceivers" who breach the roles and rules of Predator/Prey. This is what leads people to sexualize us. And that sexualization—the fact that we are reduced to the status of "sexual deviants"—is the reason why we have been historically ostracized and demonized.

Mainstream gay rights activism has largely sidestepped this central issue of sexualization. Its respectability politics stance requires us to hide or play down our queer sexualities if we wish to be accepted, not unlike how women are expected to hide or play down our sexualities if we wish to be seen as "respectable." Throughout the media, straight sexual desires and encounters are everywhere, whereas the few positive queer characters and couples that exist are almost always depicted as chaste or platonic, so as not to offend straight sensibilities. And while mainstream gay rights activism did alleviate some of straight people's concerns about being "turned queer" via gay teachers, coworkers, or neighbors, it flat-out failed to challenge their fears that they might become "corrupted" by queerness if they find us sexually attractive or have intimate interactions with us.

If we truly wish to eliminate anti-LGBTQIA+ prejudice, then our activism must confront sexualization head-on. Rather than attempting to appease the mainstream by keeping our sexual desires, relationships, and bodies out of sight and out of mind, we should instead challenge their tendency to relentlessly reduce us to these attributes. But this isn't merely an "us versus them" endeavor. Intracommunity sexualization is also quite pervasive, whether it be the gay men who deride women as "fish," the trans-exclusionary lesbians who wield the "sexual predator" trope against trans women, the self-identified "true transsexuals" who demean their nonbinary and nonheterosexual counterparts as "fakes" or "perverts," or the people across the LGBTQIA+ spectrum who dismiss asexual and bisexual individuals as merely "sexually confused." Not to mention the countless instances in which LGBTQIA+ individuals sexualize one another because of their race, class, ability, or other factors. Sexualization cuts across all demographics. While it mostly flows down social hierarchies—men tend to sexualize women, white people tend to sexualize people of color, straight people tend to sexualize queer people, etc.—it is also something that marginalized people routinely do to one another. And its constant presence hinders all of our social justice movements.

Reconceptualizing LGBTQIA+ activism as a movement to end sexualization has numerous advantages. For starters, if we are successful, then we will no longer be saddled with spurious accusations that we are "sexual deceivers," "deviants," and "predators"—charges that have long been used to justify our exclusion from society. And since our movement's focus would be on sexualization rather than on any specific identity, there would be far less identity-policing and infighting among various LGBTQIA+ subgroups. Furthermore, sexual minorities that are not explicitly named in the LGBTQIA+ acronym but that significantly overlap with our communities—such as people who are sex workers, polyamorous, or HIV-positive (to name a few)—would not be abandoned for being "too disreputable" this time around. The same holds true for other multiply marginalized queer people. In fact, an LGBTQIA+ movement that challenged *all forms* of sexualization would actually benefit all of its constituents and could facilitate coalitions across multiple social justice movements.

To be clear, I am not suggesting that sexualization is the only social force that we need to challenge. While sexualization is certainly a component of sexism, racism, classism, ableism, and so on, there are other facets to these forms of marginalization that need to be addressed directly and intersectionally. But working to eradicate sexualization has the potential to positively impact not just LGBTQIA+ people, but women and other marginalized groups as well.

9 YOU MAKE ME SICK

Discourses on sexual attraction are often centered on ideal-ized body types: certain masculine physiques and feminine figures that are routinely glorified in our culture. While many people cer-tainly find such individuals attractive, framing the matter in this way leads to universalizing narratives. For instance, some will as-sert that human beings must have been biologically programmed to find these particular traits attractive—this ignores the fact that idealized body types often change over time, and vary from cul-ture to culture.[1] Others will proclaim that everyone should strive to achieve these body types if we wish to attract other people. But this overlooks the fact that human beings find a wide variety of traits attractive.

Take my freckles, for instance. Back when I was younger, they were one of my more prominent features. It was not uncommon for my sexual partners to tell me how much they liked my freck-les—they found them "cute" or "sexy." But I have also had partners who never even mentioned them. In the latter cases, if I brought up the subject of my freckles, they would often say things like "They're fine" or "They're a part of who you are." In other words, these partners were more attracted to other aspects of my person, and had a relatively neutral attitude toward my freckles.

This variation holds true for most human traits: Some people may be enamored with my smile, my hazel eyes, my tomboyish nature, my nerdy sense of humor, my activism, my interest in science, or some combination thereof, while other people may not find any of these qualities attractive. In other words, rather than dwelling on supposedly "universally attractive" attributes, it is more useful to recognize that most human traits are considered to be *legitimate objects of desire*—that is, we accept the fact that some people (but not all) will find those traits attractive.

But not every trait is viewed as legitimate in this way. There remains a subset of traits that are deemed *illegitimate objects of desire*, in that it is widely presumed that *nobody* finds such characteristics attractive. And if an individual does seemingly exhibit attraction toward one of these illegitimate traits, most people will presume that there must be something wrong with them. So while it is perfectly okay for people to be attracted to my freckles, being attracted to the fact that I am transgender is largely considered to be beyond the pale. In fact, regardless of how many other positive traits I may have, to some, my transgender identity and body "spoil" my entire person, rendering me "undesirable" through and through.

While I will be using attraction to transgender people as my primary example throughout much of this chapter, there are other examples of this phenomenon. Previous chapters have touched on the societal consternation that has long surrounded interracial relationships, with white people who express attraction toward people of color having been labeled "degenerates" or other epithets. While this is less true nowadays, problematic attitudes regarding attraction to people of color still persist, as I will address toward the end of this chapter. Other examples of supposedly illegitimate objects of desire include people who are fat and people with disabilities; those dynamics (as chronicled by writers such as Hanne Blank, Kate Harding, Eli Clare, and Alison Kafer) bear striking parallels to how attraction to trans people is often perceived.[2] Notably, even if you are *not* attracted to a person's disability, fatness, ethnicity, or transness per se, simply being visibly partnered with such an individual may lead others to presume that "there must be something wrong with you." And no matter how much you are drawn to my freckles, or appreciate me as a whole person, many onlookers will jump to the conclusion that you must "have a thing" for transgender people.

I have written about these presumptions at length elsewhere, and I've come to refer to them as the Fetish mindset.[3] The name stems from the fact that laypeople tend to label attraction to unusual or illegitimate objects of desire as "fetishes." In psychiatric discourses, these expressions of sexual desire have historically been categorized and pathologized as "paraphilias." So if you just so happen to find me attractive, some psychologist or wannabe scientist out there may describe or diagnose you as having "gynandromorphophilia." This unwieldy term somehow manages to be one syllable longer than its referent: attraction to trans women.[4] Paraphilias have also been coined to describe attraction to people with certain disabilities, elderly people, and so forth.[5] In contrast, attraction to my freckles escapes analogous pathologizing terminology.

Admittedly, lay usage of the word "fetish" can sometimes be broader, and less pathologizing, than this. For instance, I can imagine someone who is attracted to freckles describing themself as having a "freckle fetish." I have also heard people describe themselves as having a "smart-girl fetish" or a "nose-ring fetish," not to imply that these were "disorders," but to convey that such people were their "type." But even when deployed in more light-hearted ways, the word "fetish" is invariably used to describe forms of attraction that are considered non-normative to some degree. After all, nobody ever describes themself as having a "supermodel fetish" or "rich-guy fetish," as such people are assumed to be universally appealing in our culture.

More to the point, while there is considerable hand-wringing over transgender, fat, and disability "fetishes," nobody ever describes themself as having a cisgender, thin, or able-bodied "fetish," even in cases when they date exclusively within those groups. To emphasize this asymmetry: Based on conversations with my past sexual partners, I'm pretty sure that every single one of them was also attracted to, and had relationships with, cisgender people. Yet they are the ones who are susceptible to being described as having a "transgender fetish" or "gynandromorphophilia," whereas people who purposely limit their dating pools *exclusively* to cisgender people remain completely unmarked and unlabeled.

Interestingly, the word "fetish" is derived from the Portuguese word for "artificial." This should raise some eyebrows given the previous chapter's discussion of the term "queer" being synonymous with "phony" and "counterfeit." In both cases, these phenomena are interpreted as "fake" because they fail to adhere to the Predator/Prey script and to other beliefs about who is considered "normal" and thus "worthy" of being desired. And as with lay presumptions about queerness, the Fetish mindset sexualizes all parties involved. The person who is attracted to "illegitimate objects of desire" is reduced to the status of a "fetishist," to the exclusion of other characteristics. This exclusion of other characteristics helps to explain why onlookers are so quick to assume that "fetishists" must be obsessed with, and singularly focused on, their "fetish." In reality, such individuals typically have numerous other interests, both sexual and otherwise. As with other groups who are framed as "sexual deviants," "fetishists" are routinely depicted as literal predators, as evidenced by the pejorative descriptor "chaser" that is often applied to them ("trans chaser," "chubby chaser"). In contrast, individuals who obsessively or aggressively pursue cisgender and thin people are never described as "chasers."

While the person who is attracted to me is reduced to the status of a "fetishist," as the supposed illegitimate object of desire, I am reduced to the status of a "fetish object," to the exclusion of other characteristics. This exclusion of other characteristics helps to explain why onlookers assume that my partners must be primarily attracted to the fact that I am transgender, rather than to my freckles or many other traits. Thus, the Fetish mindset constitutes yet another way in which my transgender body, identity, and experiences are sexualized by others. Furthermore, because people tend to view me as an illegitimate object of desire, they may presume that I must be "desperate" for sexual attention. This "desperate" trope is a common justification for sexual harassment and assault targeting people who are fat, disabled, or basically anybody who is (mis)construed as unattractive or "ugly" in some way.[6]

In other words, the Fetish mindset undermines us in two potential ways. First, it *desexualizes* us by creating the impression that we are unlovable and undesirable. But on the flip side of the same coin, it occasionally *hypersexualizes* us by portraying us as "objects" of other people's "fetishes," and insisting that this is the only way that we can be sexually appreciated.

The Fetish Mindset and Stigma

As with all of the previous mindsets I've described throughout this book, I do not believe the Fetish mindset accurately depicts the reality of the situation (although it does capture popular preconceptions). People who are labeled "fetishists" or "fetish objects" as a result of this mindset sometimes propose alternative views of these dynamics, although they often exist in conflict with one another. I believe that these differing perspectives can be reconciled once we recognize that stigma is what's driving these reactions. As we've discussed, a hallmark of stigmas is that some perceived flaw (such as being transgender, fat, or disabled) seems to "spoil" one's entire person. This explains why there aren't enough freckles in the world to redeem me once people find out that I'm transgender.

It's also worth noting that if two trans people, or two fat people, or two people with disabilities partner with one another, onlookers typically do *not* interpret that as a "fetish." Rather, most people will likely presume that these individuals are simply "sticking with their own kind" or (more crassly) are "unable to do any better." Regardless of the attribution, it seems odd that people are inclined to view attraction to trans people as "sick" or "perverted" when it occurs in a cisgender person, but as fairly mundane when it occurs in a transgender person—talk about sexual double standards! Here's my interpretation of this disparity: When a cisgender person partners with me, onlookers will unconsciously view them as being "contaminated" by trans-related stigma, whereas no apparent "contamination" takes place with my transgender partners, as they are already considered "spoiled" by that same stigma. Thus, the Fetish mindset serves to name this imagined contamination event: Upon expressing sexual interest in me (the supposed "fetish object"), a previously untainted and unmarked individual suddenly *has* a "fetish" and *becomes* a "fetishist."

Since stigmas are simply social beliefs that not everybody holds, this can create considerable diversity in how the people directly impacted by the Fetish mindset may conceptualize themselves and others. For example, if I personally buy into anti-trans stigma, then I will likely view my transness as a wholly negative trait that makes me undesirable in the eyes of others. Thus, I may hold out hope that I'll eventually meet someone who can "look past" my transness and love "the rest of me." If I then meet someone who is attracted to me *because* I'm transgender, I might worry that "there must be something wrong with them" and come to view them as a "fetishist."

Alternatively, if I have completely transcended anti-trans stigma, I may come to view my transness as akin to my freckles—just another trait that some people may find attractive but others will not. In this case, I would reject the Fetish mindset. This does *not* mean that I would automatically welcome all manifestations of said attraction, as I might find some expressions objectifying or sexually harassing. Rather, by rejecting the Fetish mindset, I mean that I would not view attraction to my transness as "sick" or "perverted" in and of itself.

The two scenarios I just laid out may give the false impression that stigma acts in a binary manner, being either fully present or completely absent. However, in reality, there are gradations of stigma that are important to understand if we want to fully make sense of attraction to non-normative traits and people's various reactions to them.

Destigmatization, Contagion, and Disgust

While there is a large body of research on stigma, the processes by which it may decrease or completely disappear over time have been less well theorized.[7] What follows is my own synthesis of destigmatization, drawing from research in related fields and my own experiences as a trans activist.

In a previous essay, I mapped out several different "stages of acceptance" that highlight the different ways in which marginalized groups are often viewed, and which are associated with varying levels of stigma.[8] On one end of this spectrum are groups who are viewed as *fully stigmatized*. Such groups possess some trait that is not only marked but viewed extremely negatively, so much so that it "spoils" their entire person, turning them into abominations or pariahs. On the other end of the spectrum are groups who are deemed *fully accepted*. These are typically dominant or majority groups, and they are considered unmarked with regards to the trait in question.

Through activism and shifting popular opinions, a fully stigmatized group may reach the first stage of acceptance: *toleration*. This involves a reassessment of the stigmatized trait, such that instead of being seen as completely damning, it is viewed more as a "defect," "flaw," or "unfortunate fate." While tolerated groups are often looked down upon and pitied for these reasons, they are mostly seen as human beings rather than monsters. They are also allowed to participate in society to some degree, provided that they don't make too many waves.

A group that is already tolerated may strive to reach the second stage of acceptance: *legitimization*. Rather than being viewed as a "defect," the trait is now seen as simply part of human diversity and just as valid as its unmarked counterparts. It is at this stage that calls for "equal rights" will begin to be taken seriously. While much of the associated stigma has dissipated by this point, the trait is still marked in most people's eyes and thus may garner disproportionate attention, remarks, questions, and scrutiny.

The third stage of acceptance is reached upon acknowledgment that biases against the trait may be occurring in an unconscious or systemic manner. This is often accompanied by increased recognition of these more subtle double standards, and efforts to transcend or dismantle them.

To be clear, the stages I have just outlined are by no means discrete: Over the course of my day, I may come across people who view trans people as monsters (fully stigmatized), merely defective (and thus tolerated), just as valid as anyone else (legitimate), and so forth. But I do believe these stages roughly capture the range of attitudes expressed toward marginalized groups.

Since first articulating these stages, I've become increasingly convinced that a major factor driving these differences is the degree of contagiousness that the stigma is imagined to possess. Fully stigmatized groups are viewed as highly contaminating, as even a brief encounter or loose association with them can lead one to be "tainted" by their stigma. This is why such groups are often vehemently ostracized. In contrast, when a group is tolerated, their perceived flaw is no longer considered to be quite so infectious, so it is now okay to interact with them, or to have them as acquaintances, coworkers, or family members. However, low levels of contagiousness are still presumed to exist, and may surface if you are perceived to be "too intimate" with them—such as if many of your friends belong to that group, or if you have more than a cursory knowledge about their communities and perspectives, or (most pertinent to the Fetish mindset) if you are sexually interested in or involved with a member of the group. Finally, in the case of legitimized groups, the fact that their stigma has receded means that you can be intimate with them without much fear of being seen as "contaminated." That said, because the group is still marked in many people's eyes, those intimacies may nevertheless strike some as unusual or notable.

There is one last piece to this puzzle: Researchers have described the strong connections that exist between stigma, its imagined contagion, and the emotion of disgust.[9] While there are a number of more primal triggers of disgust (rancid foods, vomit, bodily excrement, signs of death or decay), this emotion is often evoked in a host of other social and moral contexts that are entirely learned, and individually and culturally variable. For instance, while I may be disgusted upon hearing that some people eat horse meat, you may find it disgusting that I am willing to eat beef, or perhaps any meat at all. While some people experience disgust upon contemplating foreigners or immigrants, I experience disgust upon learning that white nationalists are converging on my city for a political rally. And while I may take great pleasure in expressing my queer sexuality, a religious fundamentalist might recoil in disgust upon having had a single same-sex fantasy for fear that those "dirty," "sinful" thoughts might permanently "blemish" their soul.

While the physical objects and the social and moral acts that elicit disgust may vary from person to person, what often underlies them is some kind of fear of contamination or contagion. As psychologist Paul Rozin and colleagues demonstrate, this fear of contagion is not rooted in our contemporary understanding that germs may cause infections and disease but rather relies on pre-modern "magical thinking" that adheres to the following formula: 1) a *transfer of "essence"* occurs when two objects come into contact with one another; 2) *negativity dominance:* Bad qualities are more potent than, and inevitably trump, any positive qualities an object may have; 3) *dose-insensitivity:* Even extremely brief or minimal contact is sufficient to thoroughly spread the contagion; and 4) *permanence:* Once the contagion is contracted, its effects are irreversible.[10]

Throughout his writings, Rozin provides many examples that illustrate human beings' irrational yet pervasive beliefs about such imagined contagions. Here's one of his most persuasive examples: If a friend lent you a sweater, you might wear it. But if they mentioned that it once belonged to Adolf Hitler, you'd likely recoil from it, even if you were assured that it had been thoroughly washed. In this scenario, there is no rational fear of germs but merely a "gut feeling" that you might be indirectly "contaminated" by a person or ideology that you find repugnant.

These imagined contagions explain stigmas' ability to seemingly "spoil" an entire person and to "contaminate" others. The disgust that they evoke appears to play a formidable role in perpetuating prejudice against a wide variety of marginalized groups.[11] Furthermore, they provide an explanation for many facets of sexualization, such as the belief that a single sexual experience can permanently "spoil" a person, or the sense of disgust people sometimes feel when contemplating sexual acts that they find unusual or unsavory. Such stigma and disgust appear to be the animating force behind the Fetish mindset.

I can imagine some readers insisting that the disgust that they may personally experience upon contemplating attraction to, or sexual interactions with, supposed illegitimate objects of desire (such as myself) must be a "natural" response. Perhaps it is innate and instinctual? (It's not, as children don't develop disgust until around the age of five, and it requires enculturation.[12]) Or maybe since disgust is a "gut feeling," we should trust it over other forms of judgment or reasoning. (This argument has been thoroughly refuted from both ethical and legal standpoints.[13])

No, the reason why disgust feels "natural" to us is that it is a deeply visceral emotion that elicits physiological and behavioral responses.[14] And if disgust toward transgender people was actually "biologically programmed" into human beings, then *nobody* would find us attractive, and I wouldn't have had to write a chapter debunking the Fetish mindset in the first place!

For me, the most compelling reason why our disgust toward certain people, objects, and acts is not "natural" is that we are capable of unlearning it. Back when I was in graduate school, when I first began doing research on fruit flies, I was rather squeamish about handling their larvae—they are maggots, after all, a very common trigger of disgust. But over time, I got used to them, and they no longer bothered me. In fact, I'd often completely forget that they were widely seen as disgusting until someone visiting the lab would point out how grossed out they were by the sight of them. Friends of mine in medical fields have told me similar stories about how they lost their sense of disgust toward blood, other body fluids, and bodily injuries after working with them on a regular basis. And I can assure you that this ability to unlearn disgust very much applies to the sexual realm as well.

Speaking of Maggots . . .

A few years ago, I came across a research article whose title began with a provocative question: "What do two men kissing and a bucket of maggots have in common?"[15] In the study, heterosexual men were shown a series of photos while being monitored for a physiological marker of disgust. As expected, researchers found a strong response to images predicted to evoke disgust ("maggots, rotting food, and open wounds") but not to neutral items ("paperclips, rocks, and staplers") or images of heterosexual couples kissing. However, they did find a strong disgust response to images of two men kissing or engaged in other displays of affection. (These results are consistent with a slew of similar studies conducted by other research groups.[16]) The researchers were surprised to find that this disgust response occurred across all subjects, even those who (based on self-reports) expressed little to no conscious prejudice against gay men. This result did not surprise me, however, based on some of my own personal experiences with disgust.

My first "disgust epiphany" (for lack of a better word) took place back in my early twenties, shortly after I had moved to New York City to attend grad school. My girlfriend from college and I had just broken up after a year or so of navigating a long-distance relationship, so I was contemplating dating for the first time in a while. I was paging through the *Village Voice* personal ads when I stumbled upon an ad in the "alternative" or "miscellaneous" category. The person who placed it was seeking a crossdresser (a category I resembled at the time) for an ongoing relationship. During this period, I was very much in the closet, horribly ashamed of my transness, but also hopeful to find ways of safely exploring it. The possibility of being able to express that part of myself within the context of a relationship seemed amazing to me, so I called the voice mail associated with the ad and left my message.

It didn't occur to me until the following day that the gender of the person who placed the ad was not specified. I had naively assumed it was a woman at first, since that was all I had known relationship-wise up to that point. But once I realized that it might be a man, I was forced to consider whether or not that would still interest me. While I had had sexual fantasies involving men before, they were more like reverse-heterosexual fantasies with me in the female role, and with the man not really specified. But this was very different. This was me, in real life—as someone who was navigating my way through the world as male at the time—contemplating whether I would be open to being romantically and sexually intimate with a man. As I explored the idea, it was as if floodgates had opened within me, as all sorts of thoughts and feelings rushed to the surface (as often happens with epiphanies). Among these feelings was clear excitement about the prospect of such a relationship, along with the realization that I had been suppressing a latent attraction toward men. But along with that excitement came a palpable queasiness—in a word, disgust—as I imagined myself (the real me, not a fantasy version of me) being sexual with a man. And frankly, this sense of disgust surprised me just as much as the attraction to men part, as I did not consider myself to be one bit homophobic. I had gay friends, after all!

Here's how I've come to make sense of this experience, as well as the gay-kissing/maggots study that I opened this section with:

Unbeknownst to me, I must have been in the aforementioned "toleration" stage with regards to same-sex desire. While I no longer bought into the "fully stigmatized" view that I had been socialized to believe, I still harbored sentiments that same-sex attraction and relationships were less valid or natural than heterosexual ones. Because this anti-queer stigma that I had unconsciously bought into remained at a relatively low level (as is typical of the toleration stage), it did not interfere with me associating with people whom I knew to be queer, but it did trigger disgust in me as soon as I got "too close" to it—specifically, once I began contemplating being in a "same-sex" relationship myself. However, not unlike the disgust I once felt toward fruit-fly maggots, the queasiness I initially experienced gradually disappeared as I further explored these thoughts and possibilities. While I never received a response to that first personal ad, I would eventually go on to explore similar situations. And in the years that followed, some of the most romantic, intense, and arousing intimate experiences I've had have been with men. All without a trace of disgust.

I would come to have another "disgust epiphany" years later. It happened around the time of my transition upon seeing a short documentary featuring two trans women who were life partners. Normally, when watching trans-themed films, I would identify with the trans character, who would often be in a relationship with a cisgender character. But seeing this couple prompted me to consider being in a relationship with a trans person myself for the first time. And much to my chagrin, I found myself squicked by the idea. I had already done a ton of self-reflection up to that point—work that was vital for me to even contemplate transitioning—so I immediately recognized this reflexive sense of disgust as a vestige of internalized anti-trans stigma. Over time, I was gradually able to transcend it, and nowadays, I can readily see the beauty in other trans people.[17]

In the past, when I have raised this subject of sexual desire and unlearning disgust, I have occasionally encountered reluctance or even antagonism. Some people have mistakenly assumed that I'm making the case that we are all "polymorphously perverse," capable of finding sexual pleasure in anyone or anything if we simply set our mind to it. Some have expressed fear over how this argument might be wielded by anti-LGBTQIA+ forces (for instance, telling gay men that all they need to do is "get over their disgust of women"). Still others (especially those who are determined to depict trans women as "sexual predators") have claimed that I must be trying to strong-arm people into sleeping with me by threatening to denounce them as "transphobic" if they refuse to do so. I have neither said nor implied any of these things. So to be clear, nobody should ever have to have sex with someone if they do not want to. Period. Furthermore, as I've emphasized throughout this chapter, we should expect every person to have their own inexplicable set of sexual attractions and interests, and they should be free to pursue those desires, provided that they are respectful toward, and have the consent of, all parties involved.

But what I *am* trying to convey is this: The opposite of love is not hate, nor is it disgust. It's indifference. And if you are indifferent to my freckles, or my transness, or my nerdy sense of humor, that's totally fine. But if you do consider these or other traits to be disgusting—so much so that you think that "there must be something wrong" with people who *do* find them attractive—then you might want to reflect upon why that is. And hopefully, the stories I have shared in this section may be helpful in that regard.

Exotic Others and Derivatizers

Individuals who find trans people attractive often fall into one of two broad camps. The first camp has already come to question

many taken-for-granted aspects of gender and sexuality, such as
the Predator/Prey mindset and straight assumption. Not coincidentally, they also tend to have many trans people in their lives,
often via being active in queer communities themselves, and recognize us as varied in our self-understandings, experiences, and
perspectives. In other words, they view us as human beings and
consider our transness to be but one of many traits we possess.

The second camp, by and large, lacks this background. Because
they accept Predator/Prey and straight assumption as the norm,
their fascination with us is often centered on the gender and sexual taboos that we seem to transgress. And since they know few
(if any) trans people in real life, their conceptualization of us may
be derived primarily from trans-themed pornography. Such porn
tends to cater to one of two particular fantasies: a performance of
high femininity in someone who "is really" or "used to be" male,
or an individual who is physically female except for the presence
of a "fully functional" penis. In other words, people in the second
camp are likely to reduce us to our transness, which is intertwined
in their minds with these transgressive sexual fantasies. They may
even outright refer to trans people as their "fetish."

Earlier I discussed *enforced ignorance*: the taboo I experienced
when I was younger that discouraged me from learning about
women's and LGBTQIA+ people's perspectives, and that led me
to initially "mystify" those groups. Within the humanities, this
phenomenon is sometimes called *exoticization of the Other*. While
it is not intrinsically sexual in nature—we may exoticize minorities or different cultures for nonsexual reasons—the phenomenon
is especially insidious when it is tied to erotic desires. The sexual
dynamic it creates might be described as follows: *"Wow, you're really hot because you're completely unlike what I'm used to! But your
exoticness also scares me a bit (which is also hot!), so I'm afraid to get too
intimate or familiar with you. But I sure would love to fuck you!"*

I would never denounce someone for being attracted to the fact that I'm transgender. Still, there are few forms of sexualization more exasperating than being cast as somebody else's "exotic other." This would happen to me on occasion in the 2000s, back when I was younger (and frecklier) and performing several nights a week, both with my band and as a slam poet. I'd usually out myself in trans-themed songs and spoken-word pieces. Then, after my performance, I'd be approached by a man who, almost immediately upon introducing himself, would casually mention that he was into trans porn or frequented trans pickup bars. He might even describe some of his past sexual dalliances with trans women.

Unlike the street remarks I received when presumed to be a cis woman—in which men *expected* to get a rise out of me—these men seemed completely oblivious to the possibility that I might feel uncomfortable or offended by their engaging with me in such a sexually explicit manner. To them, I was not a "normal" woman to whom standard social scripts and etiquette applied. In their eyes, I was an "exotic other"—it was almost as if I had stepped right out of one of their porn videos.

From my vantage point, there were several disturbing aspects to these interactions. I have already alluded to the first: Because these men viewed trans women exclusively as sexual beings, they tended to be sexually aggressive in their interactions. In a word, these exchanges felt sexually harassing. And I often found it difficult to extricate myself from them without triggering the "leading on"/"asking for it" charges, given that these men interpreted my openness about being transgender as a signal that I was seeking out their sexual attention.

Second, they tended to have little to no understanding about actual trans women's lives and perspectives, which bear little resemblance to the "chicks with dicks" and "female impersonator" depictions that populate pornography. As a result, such men may be heavily invested in the idea that we are "the best of both worlds" or "really a man underneath it all"—conceptualizations that most trans women find personally invalidating. Because these men are looking for someone to fulfill the role of their imagined "trans dream girl," they tend not to see us as complex human beings. In fact, they may even view our distinguishing characteristics (such as my nerdy sense of humor, or passion for science and social justice) as a distraction that interferes with their preconceived fantasy.

Within trans communities, the men who engage in these sorts of behaviors are often dismissed as "chasers" and "fetishists." While I obviously share some of these concerns, I cannot endorse the use of these particular labels, as they are strongly associated with the presumption that we are illegitimate objects of desire and that "there must be something wrong" with people who are attracted to us. In my estimation, what's problematic about these men is not that they are attracted to us but that they *sexualize* us—they reduce us to our real or imagined sexual bodies and behaviors, to the exclusion of other characteristics.

If that critique seems a bit too generic (as there are many different ways in which people are sexualized), an alternative possibility may be found in the work of philosopher Ann Cahill. In her book *Overcoming Objectification*, Cahill points out how the concept of "objectification" doesn't quite capture why sexualization can be so invalidating. She makes the case that objectification relies heavily on the specious mind/body and subject/object dichotomies, in which the former categories (mind, subject) are viewed as superior and associated with men, while the latter (body, object) are viewed as inferior and associated with women. In reality, all of us (regardless of gender) are embodied subjects who may be the object of another person's desires. Thus, we shouldn't rely on the male-centric notion that being a "body" or an "object of desire" is inherently demeaning.

That's one part of Cahill's argument. The other part dovetails with points I made earlier, namely, that when men sexualize women, it's not that they imagine us as mere inanimate objects but rather that they *expect* us to act in certain ways, preferably in a manner that they find appeasing or arousing. This perfectly captures many of my interactions with these supposed "trans chasers": They weren't merely appraising me as a "sexual object"; rather, they *expected* me to act like the trans female/feminine characters that populated their fantasies. And they were visibly frustrated when I turned out to be the nerdy, tomboyish, feminist trans woman that I am.

To account for these sorts of expectations, Cahill proposes a new term, *derivatization*, and defines it as when we "portray, render, understand, or approach a being solely or primarily as the reflection, projection, or expression of another being's identity, desires, fears, etc."[18] While that may sound like a mouthful at first, the concept is fairly easy to understand if you simply imagine removing the word "object" from "objectification" and replacing it with the word "derivative" (meaning: derived from, or based on, something else). Thus, we are *derivatized* whenever somebody presumes that we must possess certain features and will behave in particular ways that are in accordance with *their own desires*. To derivatizers, we are mere manifestations of *their fantasies* rather than complex human beings with desires of our own. I think derivatization perfectly captures what happens when other people cast us as their "exotic others," and it's my preferred replacement term for the needlessly pathologizing concepts of "fetishization" and "chasing."

One might hope that as trans people garner more acceptance and visibility within society, many of these sexualized stereotypes will gradually fall by the wayside as people acquire a better understanding of the diversity of trans people and experiences. I know a number of individuals who first learned about trans women through pornographic depictions but who nowadays have more nuanced and realistic views of us, so such evolutions are certainly possible. Alternatively, as trans people increasingly progress from the toleration stage toward legitimization—where we will remain marked in most people's eyes, but there will no longer be stigma associated with partnering with us—perhaps even more people will come out of the woodwork and seek us out as "exotic others."

The likelihood that both these trajectories may occur in tandem is suggested by the experiences of people of color. While the stigma associated with interracial relationships has significantly decreased over the last half century, many people of color still experience some combination of sexual racism and "fetishization"/derivatization. In other words, some discount people of color as potential partners due to their ethnicity, while others specifically seek them out because of the stereotypes associated with their ethnicity.

In her 1992 essay, "Eating the Other," author and activist bell hooks wrote about the then growing trend of white men actively seeking out women of color for sex.[19] Rather than subverting racism, hooks argued that such practices were merely a form of cultural appropriation that upheld the status quo:

> Within commodity culture, ethnicity becomes spice, seasoning that can liven up the dull dish that is mainstream white culture. Cultural taboos around sexuality and desire are transgressed and made explicit as the media bombards folks with a message of difference no longer based on the white supremacist assumption that "blondes have more fun." The "real fun" is to be had by bringing to the surface all those "nasty" unconscious fantasies and longings about contact with the Other embedded in the secret (not so secret) deep structure of white supremacy.[20]

Similar dynamics have been reported within white-centric gay male dating scenes, where men of color often encounter sexual exclusion, or else find themselves pigeonholed into particular sexual roles (tops, bottoms) in accordance with previously discussed racial stereotypes (Black people being perceived as "masculine" and "aggressive," and Asian people as "feminine" and "submissive").[21]

One of the most lucid analyses of this subject that I've read (even if I do not fully agree with every point) is philosopher Robin Zheng's essay "Why Yellow Fever Isn't Flattering: A Case Against Racial Fetishes."[22] The article considers the phenomenon of white men who claim to be primarily or solely attracted to Asian women. Zheng first summarizes existing debates, most centered on the following questions: Is such attraction merely an aesthetic preference (akin to being attracted to a particular hair color) and thus okay? Or is it rooted in racial stereotypes (that Asian women are especially "passive" and "submissive") and therefore morally questionable? Zheng then shifts the framing away from these "But *why* are some men attracted to Asian women?" questions, and toward a more pertinent question: What impact does this and other racial "fetishes"/derivatizations have on the individuals targeted by them?

Some of the consequences Zheng describes—being *otherized* (singled out for the ways in which you are different from "normal people") and *depersonalized* (made to feel that you are readily replaceable by another person "of your kind")—resonated strongly with my own experiences in dealing with people who derivatize trans women. Zheng also points out how, even if said attraction was purely aesthetic in nature, it is nevertheless expressed in a milieu wherein Asian women routinely face racial stereotypes and discrimination. As a result, their interpretations of said attraction will likely be shaped by those social forces and past experiences.

I can imagine some readers thinking, "Earlier you implied that it was bad to view marginalized groups as undesirable, but now you're suggesting that it can also be bad to consider them particularly desirable—how can both be true?" Well, as I said before, being "desexualized" and "fetishized" are often flip sides of the same coin: The people who avoid trans women like the plague and those who find us especially alluring are often both operating from the same premise—that trans women are sexually taboo—the only difference being that the latter find that taboo "hot" while the former do not. (And frankly, I'd rather not be anyone's taboo.)

But the other source of confusion here stems from the be-lief—found in countless advertisements encouraging us to main-tain a youthful appearance, a fit and thin figure, etc.—that being deemed attractive is an uncomplicatedly and indisputably good thing. Sure, there are social advantages to being considered at-tractive, and most of us do want to be sexually appreciated, at least by some people, or in certain contexts. But as we've seen in past chapters, attraction is often accompanied by unwanted attention, especially for those of us who are cast as "objects" of other people's desires. Furthermore, what may appear on the sur-face to be bona fide attraction may instead be nothing more than derivatization. And frankly, there is nothing enjoyable or flatter-ing about having someone fancy you for reasons that do not mesh with, or may even contradict, your own desires and sense of self.

Paraphilias and Pseudoscientific Slut-Shaming

While Robin Zheng's essay really resonated with me, I feel that its applicability to other marginalized groups may be somewhat limited. It is easier to take a hard-line stance against "fetishists" when you have other options available to you—specifically, people who desire you but don't "fetishize"/derivatize you. In contrast, groups who are widely deemed illegitimate objects of desire don't always have that option, and may feel as though they need to find a way to make things work with a "chaser"/"admirer" if they wish to experience sexual intimacy at all.

As a bisexual trans woman, I feel lucky that I've been able to find partners in that "first camp" of predominantly queer people who are attracted to trans people sans derivatization. In contrast, many heterosexual trans women find that, of the relatively few straight men willing to partner with them, many identify as being specifically attracted to trans women. And while these men may start out with highly derivatized views, this may change over time as they learn more about trans women's experiences and perspectives. For all these reasons, I am uncomfortable with objecting to such attractions and relationships outright.

While Zheng rightly focuses on the social and political ramifications of "fetishes" for those targeted by them, others who raise objections lean hard into the idea that the sexual interests themselves are "sick" and "perverted." And that is a line I cannot cross, having been on the receiving end of analogous accusations myself. Now that I'm in my early fifties, I have largely aged out of the street remarks and harassment I regularly experienced as a younger woman. But I still face relentless sexualization these days, most of it occurring online, at the hands of both women and men who specifically target me because I am an outspoken transgender author and activist. Sometimes they generically call me a "pervert." Other times a "fetishist," based on their assumption that trans women are merely "men" who are "turned on" by wearing women's clothing. The more hardcore anti-trans campaigners will call me an "AGP"—shorthand for "autogynephilia," the disproved theory I mentioned in the previous chapter that presumes that trans women transition primarily to fulfill their "paraphilic" sexual fantasies.[23]

Frankly, the specific "paraphilia" that these online harassers cite doesn't really matter in the end, as all these terms serve the same purpose: to smear their targets as "sexual deviants." Much like the use of the slurs "slut" and "faggot," these are not intended to be accurate critiques of an individual's sexual history; they're simply meant to discredit them with sex-related stigma. The only difference is that accusing someone of having a specific "paraphilia" evokes the veneer of science; it sounds more like an impartial psychiatric assessment than a crude and potentially slanderous epithet. Given this, if we wish to truly end sexualization, then we must interrogate the very concept of "paraphilias" and how they are misused by psychologists and laypeople alike. I will focus on this and related matters in the next chapter.

10 FANTASIES AND HIERARCHIES

There is far more to human sexuality than mere attraction to other people and the physical act of sex.

To illustrate this, simply recall a past sexual fantasy or real-life experience you've had, one that you found particularly arousing. It probably took place in some kind of setting, right? Most likely a bedroom, but perhaps it occurred someplace atypical (outdoors? on a table? in an airplane?). There may have been some kind of overarching narrative (a romantic date? a fling while on vacation? an illicit affair? a role-playing scenario?). Certain inanimate objects may have been involved (a gift of flowers? candlelight and mood music? a vibrator or dildo? rope to tie one up to the bedpost?). Some of these inanimate objects may have been articles of clothing (a suit or uniform? a sexy dress and heels? lipstick? lingerie? leather? latex?). And it's likely that the "sex" part of the fantasy was more involved than straightforward intercourse. There may have been foreplay (kissing? whispering sweet nothings? fondling? biting? spanking?) and specific roles or positions (were you on top or bottom? was it "missionary position" or "doggie style" or other? was it oral sex? anal sex? mutual masturbation?). While all this was going on, some of your attention may have been focused on your lover (appreciating their body, doing things to or with them), while other attention may have been centered on your own embodiment (their appreciation of you, their doing things to your body, and experiencing the rush of sensations that come with that). By the way, who was this other person? (Your life partner? someone you have a crush on? a celebrity? a faceless stranger? multiple people?)

A cursory scan of romance novels, fan fiction, erotica, pornography, and accounts of people's actual sexual fantasies and experiences will uncover all of these elements in various combinations. Given this, one might expect all of these facets to be considered legitimate expressions of sexuality, but historically, this has not been the case. As we saw in the previous chapter with supposed "illegitimate objects of desire," sexual fantasies and experiences that include some of the aforementioned elements may be stigmatized and pathologized. I will begin this chapter by critically examining this tendency and showing how it needlessly sexualizes people who engage in certain solitary or consensual sexual acts. I will then flesh out a more accurate and useful framework for thinking through this variation in sexual desires.

Paraphilias, Consensuality, and Normalcy

Richard von Krafft-Ebing, one of the late-nineteenth-century founders of sexology, first conceptualized atypical expressions of sexuality as "Psychopathia Sexualis," which translates to "sexual psychopathy." In the early 1900s, Sigmund Freud would refer to such expressions as sexual "perversions." When the *Diagnostic and Statistical Manual of Mental Disorders* (*DSM*; a compendium of all the official psychiatric diagnoses) was first published in the 1950s, they were codified under the heading "Sexual Deviations." In later editions of the *DSM*, they were called "Paraphilias," which is the term that I will use here, as it's the one most commonly used by psychologists and sexologists today. "Paraphilia" has been described as a "confused concept," and critiques have been penned detailing its many contradictions, and arguing that most sexual expressions labeled as such do not meet the *DSM*'s own criteria for mental disorders.[1] Here, rather than reviewing that body of work, I will highlight just a few of the more pertinent points.

Let's begin by looking at which sexual desires get labeled as paraphilias. The last few revisions of the *DSM* have explicitly listed diagnoses for eight paraphilias: fetishism (arousal associated with inanimate objects or specific body parts), transvestic fetishism (arousal associated with crossdressing), sexual sadism and sexual masochism (more commonly called BDSM[2]), exhibitionism, voyeurism, frotteurism (nonconsensually touching or rubbing against someone), and pedophilia. The *DSM* also allows for the diagnosis of paraphilias that are "not otherwise specified"; the current *DSM* (*DSM-5*) "Paraphilic Disorders" section mentions "telephone scatologia (obscene phone calls), necrophilia (corpses), zoophilia (animals), coprophilia (feces), klismaphilia (enemas), or urophilia (urine)" as examples, but really any paraphilia can be cited as the basis for a diagnosis.[3] And there is no shortage of potential paraphilias to choose from. *Wikipedia*'s "List of paraphilias" page contains over one hundred entries for sexual interests that have been labeled as paraphilias in the research literature.[4] There, you will find a host of Greek-and-Latin-root-derived neologisms to describe people who have an erotic interest in hair (trichophilia), body piercings and tattoos (stigmatophilia), obscene words (narratophilia), being onstage or on camera (autagonistophilia), and body odors (olfactophilia), among many others.

Upon considering this list, a few things immediately stand out. First, it's a bizarre mishmash of sexual desires that, by and large, occur in a solitary or consensual manner, and nonconsensual acts that are rightfully considered crimes (frotteurism, pedophilia, and zoophilia). Even if you find crossdressing, BDSM, or enemas to be strange or gross or what have you, I think it should be obvious why lumping people who are aroused by such things together with people who commit nonconsensual crimes is pretty messed up. For this reason, throughout the rest of this chapter, I will consider only the solitary and consensual "paraphilias."

A second thing that jumps out upon perusing this list is how utterly disconnected many of these sexual interests are from one another. Some involve attraction to certain subgroups of people (as discussed in the previous chapter); some single out specific body parts (hair, feet) but not others (face, genitals); some involve having sex with something other than a live human being; others do not involve sex at all but merely the experience of arousal in a context that most people would find to be nonsexual. There are also pretty blatant double standards built into some of these supposed paraphilias. For instance, a woman who experiences arousal upon wearing a sexy dress for her partner is not considered paraphilic, whereas a man who experiences the same would be labeled as exhibiting "transvestic fetishism." Being turned on by the sight or texture of your wife wearing a lace or silk negligee is perfectly okay, but the same reaction to her donning a leather or latex outfit would likely be flagged as "fetishism." And if the intrusion of "nonliving objects" into the sexual realm is such a concern, then why aren't there paraphilia listings for being aroused upon receiving a dozen roses or getting it on to Barry White records?

The inescapable conclusion is that "paraphilia" is simply a fancy term for sexual desires that our culture deems "not normal" for one reason or another. In fact, John Money—the psychologist who popularized the concept of "paraphilia" back in the 1980s—tacitly acknowledged this when he simultaneously proposed its counterpart, "normophilia," to describe the "condition of being erotosexually in conformity with the standard as dictated by customary, religious, or legal authority."[5] Thus, "paraphilias" (along with "perversions," "sexual deviancy," and similar terms) are socially derived categories, not scientific ones. This explains why masturbation, oral and anal sex, and homosexuality—which Krafft-Ebing, Freud, and many twentieth-century researchers pathologized—are no longer considered to be "paraphilias" now that they've become more accepted by society.

Despite "paraphilia" clearly being a social invention, a few researchers hold to the belief that there must be some kind of underlying scientific basis for the concept. Take for instance psychologist Ray Blanchard, who coined the previously discussed terms "autogynephilia" and "gynandromorphophilia" (he has a penchant for inventing new "paraphilias," especially ones that sexualize trans women). In his capacity as chair of the committee that wrote the *DSM-5* "Paraphilic Disorders" section, he tried to unite the concept's disparate diagnoses under a brand-new definition: "Paraphilia denotes any intense and persistent sexual interest other than sexual interest in genital stimulation or preparatory fondling with phenotypically normal, physically mature, consenting human partners."[6] Yikes! By this strict definition, masturbation is arguably a "paraphilia," as is any non-fondling foreplay (dirty talk, giving hickeys, perhaps even kissing), as well as being aroused by erotica or pornography. In a subsequent interview, Blanchard insinuated that if he were to "start from scratch," he would be inclined to reclassify homosexuality as a paraphilia on the basis that it is a non-reproductive sexual activity.[7]

Researchers who are determined to defend the designation have insisted that "paraphilias" share other features that make

them fundamentally different from "normophilic" sexual interests. Perhaps the most common claim along these lines is that
"paraphilias" are very rare. Not only does this claim fail to justify
their pathologization (after all, stamp collecting and speaking Es-
peranto are quite rare, but they don't appear in the *DSM*), but
numerous studies of sexual fantasies have shown that many supposedly "paraphilic" sexual interests are actually quite common.[8]
Those studies also challenge the assertions that "paraphilias" are
male-specific or entirely distinct from "normophilic" interests (as
many people experience both). Another repeated claim is that they
are "persistent" or "chronic and lifelong," which not only applies
to many "normophilic" desires but has been shown to be false for
some supposedly "paraphilic" desires.[9] "Paraphilias" are often described as being especially "intense," but recent research suggests
that they aren't necessarily experienced any more intensely than
"normophilic" heterosexual desires.[10]

Increasingly, and especially in the *DSM-5*, emphasis has been
placed on the "distress" caused by "paraphilias." This sidesteps
the fact that most, if not all, of such distress stems not from the
sexual desire itself but from its societal stigmatization. And list-
ing these sexual desires in the *DSM* most certainly contributes to
this stigmatization. Furthermore, many straight people also experience distress related to their heterosexuality—in fact, distress
about heterosexual attraction, relationships, and sexual endeavors
is perhaps the most common lyrical theme in contemporary popular music!

In their 2005 article "Does Heterosexuality Belong in the
DSM?," clinical sexologists Charles Moser and Peggy Kleinplatz
make a convincing case that "heterosexuality meets the [DSM]
definitions of both a mental disorder and a paraphilia, at least as
well as the other listed paraphilias."[11] The intent of their argument was not to push for heterosexuality's inclusion in the *DSM*

but rather to promote the depathologization of BDSM and other consensual sexual interests. But I think their article also provides a teachable moment for straight, non-kinky folks to consider what the ramifications might be if *their* sexual interests were similarly pathologized. The mere fact that a solitary or consensual sexual interest is listed in the *DSM* or described as a "paraphilia" in the research literature has been wielded against sexual minorities in the courts, in healthcare settings, and in conservative political campaigns.[12] By this point in the book, it should be clear why calling people who behave consensually "perverts," "deviants," or "paraphilic" is not only sexualizing but contributes to sex-negativity more generally.

Thankfully, the fields of psychology and sexology have been gradually moving away from pathologizing solitary and consensual expressions of sexuality, and toward viewing them as a part of human variation.[13] Unfortunately, within society more generally, there is still a strong tendency to judge expressions of sexuality based on an imagined "normal" versus "perverted" distinction, and to sexualize those whose desires fall into the latter category. So, with the rest of this chapter, I will offer an alternative (and less pathologizing) way of thinking through these matters.

A Sexual Elements/Meanings Framework

Rather than rely on the confused concept of "paraphilia," I think it's far more useful to think of varied sexual interests in terms of *sexual fantasies*, for which there is many decades' worth of research. For most of us, our sexual fantasies run the gamut: We sometimes have fairly "normal" fantasies of having straightforward sex with someone we find attractive, while on other occasions we may have atypical or unconventional sexual fantasies of one form or another. The latter fantasies do not make us a particular type of person—an "atypicalphile" who suffers from "unconventional-philia"—any more than daydreaming about winning the lottery or eating a special meal makes us "lotteryphilic" or is a sign of "tastydinnerphilia."

Just as we might page through a cookbook or peruse the Food Network if we are hungry, we may seek out romance novels, erotica, or pornography if we are horny. If we especially like a particular food or sexual interest, we may specifically seek it out in the aforementioned media; other times, something we read or see there might spark a new interest or craving that we hadn't experienced before. In some cases, our food- and sex-related fantasies may compel us to seek out those experiences in real life. Sometimes such endeavors are mere experimentation, akin to those TV shows where the host seeks out "bizarre" foods simply for the sake of trying them. Other times, we may enjoy a particular sexual experience so much that we repeatedly seek it out, akin to that favorite dish we always order from a nearby restaurant. Still other times, our fantasies remain relegated to our imaginations, either because they are unattainable or because they are deemed socially unacceptable.

I am most certainly not the first person to draw an analogy between food and sex, as they share obvious parallels. Both evolved to serve a necessary survival function (sustenance and reproduction, respectively), but nowadays our preoccupations with them are largely centered on the pleasure we experience from them. While gustatory pleasure is clearly rooted in biology, one cannot predict an individual's favorite ethnic cuisine or pizza toppings by simply examining their taste buds or the DNA sequence of their taste and smell receptors. While food preferences are influenced by the culture we're immersed in, it is not uncommon for us to dislike foods we were socially encouraged to eat, or to appreciate ones we've never had before or were actively discouraged from consuming. Some differences in taste are shaped by individual experience: the special meal that your grandmother used to make, or the food you can no longer tolerate because of that one time you got sick. Some people appreciate intricate, unique, or novel foods, while others are more "meat and potatoes" type people.

Foods can also have symbolic meanings that go well beyond the nourishment they provide: a communion wafer, champagne and caviar, a birthday cake, or a family recipe that's been passed down for generations. Furthermore, the meanings that we associate with particular foods can change depending upon the context: Whipped cream implies wholesome celebration when it tops a slice of birthday cake, but means something else entirely when you're squirting it onto and licking it off your lover. A similar mix of forces—shared biology, individual biological variation, culture, personal experience, disposition, symbolic meanings, and likely other factors—are bound to influence our sexual interests in diverse ways as well.

Pleasure itself varies greatly in the human population. For reasons that elude me, some people immensely enjoy running marathons, gambling, knitting, meditating, doing crossword puzzles, bungee jumping, listening to techno music, and combing beaches with metal detectors. But this is absolutely fine, because they probably cannot fathom why I experience so much gratification from listening to old They Might Be Giants albums or penning pointed critiques of the concept of "paraphilia." (Even I have trouble fathoming the latter!)

I'm sure you can invent plausible biological or evolutionary hypotheses to account for these phenomena in a more general sense. (They release endogenous dopamine or endorphins! Problem-solving skills have been evolutionarily selected for!) But I highly doubt that you can sufficiently explain why any given person gravitates toward any specific hobby or endeavor while remaining uninterested in activities that others find enjoyable. This diversity and inexplicability are inherent to how pleasure works in human beings. And frankly, the expectation that our sexual desires should be some kind of exception to all this is nothing short of perverse (in the nonsexual sense of the word, of course).

In the previous chapter, I used the phrase "objects of desire" to refer to people and traits that individuals may find attractive. I began this chapter with a list of other *elements* (settings, narratives, inanimate objects, apparel, acts, roles, scenarios, positions, sensations, our own embodiment, etc.) that some onlookers may find extraneous because they are separate from the "object of desire" but may nevertheless supplement, facilitate, or evoke arousal in us. In other words, these elements are "turn-ons" for us, even though we are not attracted to them per se: If you masturbate to a Victoria's Secret catalog or fantasize about joining the "mile-high club," it does not mean that you literally want to fuck lingerie and airplanes, respectively. (I feel the need to make this distinction explicit because some researchers in the Blanchardian tradition have promoted theories that seem to conflate these elements with actual objects of desire.[14])

So why do these varied elements have sexual valence? Well, it's because they have *sexual meanings* associated with them. For instance, for many centuries now, giving someone flowers has signaled romantic or sexual interest in them. Of course, there is nothing inherently sexual about offering someone severed plants as a gift, just as the letters "L-O-V-E" or "S-E-X" arranged in that precise order have no inherent meaning. However, having been raised in our culture, most of us understand what these signifiers mean, and we may experience very real emotions, as well as sexual arousal, when they are conveyed to us.

Many of the sexual meanings that move us stem straight from the mindsets I've described in past chapters. For instance, romantic narratives that involve male chivalry or damsel-in-distress-type scenarios seem to eroticize the Opposites mindset's assumptions that men are "strong," "tough," and "independent," while women are "weak," "fragile," and "dependent." Similarly, the Predator/ Prey mindset may lead us to eroticize the idea that, during heterosexual sex, the man "takes" the woman or that she "surrenders" to him. And, as we saw in the previous chapter, the Unmarked/ Marked mindset may lead us to view an individual who is marked in our eyes as especially "exotic" or "mysterious," and this may fuel our desire for them.

Aspects of all these mindsets come together in a previously mentioned sexual element: lingerie. Typically, such items are made out of lace or other delicate fabrics, which seem to emphasize the idea that the woman who is wearing them is "fragile" and "vulnerable." Lingerie is generally considered to be a purely "ornamental" item of clothing, which plays into the idea that the woman who wears it is an "exotic object" for others to appreciate. And because these items are often sheer or skimpy, lingerie may seem to "invite" sexual attention or signal that the woman is "asking" to be "ravaged."

Because of all these associated sexual meanings, a lover may become even more aroused by the sight of their female partner wearing lingerie than they would if she was wearing something else or completely naked. Yet few, if any, would describe being sexually aroused by the sight of a woman wearing lingerie as "perverted," even though it clearly involves an inanimate object. Why is this? Well, it's because the sexual meanings commonly associated with "lingerie" and "woman" seemingly align with one another, so their pairing makes sense to us. In contrast, the sight of a man wearing lingerie may strike people as "perverted," not because the act itself is "unnatural" (as there is nothing natural about any human being wearing lingerie!) but because the sexual meanings seem all wrong: *He's not supposed to be the "sexual object,"* *or "ornamental," or "vulnerable"!* I purposely used lingerie in this example because we have already discussed how all clothing is artificial, and the social (and sometimes sexual) meanings we ascribe to such items are arbitrary. In other words, there is no reason, aside from convention, why the signifier "lingerie" couldn't instead mean "powerful" or "aggressive," at least in some people's minds. Similarly, since the meanings associated with the Opposites and Predator/Prey mindsets are also superficial and subjective, there is nothing stopping people from reimagining "man" as "vulnerable," "ornamental," or a "sexual object."

Once we recognize that all the previously discussed sexual elements may have real (if arbitrary) sexual meanings associated with them, then it's not too much of a stretch to accept that some people may feel arousal in response to imagining or experiencing these elements on their own, independent of an object of desire. Or that some people may project sexual meanings onto elements that most people do not perceive as sexual. Or that they may prefer seemingly "mismatched" sexual meanings, as in the man-wearing-lingerie example. In other words, the sexual elements/meanings framework I have just described provides a nonpathologizing explanation for both typical and atypical sexual fantasies and desires.

Eroticizing Hierarchies (to Varying Degrees)

Many studies of sexual fantasies have been conducted over the years; here I will mostly be drawing from recent studies by Christian Joyal and colleagues, and two book-length analyses: Justin Lehmiller's *Tell Me What You Want*, and Emily Dubberley's *Garden of Desires: The Evolution of Women's Sexual Fantasies.*[15] These studies all find considerable overlap between women's and men's fantasies—that is, they share many of the same elements. But one commonly reported gender difference is that men's fantasies tend to be more focused on the person they are attracted to, whereas women's fantasies are often centered more on being the object of other people's desires.[16] In fact, in some women's fantasies, the desiring person is often nondescript or even irrelevant; as Dubberley puts it, "For some women, the idea of being viewed as a sexual object—and possibly nothing more than that—can be arousing."[17]

Such trends seem to arise from the Predator/Prey mindset, with many men and women internalizing the "sexual aggressor" and "sexual object" roles, respectively. Those who are inclined to view sexual matters strictly in terms of innate biology might reflexively disagree with my assertion here, to which I'd respond, "What evolutionary purpose is served by women eroticizing themselves as the sexual object of a faceless person?" Furthermore, the idea that men and women are somehow "biologically programmed" to experience sexual arousal in these disparate ways is undermined by the many exceptions to these trends, as I will discuss shortly.

My own personal experiences are consistent with this Predator/ Prey-influences-our-fantasies hypothesis. Specifically, when I was younger and moving through the world as male, in my heterosexual relationships, very little of my erotic attention was centered on my being the object of my partner's desire. I mean, I certainly *appreciated* the fact that they were attracted to me, but I never really dwelled on the specifics. But since my transition, while I still experience sexual attraction toward my partners, the attention they place on my body—their desiring of me—has become far more sexually salient for me. And how could it not be? We live in a culture where drastically different sexual meanings are relentlessly projected onto female and male bodies. I might consciously understand that these meanings are socially derived rather than inherent to the bodies themselves, but I cannot entirely ignore these meanings. In fact, it would be unwise of me to do so, given that they shape how my partners and other perceivers are likely interpreting me.

Back when I was male-bodied, I had lovers touch and feel my chest, but that experience was phenomenologically different from what I experience now when a lover fondles my breasts. There are physical differences, to be sure, but there's also an intense visceral sense of a private boundary being crossed that wasn't there before, and real feelings of vulnerability that come with that.[18] These feelings aren't merely "in my mind"; they're in *most people's minds*, as we as a society attribute very different meanings to breasts versus chests. And having been on both sides of heterosexual intercourse, while they may both be pleasurable, they are not quite analogous. Once again, aside from the obvious physical differences, there are the ever-present connotations associated with "penetrating" versus "being penetrated" by someone. In an earlier chapter, I commented that penetration sex could theoretically be described in terms of the woman's vagina "consuming" the man's penis. I've actually tried this a couple of times—imagining the act that way as it was happening—but I found it really hard to do! It felt as if I was swimming against the current, with all the more standard sexual meanings continually rushing past me.

Of course, those standard sexual meanings may not apply to everybody. I'm sure there are some people who find "vaginas consuming penises" sexual fantasies quite compelling. And since these meanings aren't intrinsic to the elements themselves, there is always a possibility for change, for new associations to be made. For instance, as with all trans people who transition, it's not as if I simply woke up one morning with a "fully female" body with all new meanings attached to it. Just as the physical changes were gradual during my transition, so too were the changes in meaning that accompanied them. Sometimes these changes stemmed from my own reconceptualization of myself, other times from the new ways in which other people were reacting or relating to me. It was not a conscious or deliberate process on my part but rather an experiential and embodied one. In some of her writings, Talia Bettcher analyzes the various ways in which trans people sometimes "recode" our bodies as we reconcile our own internal understandings of ourselves, while navigating a binary world full of "opposite" gendered and sexual meanings.[19] Having experienced this myself firsthand, I've learned not to take such sexual meanings at face value, as they may differ significantly from person to person.

Returning to the aforementioned sexual fantasy studies, another gender difference that is sometimes reported is that men's sexual fantasies are more likely to involve dominance (being in control over others), whereas women's fantasies are more likely to involve submission (surrendering control to someone else).[20] This too could be interpreted as an obvious extension of Predator/Prey logic, in which men are supposed to make all the moves while women merely react or acquiesce, and where the connotations of "male conquest" and "female surrender" are often found in even the most mundane expressions of heterosexual sex. Submission fantasies can range from scenarios of being "overpowered" or "taken" by someone you actually fancy, to "rape" fantasies where nonconsensuality is built into the imagined scenario.[21] Dominance and submission fantasies may also include various elements that fall under the BDSM umbrella, such as bondage, discipline, and the giving or receiving of pain. They may also involve implicit or explicit humiliation, often invoking previously discussed forms of sex-related stigma, such as slut-shaming, feminizing slurs, or emphasizing that the submitting person is being "used." In other words, dominance and submission fantasies seem to *exaggerate* and *eroticize* the unequal power dynamics and sexual stigma associated with the standard Predator/Prey roles.

The existence of submission and forced-sex fantasies has raised concerns that the women who experience them are unquestioningly buying into rape culture or male-centric views of sexuality, but the reality is more complicated than that. For instance, nearly all women who experience these sorts of fantasies state that they would not want them to come true in real life and that they also experience more conventional and consensual fantasies; the biggest predictor of whether any given woman is likely to experience forced-sex fantasies is her openness to sexual experiences more generally.[22] Then there's the fact that many men also experience submission and forced-sex fantasies, while a significant number of women experience dominance fantasies.[23] Sometimes these Predator/Prey role reversals even extend into the realm of embodiment: In Lehmiller's study of over four thousand Americans, he reports that "about one-quarter of men and women had fantasized about cross-dressing, and nearly a third had fantasized about trading bodies with someone of the other sex."[24] In Dubberley's more qualitative study, she provides numerous examples of women's sexual fantasies of having a penis or outright being men in a variety of sexual scenarios.[25] (For context, transgender people comprise less than 1 percent of the U.S. population, so the overwhelming majority of individuals who report having these fantasies are cisgender.)

While the prevalence of the latter fantasies defies simplistic "biological sex differences" or "brainwashed by the patriarchy" explanations, they can be accounted for via my sexual elements/ meanings framework. Specifically, Predator/Prey imparts different sexual meanings upon male and female bodies and their associated "aggressor" and "object" roles. While some people strictly adhere to their assigned roles, others may experiment with rearranging these sexual elements in novel ways, especially within the relative safety of their own fantasies. If we recognize that sexual fantasies provide a source of escapism, rather than perfectly reflecting some kind of "deepest wish" or "core self," then it shouldn't be surprising that some people choose to inhabit different bodies, personalities, or roles that aren't typically available to them in real life, as is the case for many of Lehmiller's and Dubberley's subjects. From this perspective, it makes sense that someone who is usually expected to make all the moves might appreciate fantasies in which they are the passive or pursued party, just as someone who is expected to be passive and pursued might enjoy imagining themself as the sexual initiator for a change.

People often presume that "sexual object" and submission fantasies are inherently disempowering and degrading—I believe this misconception stems directly from Predator/Prey thinking, so I want to push back on it a bit. Some of my most fulfilling sexual experiences have been in relationships where there were no set roles: We both desired one another and enjoyed being each other's object of desire, simultaneously. Both these states of being can be beautiful and feel empowering. Predator/Prey artificially cleaves these two states from one another and privileges the desiring party over the one who is desired—the former is imagined as the sexual subject whose desires are being fulfilled, while the latter is deemed an "object" who lacks desires of their own. But we need not buy into these asymmetrical sexual meanings. We are all sexual subjects in our own right. And enjoying the experience of being sexually appreciated by somebody else does not negate that, nor does it nullify any other concurrent desires we may have. This is especially true when it comes to sexual fantasies, which exist solely for the benefit of the person who is imagining them, and within which it is possible to explore being desired by other people in contexts that might otherwise feel uncomfortable or unsafe were they to occur in real life.

As for submission fantasies, I believe that many of them can be understood in terms of stigma management. The Predator/Prey mindset stigmatizes pretty much everyone who doesn't strictly adhere to the canonical straight male "sexual aggressor" role—this includes women, queer people, men who have interests that are culturally coded as feminine, and people who are "marked by sex" in other ways. Those of us whose identities or sexualities fall into these categories often face a conundrum in that what we desire also has the potential to disgrace us in the eyes of others. There are at least three strategies for dealing with such situations. One is to outright reject these social meanings. As a bisexual trans woman who no longer subscribes to queerphobic and misogynistic stigma, I would argue that this is the most efficacious route in the long run, but it doesn't usually happen overnight. In my case, it took years of questioning and unlearning to overcome these forms of stigma.

Individuals who have not fully transcended Predator/Prey stigma may turn to two other strategies: *mitigating* or *merging* stigma. One way to mitigate sexual stigma is through submission fantasies. The logic is simple: If an imagined party forces you to take part in a stigmatizing yet desired act, it can help lessen the guilt associated with it. In her study, Dubberley recounts the stories of women who turn to submission fantasies in order to escape the shame they were taught to feel for having sexual desires;[26] many LGBTQIA+ people I've talked to have shared similar anecdotes about their early queer-themed fantasies.

Alternatively, the "merging stigma" approach involves associating those feelings of shame with the experience of desire or pleasure itself. In other words, the stigma becomes eroticized to a degree, at least within the context of the submission fantasy (whereas real-life stigma likely remains unwanted). For instance, within these fantasies, a woman might eroticize being called a "slut," or a man might eroticize being called emasculating or feminizing slurs.[27] While this merging-stigma strategy may seem counterintuitive on the surface, it often provides a first step toward uncoupling the desire from the accompanying shame. Many people I've spoken with have told me that exploring such submission fantasies has helped them process the anxiety or trauma they experienced associated with the sexual stigma in question.

To be clear, I am not attempting to attribute singular "causes" or "motives" to any specific sexual fantasies. Returning to my earlier taste metaphor, the two of us may enjoy the same food item, but for somewhat different reasons, and we may have very different palates otherwise—the same holds true for our sexual interests. Rather, my main point in this section has been to highlight how the Predator/Prey mindset often influences our sexual desires, albeit not necessarily in a straightforward fashion. While many people have conventional Predator/Prey-type fantasies, others may experience more extreme or exaggerated versions, partial or complete role reversals, or novel rearrangements of sexual roles and meanings.

While I have focused on the influence of Predator/Prey in this section, these are not the only types of sexual fantasies that people have. Lehmiller lists "passion and romance," "novelty, adventure, and variety," "multipartner sex," "nonmonogamous relationships," and "taboo and forbidden sex" as other frequent sexual fantasy themes.[28] Other sexual fantasies may be less readily classifiable. For example, Dubberley has an entire chapter on "Esoteric Fantasies," which includes her female subjects having sexual fantasies about pregnancy, paranormal activities, and other scenarios.[29] Relatedly, there is a popular Internet meme known as "Rule 34" that goes something like this: If you can imagine something, then there's almost certainly porn about it. When confronted with previously unheard-of or seemingly unusual sexual interests, we may find ourselves reflexively trying to craft highly individualized explanations for why person X is turned on by particular thing Y, but there's really no need to do this. Far more often than not, it makes more sense to chalk up this sexual diversity to human beings' ability to make unexpected associations between various objects, elements, and meanings.

Feminist Debates About Sexual Hierarchies

I began this chapter by making the case that we should stop pathologizing other people's solitary and consensual sexual interests via sexualizing terminology such as "paraphilic," "perverted," and "deviant." But in the previous section, I described how some of our sexual fantasies and desires seemingly draw from Predator/Prey dynamics. Given the many problems associated with the Predator/Prey mindset—particularly the fact that it creates hierarchies of sexual "subjects" and "objects," of those who "take sex" and those who are "taken"—it seems reasonable to ask whether the latter sexual fantasies are problematic in their own right, and thus worthy of critique or intervention. Indeed, this question dovetails with the previous chapter's discussion of how marginalized individuals are often "fetishized" and viewed as "exotic others" by those in the dominant group—a phenomenon that also relies upon and potentially exacerbates previously existing social hierarchies.

Within feminism, opinions about these matters tend to be clustered into one of two camps. During the "feminist sex wars" of the 1980s (yes, they were really called that), these camps were self-described as "anti-pornography" and "pro-sex"; they still exist today, although not necessarily under the same names. The anti-pornography camp strongly opposed pornography, BDSM, sex work, and butch/femme roles on the basis that they all supposedly reinforced sexual hierarchies based on male/masculine dominance and female/feminine submission. The pro-sex camp challenged the universality of those claims and further argued that—especially for women and sexual minorities, whose desires are erased in our culture—asserting one's sexuality is also crucial for challenging those hierarchies. While these two camps are often conceptualized as being in opposition to one another, this need not be the case. An observation I made in an earlier chapter—that the anti-pornography position tends to be centered on reducing objectification, while the pro-sex position is focused more on reducing sexual stigma—offers a possibility for reconciliation or, at the very least, a better understanding of where each party is coming from. After all, sexual stigma and objectification are both serious problems that impact women and other marginalized groups. Perhaps there are ways to take both into consideration or to reduce both simultaneously.

Let's begin by dispensing with some of the more untenable sentiments on both sides. There are some people in the pro-sex camp who will make broad claims about how pornography, BDSM, or even sex more generally is liberating and empowering, thus implying that it is inherently good. However, over the course of this book, I've detailed numerous ways in which expressions of sexuality can be difficult or downright bad, the most obvious example being acts of sexual violence. Given the ever-present specter of sexualization in my own life, I would describe sex as being far more *complicated* than it is wholly positive. For me, sex has been a source of pleasure, but one that I had to keep secret for many years because my desires were deemed queer. It's been finally feeling comfortable in my own skin upon transitioning, only to have strangers make degrading street remarks about my female attributes. It's been hitting it off with someone on a dating website, only to be met with radio silence when I ask them if they've read the part of my profile where I mentioned that I am trans (clearly they hadn't). It's been interacting with men who were quite attracted to the fact that I'm trans but who weren't interested in anything else about me. It's been writing a book about sexuality and sexualization—two important subjects that I care deeply about—knowing full well that no matter what I say, or how carefully I say it, anti-trans campaigners will likely twist my words, or perhaps even the very premise of this book, in order to smear me as a "pervert."

In addition to these sorts of sexualization-related complications, not every person wants sex. Some people are asexual. Others may simply not be in the mood, or may be getting over a relationship or bad incident, and sex is the furthest thing from their minds. For such individuals, blanket statements about sex being inherently liberating and empowering may feel disingenuous or even derogatory, as they insinuate that people who are not having sex must be unliberated and disempowered. Despite all of the sex-negativity that exists in our culture, there is also a pervasive sense of *compulsory sexuality* in that most of us are expected to have sexual desires of some kind or another.[30] Compulsory sexuality can be seen in how a lack of sexual arousal or interest in other people has long been pathologized in the *DSM* and even categorized as a "paraphilia" by some researchers.[31] The presumption that people *should* want sex is also sometimes invoked to pressure individuals into having sex that they do not want. In other words, the accusation that "there must be something wrong with you" is often levied against people who eschew sex, just as it is against people who want "too much" sex or the "wrong kind" of sex.

Given all this, rather than promote an unqualified "pro-sex" position, it would be more accurate for us to recognize that many people's experiences with sex are better described as *ambivalent* in that they can evoke both positive and negative feelings, often simultaneously. The sexual elements/meanings framework I've shared here is better able to accommodate this ambivalence, as a sexual expression that has exclusively positive connotations for one person may be associated with negative or mixed meanings for another.

Turning to the anti-pornography side of the debate: While I am just as concerned about sexualization and sexual violence as anyone, I cannot endorse the position that all acts that seemingly resemble sexual hierarchies are inherently oppressive, and thus should be discouraged or condemned. There is an obvious "eye of the beholder" component to these sorts of claims: While a butch/femme lesbian couple may strike some anti-pornography feminists as merely "mimicking" or "reinforcing" a patriarchal sexual hierarchy, the couple in question may understand themselves as "subverting" those norms. For instance, they may see themselves as challenging the notion that sex requires a cis male penis, or that women cannot be legitimate sexual initiators. And frankly, many straight people would likely agree with this couple's assessment.

Furthermore, how exactly does one distinguish between oppressive "hierarchy-reinforcing" sex and more egalitarian expressions of it? If the sex in question involves one person on top and another on the bottom, is it hierarchical by default? Or what if one partner has considerably more social status than the other—whether due to differences in gender, economic class, ethnicity, age, ability, or some other factor—does that automatically disqualify their sex from being equitable? While I think many people would answer "no" to these hypotheticals, some would be inclined to say "yes," illustrating how subjective these sorts of determinations can be. In fact, the only thing that I feel confident in saying is that, while every person may draw the line between "good equitable sex" and "bad oppressive sex" in somewhat different places, they will invariably do so in a manner that ensures that their own sexual desires fall squarely into the "good" category.

While the Predator/Prey mindset that I have described throughout this book shares numerous observations and similarities with the anti-pornography feminist perspective, there are crucial distinctions. According to some renditions of the latter, the male dominance/female submission hierarchy is a totalizing force that pervades all aspects of society and wholly determines our sexualities, and the only way to overcome its pull is to purge every vestige of it from our lives. In contrast, the Predator/Prey mindset is a collection of shared assumptions that most of us learn early on in our lives, and that helps shape our understanding of gender, sexuality, and navigating romantic and sexual encounters. While some people tacitly accept Predator/Prey's dynamics and script as simply the way things are, many of us come to question it, or at least parts of it, over time. Some of us ultimately discard it, turning instead to other frameworks to make sense of sex, gender, and sexuality. Because most of us are exposed to Predator/Prey thinking during our formative years, it may be one of numerous factors that can influence our burgeoning sexualities. As a result, even those of us who later consciously disavow Predator/Prey as a way of interpreting the world may nevertheless find that certain aspects of it continue to sexually resonate with us, albeit not in a totalizing manner. For instance, we may find ourselves reappropriating or recombining some of its sexual elements and meanings in various ways, leading to the panoply of Predator/Prey-adjacent or -inspired sexual fantasies detailed in the previous section.

Perhaps nowhere is the disparity between these two models more evident than in their considerations of BDSM. Anti-pornography feminists have decried BDSM as "deviant," "patriarchal," and "anti-feminist" on account of its seeming to reproduce hierarchies involving objectification, submission, and dominance.[32] This strikes me as an extremely literal reading that overlooks people's lived realities. Take, for instance, a hypothetical queer woman named Jess who is feminist, social justice–minded, and critical of hetero-male-centrism and Predator/Prey dynamics in society at large, but who occasionally engages in BDSM with consenting partners. (This describes most people I personally know who are into BDSM, given my involvement in queer women's communities.) As is emphasized in virtually all BDSM "how to" guides, Jess and her partners always begin with open communication: discussions about likes, dislikes, boundaries, safety, and what will happen during any given "scene." They have a "safe word" so that either party can end the scene if they feel uncomfortable, plus they check in with one another both during and afterward. Like many BDSM practitioners, Jess sometimes refers to it as "role-playing" (temporarily inhabiting a role) or "power exchange." The latter phrase acknowledges that all individuals have autonomy and agency and that, for the duration of the scene, one party willfully cedes that power to another. Jess has absolutely no desire to nonconsensually project any sexual hierarchies onto other people; rather, she limits her explorations of these sexual roles and meanings with particular individuals in very specific, highly controlled and negotiated environments.

Admittedly, this is not every person's experience with BDSM. There are people for whom BDSM plays a far bigger role in their relationships, people who are into BDSM but not especially feminist, and occasional bad actors who play fast and loose with communication and consent. But Jess's example highlights how the anti-pornography stance on BDSM often fails to see the forest for the trees. In my estimation, the main problems with Predator/Prey thinking are its shared assumptions and its nonconsensual shoehorning of all people into very specific and sometimes stigmatized sexual roles. Jess's approach to sexuality—especially the honest communication, setting boundaries and safe words, and not judging people for their unconventional desires—circumvents

Predator/Prey's primary pitfalls. This is not to say that Jess's expressions of sexuality are "righteous," "exemplary," or "liberated and empowered," as no expressions of sexuality are these things. But to lump Jess in with men who actually do view and treat women as mere sex objects, because your litmus test for oppressive sex is "eroticizing hierarchies," seems profoundly misplaced to me.

A similar conflation of the sexually complicated with the indefensibly oppressive can be found in anti-pornography feminist stances on sex work and pornography itself. Both these phenomena are fairly diverse. Sex work includes remote work (webcam models, phone sex operators), performative work (stripping, pornographic modeling and acting), and more direct sexual activity (various forms of prostitution). The standard anti-pornography position is that sex work should be prohibited because it treats women like "objects that can be bought and sold." Those who hold this position will often conflate sex work with sex trafficking—cases in which actual abduction, forced labor, and sexual slavery may be involved—even though these are very distinct things.[33] In contrast, sex workers' rights activists emphasize the fact that sex work is *work*: Within a capitalist system, most of us sell our bodies, physical abilities, talents, and time to employers in exchange for some kind of financial compensation. Some jobs may be more dangerous, dirty, or demeaning than others; sex work is no different in this respect except that it is heavily stigmatized and quite often criminalized.

Anti-pornography feminists have also called for prohibitions on pornography on the basis that it constitutes and/or promotes female subordination, dehumanization, and sexual violence against women.[34] While some forms of hardcore pornography certainly do depict female characters in a degrading fashion, this is by no means ubiquitous. For example, there's plenty of pornography (softcore, amateur) that simply portrays naked bodies and people having sex sans degrading overtones. There is also queer porn that caters to sexual minorities, in which the sexual subject may be a woman, or the object of desire may be a man. Contemporary studies have shown that people who consume pornography are not any more sexist on average than those who do not, and that their reasons for viewing porn are actually quite varied and often benign.[35] Psychologist David Speed and colleagues summarize their study's findings this way: "People do not react in uniform ways to pornography."

It is well accepted in literary and media studies that audiences may interpret the same "text" in different ways, and pornography is no exception. While the average adult who watches pornography is likely to understand it as fiction that does not resemble real life (cue pizza delivery guy jokes here), an adolescent with no sex education may presume that it depicts what sex actually entails. And while many men consider mainstream female porn actors to be distinct from "average women," they may watch minority porn actors and presume that they are somehow representative of their entire group. Once again, pornography is neither wholly good nor bad; rather, it's complicated.

It's understandable why some feminists might want to critique certain aspects of pornography or sex work. But it seems excessive to portray these phenomena as uniformly and irredeemably oppressive, and to allege that they harm *all women*, when in fact only a fraction of women are directly impacted by them. A similar overreach can be found in certain feminist accounts of objectification in which, rather than focusing on how objectification invalidates the individuals who are directly targeted by it (especially those who are multiply marginalized), they extrapolate about how such instances essentially dehumanize *all women*. Sometimes these assessments use epidemiological terms such as "exposure" and "prevalence," and raise fears about how sexualized media depictions may "infect" or "corrupt" young girls, while paying significantly less attention to their impact on young boys (presumably because the latter are viewed as less susceptible to this "corruption").[36] It seems to me that what these accounts are describing is *sexual stigma*, with its contagion-like properties of contamination, negativity dominance, dose-insensitivity, and permanence.

Elsewhere in my writings, I have critiqued a recurring claim within feminism and LGBTQIA+ activism that certain individuals "reinforce" the marginalization experienced by the rest of the group when they behave in particular ways. I have debunked this from multiple angles, pointing out how it ignores the gender and sexual diversity inherent within any group, and how it shifts the blame away from the unmarked group's sexist acts and toward policing marked individuals' reactions to that sexism. Such claims also create new stereotypes—steeped in arbitrary assumptions about whether any specific behavior "reinforces" or "subverts" said marginalization—to which the marked group is now expected to adhere.[37]

Despite their specious and counterproductive nature, these "reinforcing" accusations are constantly invoked, often along with outrage directed at these supposed "reinforcers." For example, I have witnessed women express palpable anger upon seeing other women who are dressed in an especially feminine or sexy manner, and gay individuals express similar indignation toward their counterparts who dress in drag, or in leather, or who say or do anything that can be interpreted as "sexual" in any way. This is respectability politics at play.

While I disagree with these condemnations, I understand why they arise. When we are "marked by sex" in some way, the sanctioned method to gain respectability and be taken seriously is for us to play down or cover up our "sex." So when someone else who shares our marked trait seemingly "flaunts" it, we may feel implicated by their actions. In some cases, our fears may be valid, as people do sometimes hold up one member of a marginalized group as an example of what the entire group is supposedly like. But this is less true for more tolerated marginalized groups, whose members society often divvies up into the "good ones" and "bad ones." The "good" members are expected to join in on the dominant group's critiques of the "bad" members, as seen when "good girls" slut-shame their female counterparts, or "respectable" queer people deride their more "flamboyant" counterparts.

All people who are "marked by sex" in some way face a double bind. Feminists have articulated "virgin" versus "whore," but more generally it can be conceptualized as the *ashamed/shameless double bind*.[38] Society expects us to be *ashamed* by the sexual stigma that others project onto our bodies and behaviors. If we refuse to buy into that stigma, then we will be misconstrued as *shameless:* immodest, unseemly, and insensible to disgrace. Both paths have drawbacks. The "ashamed" side of the double bind is characterized by having to hide or repress our marked traits, and experiencing self-consciousness or even fear, as said traits could be uncovered or revealed at any moment. The "shameless" side of the double bind renders us vulnerable to increased scrutiny as well as accusations that we are "asking for" any unwanted attention that we receive.

The anti-pornography camp's tendency toward prohibiting certain sexual expressions, and the pro-sex camp's tendency toward celebrating those same expressions, can be read as different reactions to this double bind. While both are understandable responses—in fact, they're the only two responses allowed according to the double bind—neither will ultimately undermine or undo sexual stigma. Because that stigma does not actually reside in our bodies and behaviors, but rather in the minds of those who judge us.

If we wish to truly bring an end to Predator/Prey and other sexual hierarchies, that work begins by changing the way that we—*you, me, and everybody*—perceive and interpret other people.

On Being Ethically Sexual

Making sex more equitable—or, at the very least, less harmful—is a worthy goal. But as we've seen over the course of this chapter, it will not be achieved via a rigid one-size-fits-all solution given the diversity in our sexual palates, our differing interpretations of sexual objects and elements, and the fact that we are all socially situated in various ways. The sexual landscape looks very different to me as a bisexual trans woman than it probably does to most readers. And because I am unmarked in numerous ways (white, able-bodied, middle-class), I am not subjected to many of the obstacles and forms of stigma that others face. So rather than promote some kind of overarching "road map" or "rule book," what follows is a flexible set of guidelines that should accommodate most people's sexual interests and concerns.

The first guideline is to *reject nonconsensuality*. It should be self-evident by this point why engaging in sexual activities with individuals who do not or cannot consent is reprehensible (not to mention illegal). But there are other ways in which nonconsensuality may play out in our sexual lives. I previously introduced the concept of *derivatization*: when we view other people as mere derivatives of our own thoughts and desires, and expect them to behave accordingly. Derivatization encapsulates precisely what's wrong with nonconsensual objectification—namely, it involves treating others as mere extensions of ourselves rather than as distinct individuals with desires of their own. At the same time, this term doesn't discount the legitimate pleasure that can come from being appreciated as the object of somebody else's desire in other contexts, such as consensual relationships or solitary fantasies. We should avoid derivatizing other people, as it both invalidates the targeted person's perspective, and simultaneously denies the significant differences in sexual interests and interpretations that exist within the population.

Or, to put it differently, while nonconsensuality is sometimes driven by a deliberate disregard for the other party's wishes and well-being, it may also take the form of assuming that the other party must want the exact same things we want, or expects the same things we expect, due to a lack of imagination or consideration on our part. Therefore, rejecting nonconsensuality also requires us to ditch our reliance on assumptions, and to turn instead to honest and direct communication, in order to better understand our potential partners' perspectives and desires.

The second guideline is to *stop divvying up sex into "good" and "bad" categories*. Obviously, we each have personal preferences in these regards, in much the same way that certain foods may taste pleasant or unpleasant to us. However, we should refrain from intellectualizing these preferences and projecting them onto other people, as we saw with the psychologists who divide up the sexual world into "normophilic" versus "paraphilic," or the anti-pornography feminists who do the same with "egalitarian" versus "hierarchical" sex, or the many religious institutions that sanction "reproductive" sex while denouncing "non-reproductive" forms. Sexualization is steeped in the notion that certain sexual bodies and behaviors are inherently "bad," and thus deserving of condemnation and public shaming. Moving away from judging sex and sexuality in terms of good versus bad will not only reduce sexualization but will hopefully allow us to better embrace ambivalence: understanding that a sexual experience that is positive to one person may be negative for another and may evoke mixed feelings in a third.

This brings us to the third guideline: If we wish to live in a world where our solitary and consensual sexual expressions are not routinely policed by others, then it becomes incumbent upon us to *self-examine desire.*[39] After all, the social hierarchies, norms, and meanings that arise from the mindsets and forms of marginalization I've described throughout this book may be among the numerous factors that contribute to our sexualities. Thus, if we wish to be ethically sexual, then we should reflect upon our likes and dislikes, and question whether our predilections may be by-products of these social forces. The purpose here is not to uncover some kind of unspoiled "natural sexuality" underneath all the conditioning, as no human activity or interest exists entirely outside the social realm. Nor is it to completely "remake" our genders or sexualities, as past attempts at "conversion" and "reparative" therapies (largely inflicted upon LGBTQIA+ people) have proven to be ineffective and traumatizing to those subjected to them. Rather, what I suggest here is that if we do come across facets of our sexuality that may be unjust or infringe upon others, then we may want to reconsider our relationship to them.

We tend to be most conscious of our self-examining in cases where what we desire is generally considered to be taboo or morally suspect. In some cases, this "moral incongruence" may lead us to view our desires as "addictive" or "compulsive"—labels that people rarely if ever apply to desires they deem normal and healthy.[40] Upon further introspection, we may come to the conclusion that, while what we desire is stigmatized, it does not negatively impact others and thus is ethical; this is the conclusion that many LGBTQIA+ people ultimately arrive at. Or, if the desire involves some degree of nonconsensuality, we may choose to abstain from it entirely, relegate our explorations of it to solitary sexual fantasies, or seek out more consensual outlets for it. For instance, those who enjoy dominance and submission fantasies may explore them within the context of BDSM, following the consensual guidelines I described in Jess's example in the previous section. In some cases, nonconsensual aspects of desire can be circumvented through shifting sexual meanings. To draw on an earlier example, someone who initially experiences a highly derivatized attraction to trans women (viewing us mere "sex objects" or as "really a man underneath it all") may eventually come to see us as fully fleshed-out individuals and find us attractive for less invalidating reasons. These are but a few examples; people may come to make sense of their desires in other ways as well. If there is one take-home point here, it is always maintaining a clear distinction between our own sexual fantasies and other people's lived realities, and not recklessly subjecting the latter to the former.

Self-examining can be trickier in cases where our desires align with societal norms, as this often leads us to view them as "natural" and thus beyond reproach. But just because a desire is deemed "normal" by society doesn't mean that it's not worth examining. For instance, a woman who is attracted to cocky and aggressive men may wonder to herself whether this is primarily an aesthetic preference for her, whether it is influenced by Predator/Prey dynamics, whether part of the appeal is that her attraction to such men is culturally validated, and/or other possible reasons. There aren't necessarily any right or wrong answers here, just that we may learn something new about ourselves through contemplating our predilections and life choices, whether sexual or otherwise. Similarly, this woman might ask herself whether there are certain groups of people that she immediately rules out of consideration, and if so, why. Does she refuse to partner with people who are shorter than she is? Or those from a lower economic class? Or people of color, or people with disabilities? Does she find herself feeling disgust, rather than indifference, upon contemplating attraction to some of these individuals? Or does she find some of them attractive but would simply be embarrassed to be seen in public with them?

We often like to talk about attraction in terms of personal preferences: our appreciation of individuals who share things in common with us or who have certain distinguishing characteristics that we find appealing. But in truth, we are often driven by social status as much as anything else. Such dynamics are especially evident in conventional heterosexual relationships, where being partnered with an especially feminine woman or masculine man bolsters one's own masculinity or femininity, respectively, in the eyes of others. In stark contrast, pairing with someone who is gender-atypical or openly bisexual might seem to call your own gender and sexuality into question. After all, what does it say about you if you're not able to attract a "real" woman or man? But even outside heterosexuality, there is a twisted societal expectation that our partners must be a reflection of us in some deep or profound way. If our partner is conventionally attractive, or wealthy, or successful, then that enhances our own social status. Or if we partner with someone who is deemed "below our station," then people may view that as an indication that we must possess some hidden flaw.

There was a time in my teen and early adulthood years when I uncritically bought into this "reciprocal status" relationship ideology. I (embarrassingly, in retrospect) thought of it in terms of only wanting to partner with people whom I considered to be "my equal." I didn't really start questioning this ideology until I became more open about my transness, at which point it dawned on me that, since my gender would likely "reflect poorly" upon my partner's status, it would be hypocritical for me to not date people out of fear that they might correspondingly "reflect poorly" upon my status. Once I stepped outside this reciprocal status ideology, it became glaring to me how much it severely limits our potential partner choices, and how much it exacerbates existing social hierarchies.

We are all aware of this reciprocal status phenomenon to some extent, especially when presented with conspicuous juxtapositions of it. We poke fun at the upper-crust family who look down their noses at the genuinely likable working-class boyfriend their daughter has brought home to dinner. Or we might ridicule the "gold digger" who marries a man for his money, or the older man who has a new "trophy wife." Or we may mock the rock star who leverages his celebrity status to attract a never-ending stream of "groupies." We can readily discern and are often critical of these power dynamics when they take on such exaggerated forms. So perhaps it's worth considering whether we ourselves are engaged in smaller-scale versions of them.

To reiterate: I would never tell anyone who they should, or shouldn't, be attracted to or partner with. Everyone gets to make that determination for themselves. Which is why it is essential for us to do the bare minimum of self-examining our own desires. Not out of pity for those who are deemed "lesser," but for the opportunity to grow beyond the restrictions that cultural norms have set for us.

The last guideline I will offer here is *severing sex from stigma*. Colloquially, people often use the words "shame" and "stigma" interchangeably to refer to feelings of embarrassment or disgrace regarding some aspect of their person. Pro-sex advocates will often tout the importance of overcoming shame, sometimes making it sound as though it were primarily an internal feeling that we simply need to "let go of" or "move beyond" if we want to be sexually liberated. And sure, there is some truth to these tales of overcoming internalized shame, as I've recounted in my own personal stories throughout these pages.

But stigma is a far more powerful and accurate concept for describing our culture's attitudes toward sex and sexuality. It accounts not only for our internal feelings of distress but also for other people's negative reactions to us. While I may reject my own internal negative feelings, that does nothing to stop the onslaught of ostracization, disgust, and contempt that others may express toward me. While I got over most of my own sex/gender-related personal shame twenty or so years ago, I am still dealing with the various forms of stigma that others continue to project onto me.

While our internal sexual shame may be invisible to outsiders, sexual stigma has many telltale signs. First and most blatantly, it's often imagined to be "contagious," and those who are supposedly "infected" are routinely described by a series of pejoratives that should be familiar to readers by now: contaminated, corrupted, tainted, soiled, spoiled, polluted, dirtied, degenerate, and so on. Second, while sex and sexuality are complicated, and may evoke positive or ambivalent feelings in us, sexual stigma is envisioned as wholly negative. Third, while sexual acts are always fleeting or transient, sexual stigma is presumed to be permanent. Sexual stigma is the reason why we describe people who are sexually un-aware as "innocent" and virgins as "pure," but as soon as they come into contact with sex or explore their own sexualities, we imagine them as having been "corrupted." Sexual stigma is what leads us to describe people who've supposedly had "too much sex," or the "wrong kind of sex," as being "consumed," "used up," or "ruined" by the experience.

Sexual stigma may be distributed asymmetrically throughout the population—impacting women far more than men, and marked groups more so than their unmarked counterparts—but its presence is felt to some extent by everybody. Stigma is what makes sex feel forbidden and taboo. Its existence is what leads people to believe that sex is not merely "dirty" but "dangerous" and "deadly." Across several studies, researchers have shown that people greatly overestimate their chances of contracting or dying from STDs compared to other nonsexual diseases or activities, and that sex-related stigma seems to be driving this discrepancy.[41] The idea that sex is not just "dirty" but "deadly" can also be found throughout the media. The website *TV Tropes*, which chronicles common TV and movie themes, has several listings for the recurring trope of sex instigating a character's death or demise ("Death by Sex," "Downfall by Sex"), including its alarming regularity when the character in question is a sexual minority ("Bury Your Gays," "Disposable Sex Worker").[42]

If we want to be ethically sexual, then it is crucial that we sever this imagined link between sex and stigma. It's not enough for us to transcend our internalized self-directed stigma. Rather, we must confront our own perceptions and interpretations of others. We must stop projecting various forms of sexual stigma onto other people's bodies and behaviors, onto their fantasies and desires, and onto their solitary and consensual sexual expressions. In addition to refusing to stigmatize people for their sexual activities, proclivities, and histories, we must also reject stigmatizing people for their lack of sexual desires and experiences.

If we can effectively reduce sex-related stigma across society, then the topic will no longer be considered so taboo. And it will become far easier to access legitimate sex-related information and resources rather than relying largely on hearsay, innuendo, and intentionally salacious or sensationalistic media productions.

If we can finally sever the ties between sex and stigma in our minds, then we can more readily share nuanced stories in which sex and sexuality are complicated, and in which characters have ambivalent relationships to them. Instead of heavy-handed metaphors about how sex "kills," "contaminates," or "ruins" people, perhaps we can tell more subtle and more complex stories about sexuality, exploration, and resilience.

11 RETHINKING SEX AND CHALLENGING SEXUALIZATION

In the opening paragraphs of this book, I highlighted how people of differing research and experiential backgrounds tend to tell very different narratives about human sexuality. In the chapters that followed, I shared my own rendition, emphasizing four main ideas: 1) that unconscious mindsets shape the way we perceive sex, gender, and sexuality; 2) that sexualizing people—reducing them to their real or imagined sexual bodies and behaviors—is a recurring tactic that is used to invalidate people across genders, particularly those who belong to marginalized groups; 3) that stigma plays a crucial role in sexualization and sex-negativity; and 4) that these perceptual and social forces influence our sexual desires and histories to some degree. I'll be the first to admit that there is more to human sexuality than just perception and interpretation. But as I have shown, the latter facets do play an important role, one that should not be so readily overlooked.

Of course, I am not the first person to raise concerns about sexualization. Most past accounts have focused on its impact on women or on specific minority groups, often framing it as but one manifestation of the marginalization that these groups more generally face. There are some advantages to conceptualizing sexualization in terms of misogyny, racism, homophobia, and so on, as each form of marginalization is unique and helps shape how said sexualization may play out—for instance, through specific stereotypes or systemic forces. But there are also disadvantages to examining them on an individual basis, an obvious one being that some of us exist at the intersection of multiple forms of sexualization.

If we fail to understand how all these forms of sexualization are interconnected, we may propose solutions that wind up being at cross-purposes with the concerns of other groups. This is what happened with the SlutWalks of the early 2010s, in which many women publicly dressed as "sluts" and marched together to protest the roles that slut-shaming and victim-blaming play in perpetuating rape culture. Among the critics of this approach were Black women who pointed out that they are routinely hypersexualized (and sometimes criminalized for it) no matter how they dress or behave. Another example can be found in how feminists who condemn porn often find themselves at odds with LGBTQIA+, fat, and disabled feminists who produce sexually explicit art to challenge the sexual invisibility and stereotypes of undesirability they constantly face. Within trans communities, some trans women wield terms such as "chasers" and "fetishists" to denounce the way that they are nonconsensually exoticized and derivatized by certain men, whereas other trans women denounce these terms because of the way they stigmatize their legitimate male partners. In all of these cases, it's not that one group is necessarily right and another wrong, but rather that sexualization can take different, and sometimes seemingly antithetical, forms.

When we observe sexualization through the lens of a specific form of marginalization, or through the experiences of a particular subgroup, we will always obtain an incomplete picture, as the underlying mindsets that are driving sexualization are obscured from those vantage points. As I have detailed, these mindsets are unconscious and pervasive—they are the proverbial water that we are all swimming in. Impassioned calls to prohibit, subvert, or celebrate particular sexual expressions may sound promising on the surface, but they are akin to encouraging us to swim in one direction or another. While such calls may have tangible effects on people's lives, for better or for worse, they will not significantly impact the water itself. If we are serious about reducing *all* forms of sexualization, then we must begin by acknowledging the water. Only upon doing so can we actively work to drain the pool. Or escape the fishbowl. Or whatever metaphor you prefer for eliminating these sexualizing mindsets once and for all.

In earlier chapters, I articulated the Two Filing Cabinets and Opposites mindsets, which lead us to divvy up all people into two distinct sexes, and to expect them to behave in complementary or contradictory ways. Most forms of sexism can be traced back to these mindsets, so transcending them is vital if we wish to ultimately achieve sex/gender equity. The Unmarked/Marked mindset leads us to view marked and marginalized individuals as inherently conspicuous and questionable—they are "public spectacles" that seem to "invite" our attention and scrutiny. Many aspects of sexualization arise largely from this mindset—including attributing sexual motives and meanings to other people, and presuming that they are "asking for" any sexualization they receive. Perhaps no mindset fuels sexualization more than Predator/Prey, which constructs people as either "sexual objects" who *are* or *have sex*, or "sexual aggressors" who strive to *take that sex* from them. This mindset imparts sexual stigma onto those cast in the "sexual object" role, as well as those who fail to adhere to Predator/Prey roles, scripts, and ideals. Depending on the context, these individuals may be misconstrued as "fakes" and "deceivers," as "hypersexual" and possibly "predators," as "deviants" and "perverts," as "undesirable" and mere "fetish objects," or some combination thereof.

The first step toward dismantling all these mindsets is to learn to recognize them, to become consciously aware of when we are employing them, and to refrain from relying on them when assessing other people. As with unlearning any unconscious habit or tendency, this can take time, and progress may be gradual. Even after years of contemplating and critiquing these mindsets myself, I still sometimes feel surprised when someone behaves in a gender-atypical fashion, or find myself paying undue attention to someone who is marked in my eyes, or needlessly interpreting somebody else as "excessively sexual." The important point is that, upon catching myself doing these things, I immediately realize that these are faulty assumptions on my part rather than problems stemming from the person in question. And rather than reducing them to a mere sexual being, I can work to see them as a whole person with many attributes. If we were all willing and able to do this, then sexualization would diminish accordingly.

Some people propose untenable notions of what a world without prejudice might look like. For instance, there are feminists who have argued that we should strive to be "gender free," or to eliminate gender altogether.[1] Similarly, those who hold simplistic views of racism will often tout a "color-blind" approach wherein we refrain from taking a person's ethnicity or skin color into account. Both these approaches fail to adequately grapple with the fact that human beings express natural diversity in these regards, so it's inevitable that we will discern such variation. And pretending not to notice, or refusing to consider, said differences will only allow unconscious and implicit biases to fester. Thus, rather than

denying this diversity, our goal should be to refrain from projecting unwarranted assumptions, stereotypes, and value judgments
upon these differing traits, and to abstain from policing and punishing individuals for falling outside the "norm."

In addition to this self-work, it is crucial that we spread the
word about these mindsets. A major impetus for me to write this
book was to share this knowledge with others in the hope that
it might help readers better counter sexualization in their lives,
and in our culture more generally. While these mindsets incorpo-
rate concepts that people may already have some familiarity with,
thinking of them in terms of *our own perception and interpretation*,
rather than simply as obstacles that certain groups face, represents
a productive change in perspective.

I am not proposing that challenging these mindsets is sufficient, or that this work should completely replace previous frameworks for countering sexualization. In my book *Excluded*, I make a
distinction between "top-down" and "bottom-up" approaches to
social justice activism that seems relevant here.[2] Top-down efforts
are focused on a particular ideology or "ism" that impacts a specific marginalized group. While such approaches may be effective
in articulating the obstacles faced by the group in question, they
are ill-equipped to make sense of other forms of marginalization.
As history has shown, someone who is well versed in how sexism
works may nevertheless remain ignorant of or ill-informed about
the intricacies of racism, or ableism, or homophobia (and vice
versa). In contrast, bottom-up approaches focus on the recurring
mindsets and tactics that enable all forms of marginalization. So
even if you are unfamiliar with transphobia, you may relate to the
fact that trans people face undue attention and scrutiny because
we are marked, or that, like all marginalized groups, we are routinely sexualized. While it is often useful to focus on these com-
monalities, the specific predicaments faced by each marginalized

group tend to get lost in the shuffle via this approach. This is why I have argued that top-down and bottom-up approaches must be utilized in concert if we wish to combat society-wide problems such as sexualization.

In other words, the mindsets I've outlined here represent a complementary strategy and are not intended to negate or replace previous frameworks. I imagine that many people will continue to organize around the concept of rape culture or analyze the particulars of how racism, transphobia, ableism, etc. inform the sexualization faced by certain communities. This is all important work. That said, pairing that work alongside challenging the underlying mindsets that drive them will allow us to achieve far more together.

If there are criticisms of this complementary approach, I imagine they will likely come from "single-issue" activists and those engaged in "respectability politics." Their goal is to lift people who are "just like them" up out of marginalization so that they can become fully assimilated members of the dominant group. For them, social justice is a zero-sum game in which there must always be *some people* who will remain marginalized (and sexualized). As a result, they may see the complementary strategy that I propose here as somehow "undermining" their efforts or "taking away" from the progress they have already made. While I agree with them that our goals are incompatible, I believe that they have it backward: They are the ones undermining intersectional efforts to end marginalization and sexualization, not the other way around. And personally, I don't want to be a part of any movement that requires me to sexualize other people for supposedly being "beneath" me, or presumably being my "enemy," in order for me to personally escape sexualization. That is a Faustian bargain that I want no part of.

Having said all that, because top-down and bottom-up strategies take significantly different approaches—with one focusing on

the concerns of particular subgroups, and the other striving to reduce sexualization across the entire population—there will sometimes be tensions between them. So with the rest of this chapter,
I want to suggest potential future directions with regards to sex,
sexualization, and social justice, while also considering potential
complications and contradictions that may arise along the way.

Going Off Script

Arguably, no factor enables sexualization and sexual violence more
than the Predator/Prey script. Men who make street remarks or
engage in sexual harassment often invoke the script's "men are supposed to make the first move" premise as cover for their actions
("It was merely playful flirting," "I was just trying to gauge her
interest"). Men who wish to plow forward despite a woman's reluctance often take advantage of the script's reliance on tacit signaling
to levy accusations of "teasing," "leading on," and "sending mixed
signals." The very conceptualization of men as "sexual aggressors"
often leads people to excuse their nonconsensual behaviors, as such
brashness is presumed to be "in their nature." In addition to these
problems, the script's built-in assumptions regarding which sexual
acts are "on the menu," and that all parties are presumed to be
straight by default, denies sexual diversity and leaves gender and
sexual minorities especially susceptible to accusations of "deception" or "perversion." Even people who prefer asymmetric sexual roles—whether aggressor/object, top/bottom, butch/femme,
dominant/submissive—should be able to discern the pitfalls and
potential dangers associated with the Predator/Prey script.

To date, most proposed solutions to these problems have
hinged upon the concept of consent. Some feminists have rec-
ommended "no means no" approaches, emphasizing that, despite
whatever (possibly phantom) signals a partner may appear to send,

an explicit "no" overrides them all. More recently, "yes means yes" approaches have emphasized that a lack of "no," or even a partner's reluctant acquiescence, is insufficient to move forward; rather, all parties must enthusiastically consent to everything that's happening. Critics of consent sometimes complain that these requirements remove the elements of "surprise" and "spontaneity" from sex. Of course, most people who've had bad sexual experiences can attest to the fact that spontaneity and surprise are not always good things. Furthermore, it's hard to make a convincing case about the importance of spontaneity when you are already following our culture's standard sexual script, replete with preordained steps and consummating acts.

While consent is crucial, it is not by any means a panacea. Others have detailed numerous potential shortcomings of relying solely on consent.[3] The one that I wish to focus on here is that, while consent may provide a necessary brake to prevent unwanted sex from occurring, it does nothing to fix the other problems inherent in the Predator/Prey script, such as its assigned roles, assumed beats, and preconceived sexual meanings. Thankfully, there are previously established workarounds for these issues. As I have described, in sex-positive settings (such as many queer women's, BDSM, and polyamory settings), direct and honest communication is generally promoted so that all involved parties can discuss mutual interests and negotiate roles, acts, boundaries, and so on. Explicit discussion and negotiation are common in these settings precisely because the Predator/Prey script does not accommodate these ways of being intimate, so it becomes necessary for the involved parties to establish their own ground rules. But there is no reason why these same methods cannot be incorporated into more "typical" sexual settings and situations.

Rather than referring to this strategy as "that honest and direct communication thing that sex-positive people do," I have come to think of it as *going off script*. I like this phrase as an intervention, as saying to a prospective partner "Let's go off script" makes it clear that Predator/Prey is a sexual script with its own set of conventions, and that people can agree to toss it aside. I also like how "off script" evokes improvisation, which requires *collaboration* in order to be effective. For instance, if I was an actor on a film set where everyone else was dutifully following the script, but I single-handedly decided to veer off it, I'd likely be seen as a "bad actor" in both senses of the term. Conversely, on a set where improvisation is encouraged, if I were to insist on following the script word for word, despite my colleagues' attempts to expand upon or elaborate on it, I would again be seen as a "bad actor" for not cooperating. In other words, improvisation can only work if all parties are in agreement on what they are attempting to create together. Thus, going off script involves listening and responding to one another, and it quickly falls apart if one party is determined to dominate or upstage the other.

Speaking of improvisation, one of my favorite essays on the topic of sex and sexualization is Thomas MacAulay Millar's "Toward a Performance Model of Sex."[4] In it, Millar critiques our current "commodity model" of sex, which is his term for the notion that women *have sex* and that men strive to *acquire that sex* from them, as I've recounted in Predator/Prey. He contrasts that with his proposed "performance model," which is akin to how we view musicians and other performers. Millar points out that while a woman who sleeps with lots of people is often derided as a "slut" (because she's seen as *giving away her sex*), we would never describe someone as a "music slut" if she happens to play in multiple bands or jams with random musicians she hardly knows. Furthermore, if you are a musician, you would never expect other musicians to automatically play with you just because they've performed with other people in the past, nor would you contemplate "forcing" someone to play with you—the very idea sounds farcical given that making music with someone else is an inherently collaborative affair.

Pertinent to the case I am making for going off script, Millar writes, "Musicians have to choose, explicitly or implicitly, what they are going to play: genre, song, key, and interpretation." In other words, the music we make together will ultimately lie at the intersection of our musical interests but is unlikely to include elements that one party enjoys but the other dislikes. Millar goes on to describe how every musical collaboration can be unique, a result of each individual bringing their own talents, tendencies, and tastes to the table. Thinking of sex in terms of going off script offers a similar panoply of possibilities.

Because Millar makes an analogy with performance, and I have made one with improvisation, some readers may mistakenly presume that I'm insinuating that sex is something that we should make up on the fly as we go along. For some, the old comedy adage "yes, and"—which discourages improv performers from rejecting the premises (or "first moves") forwarded by their collaborators—may spring to mind and appear to contradict consensuality. So to clarify, my "going off script" metaphor is meant to highlight the importance of *collaboration*—compatibility and working out what's going to happen beforehand—rather than performance or improvisation per se. Notably, the most amazing musical performances and improvisations that I've personally been a part of were with my band Bitesize, precisely because we had many conversations about what we wanted to achieve together musically, and over time we became familiar with one another's preferences and tendencies. That is to say, we collaborated very well together. While "going off script" may not be a perfect metaphor (and I am open to other suggestions), I do like how the phrase emphasizes that the taken-for-granted alternative (Predator/Prey) is a strict script with set roles and rules, and little to no wiggle room for other possibilities.

While I believe that "going off script" can vastly improve sex and relationships while fostering far more sexual diversity and equity, I imagine that it might take some time for it to become adopted in more mainstream settings. One likely bottleneck is that people first need to learn that Predator/Prey is in fact a script rather than a purely natural expression of sexuality. As people become more familiar with the idea of sexual scripts, and the arbitrary and often invalidating rules associated with this particular script, it will become easier for them to contemplate alternative ways of being sexual.

A second hurdle is that many people find honest communication about sex to be challenging, largely due to fears that they will face stigmatization if they openly express their desires. This is why, in my guidelines on being ethically sexual, I emphasized severing sex from stigma, and refraining from divvying up sex into "good" and "bad" categories. If we can be assured that our partners will not judge us negatively for our solitary and consensual fantasies and desires, then openly sharing them will become dramatically easier. There is already a large body of sex-positive literature and media offering advice on how to talk about sex and communicate with our partners. And many people currently practice going off script in various contexts, even if they don't call it that. So I see no reason why these techniques can't catch on more generally.

I don't expect there to be 100 percent adoption of going off script any time soon, as too many people currently take the Predator/Prey script for granted, and some are especially invested in its male-centric and heteronormative relationship structure. Their reluctance isn't necessarily a problem for those of us who do choose to go off script, provided that we can readily distinguish between the two groups. This is why I like the idea of an expression along the lines of "going off script" (or some alternative), as it provides a convenient way to signal to others that we do not subscribe to Predator/Prey, so they shouldn't expect us to play by its rules. If it became commonplace enough, it could even serve as a way to quickly signal to someone who attempts to make a proverbial "first move" that we are not interested, at least not on those terms.

I can imagine some people asking, "But Julia, what's to stop someone from ignoring another person's pronouncement of being off script? Or pretending to go along with being off script at first, only to take advantage of the situation later?" Well, unfortunately, these things already happen within the context of Predator/Prey. In other words, no matter what the sexual script or mutually established ground rules, there will always be a few "bad actors" who are only in it for themselves, and who refuse to respect or cooperate with other parties. Therefore, in addition to moving away from Predator/Prey, we need to address the crucial issue of bad actors.

Bad Actors and Me Too

In surveys of non-incarcerated U.S. men asking if they've ever "had sexual intercourse" with or "taken advantage" of a woman in instances where she either said no, or was too intoxicated to say no, or that involved physical force or threats—all of which meet the legal criteria for sexual assault—between 5 and 11 percent answered yes, with many admitting to multiple incidents.[5] Back when I was younger and still moving through the world as male, I would have been astounded by how high those numbers are. But nowadays, I am not so surprised. I have seen too many statistics on the prevalence of sexual violence and heard too many stories from sexual assault survivors, plus I've experienced two attempted date rapes myself since transitioning. In accordance with most survivors' experiences, there was nothing at all unusual about the men who tried to date rape me. Both seemed nice at first, and neither gave off creepy vibes or warning signs of any kind. The only characteristic that they shared was that, at a certain point, both tried to sexually push forward after I had already set very clear boundaries. After I had said "no."

There is a huge disconnect between our cultural conceptualization of "rape" and the almost mundane manner in which sexual violence plays out in many people's lives. The word "rapist" often conjures up images of monsters and sociopaths. But that description doesn't seem to fit either of my assailants, nor does it readily apply to 5–11 percent of all men. People routinely express disbelief upon hearing that a man they know personally has sexually harassed or assaulted someone. It seems to me that this "rapist equals monster" conflation is doing a lot of the heavy lifting here. It essentially makes it impossible for us to reconcile the seemingly nice and normal person we know with the horrific acts that they have purportedly committed. Which is why, had I reported either of my attempted date rapes, I'm sure people close to those men would have reflexively assumed that I was making the incident up, that I was the one truly at fault, or that it must have been some kind of miscommunication or misunderstanding. In actuality, both men were well aware of the boundaries they were crossing.

So instead of equating people who perpetrate sexual violence with "monsters," it might be more useful to compare them to reckless drivers. We all understand that while reckless drivers may seem nice or normal in non-driving contexts, their actions on the road can be injurious to others. They are also fairly common: Nearly every time I am driving on a highway, someone will barrel past me going well beyond the speed limit, zipping in and out of lanes as they go. These people are "bad actors" in the sense that they knowingly deviate from the rules that everybody else is following, putting other people at risk in the process, in order to attain a short-term gain for themselves.

Reckless drivers often have ready-made rationalizations for their actions, two of the most common being that "everybody does it" (to varying extents), and that it's a "victimless crime" (provided that no one gets hurt, of course). Both excuses seem to have obvious parallels with bad actors who commit acts of sexual violence, especially those who rely on Predator/Prey thinking to justify their behaviors. The idea that "sexual aggressors" are supposed to keep pushing forward if they want to ultimately "get sex" may lead bad actors to presume that all men are engaging in the same boundary-crossing behaviors that they are. As for the "victimless crime" parallel, the combination of seeing themselves as sexually invulnerable, while also viewing sex as an unqualified good thing, may lead bad actors to discount the seriousness of their sexual improprieties, or else to euphemize them as "just sex" rather than acts of violation.

No analogy is perfect. And this one certainly doesn't apply to every instance of sexual violence, as some assailants do enjoy inflicting harm on their victims rather than rationalizing that harm away. But I do think this "reckless driver" analogy can account for many bad actors' relationship with sexual violence. More importantly, this analogy provides some insight into how we might attenuate the problem. Educational campaigns to reduce reckless driving may sway newer drivers who are still in the learning process, but will have a more limited effect on drivers who are well aware of the rules of the road, but who consistently break them anyway. However, the one thing that *does* mitigate reckless driving is the fear of getting caught. If there were no speeding tickets, or harsher sanctions for repeat offenders (losing one's license, time in jail), then far more people would engage in reckless driving than currently do. And the same is almost certainly true for sexual violence.

Until recently, bad actors could be pretty sure that they'd likely get away with sexual assault. There are numerous reasons for this, a few of which we've covered already: The Predator/Prey script provides them with plenty of cover for their actions, plus many people will be disinclined to view them as "monsters." And given the prevalence of victim-blaming, plus the significant stigma associated with being sexually violated, there are huge disincentives for victims of sexual assault to come forward. In a previous essay entitled "He's Unmarked, She's Marked" (my play on "he said/she said"), I further argued that because women are marked relative to men, our accounts may be viewed as inherently questionable— for instance, a woman's motives, memory, manner of dress, past sexual history, and alcohol consumption may come under scrutiny, while similar questions may not be posed to him at all.[6] By the same token, the accounts of multiply marked individuals are bound to be questioned and scrutinized to an even greater degree. Given this environment, it's no wonder that bad actors have historically felt free to commit acts of sexual violence with little to no consequence.

This is precisely why "Me Too" was considered to be a watershed moment. The phrase was coined by activist Tarana Burke in 2006 to help raise awareness about, and create solidarity among, survivors of sexual assault. It went viral in the form of the social media hashtag #MeToo in October 2017 in the wake of an exposé detailing numerous allegations of sexual assault against film producer Harvey Weinstein. In the months that followed, there was an outpouring of Me Too stories—mostly from cis women but also from cis men and trans people—many of which centered on male celebrities and other men in positions of power who had been accused of "sexual misconduct," a broad term favored by the media because it avoids legal implications. Rather than delve into all the specific bad actors and incidents,[7] I want to highlight three relevant points. First, for almost every bad actor who was impli-cated, numerous victims came forward, indicating that (as with my reckless driver analogy) they were repeat offenders who had been getting away with it for quite some time. Second, virtually all of the bad actors initially denied the charges, often vehemently, and the few who eventually admitted to their actions only did so after enough victims had come forward as to render their deni-als implausible. Third, likely due to the sheer numbers of victims who came forward, the general public finally began to take their stories seriously, which resulted in these bad actors finally being held accountable for their actions, typically in the form of losing their jobs.

While the Me Too moment hinted at the possibility for long-term change, some of the responses to it were disappointing, especially in light of the sexualizing mindsets that I've detailed in this book. For starters, much of the media coverage depicted Me Too as if it were a "battle of the sexes," in which progress for women was pitted against the interests of men. This oppositional framing erases stories about sexual violence that do not fit the classic male-assailant/female-victim template. Furthermore, this oppositional framing helped foster the premise that if we "Believe Women" (as the catchphrase went), then men must be negatively impacted by default. But this isn't true at all. In fact, men who aren't bad actors mostly stand to gain from this. After all, men often find themselves having to navigate the "any man could po-tentially be a sexual predator" stereotype, which can significantly complicate their lives. That stereotype persists not merely because of Predator/Prey thinking, but also because of women's (and other victim's) real-life experiences of sexual violence at the hands of men. Therefore, keeping potential bad actors in check and sanc-tioning them for their offenses is not merely beneficial to women but also in men's long-term interests.

The assumption that believing women must automatically hurt men typically hinges on concerns about false accusations, for which there is some truth but far more disinformation. Let's examine the numbers. Studies indicate that somewhere between 2 and 8 percent of sexual assault allegations are false. (Phrased conversely, 92–98 percent of allegations are true.) Since a mere fraction of men will ever be accused of sexual assault in their lifetime, this means that only a very tiny percentage of men in total (surely less than 1 percent) will ever face a false sexual assault allegation. In contrast, we know that the number of men in total who have actually committed sexual assault is 5–11 percent—a far larger number. And it's in the latter group's interest to play up fears of false accusations—which is exactly what the aforementioned bad actors did via denying what turned out to be real charges against them. In other words, not only are most men's fears about false allegations overblown, but they contribute to a smokescreen that helps shield bad actors from facing consequences, and further deters legitimate victims from coming forward.

People sometimes cite the 2–8 percent statistic in order to downplay concerns about false allegations, and then move on. But I want to take a moment to address the issue, not only because it can be harrowing for the relatively few who are legitimately wrongly accused, but also because some people are more susceptible to it than others. As we've seen, certain marginalized groups (particularly men of color) have historically been stereotyped as "sexual predators," and are falsely accused of sexual violence at disproportionately higher rates. And given that all marginalized groups are marked, and thus viewed as inherently questionable and suspect, their claims of innocence are more likely to be discounted than similar claims by their unmarked counterparts. I never once saw any of these points raised by the largely straight, white, able-bodied, middle- and upper-class men who were most vociferous about false rape allegations. This suggests to me that they were less concerned about the reality of this issue than with protecting themselves.

In addition to considering the person targeted by false accusations, there has been significant research into who tends to make these false claims, what their motives are, and what forms they usually take (spoiler alert: They're not the "vengeful ex-lover" or "post-sex regret" scenarios that many presume).[8] For all the above reasons, it should be possible for us to have nuanced discussions about false sexual assault accusations. But this can only happen if people stop invoking the notion every single time any victim comes forward.

Some objections to Me Too trivialized incidents of sexual harassment that fell short of sexual assault. On multiple occasions, I observed people emphasizing how a bad actor they personally favored had "merely" groped women, or masturbated in front of them, and how this was very different from what Weinstein had done. To which I'd respond, "Sure, most of us are capable of distinguishing between these acts, but we also find them *all* to be serious breaches of bodily autonomy and boundaries." Another often-heard complaint was "I'm not sure what I can even say or do around my female coworkers anymore." If this were a sincere question, I would tell them to simply look up their workplace's sexual harassment policy and see what it says. But typically they were not sincere; they were mere insinuations that sexual harassment claims are inherently spurious or frivolous. I also heard men say things like "Now I'm worried that any little thing I do might be misinterpreted as sexual." Of course, this is precisely what women routinely have to deal with as a result of phantom invitations! Rather than trivialize this complaint, I entreat any man who feels this way to join us in working to dismantle the Predator/Prey script so that we can all finally be free from having "tacit signaling" leveraged against us.

A lot of the debates that swirled around Me Too dwelled on whether the punishment for any given bad actor was proportionate or whether they deserved a second chance. This second point is complicated by the fact that so many of them were repeat offenders who had continued to act without remorse over the course of many years. I am not a sexual violence policy or legal expert, so I am not about to weigh in on the specifics here. But what I do know is that there needs to be at least *some* accountability for people who perpetrate sexual violence; otherwise bad actors (much like reckless drivers) will continue to commit said acts with impunity.

Finally, some of the arguments I make in this book—particularly regarding how the "sexual predator" stereotype has historically been used to sexualize various marginalized groups—could potentially be misappropriated by bad actors. For instance, if a victim were to come forward with her Me Too story about him, the bad actor might claim that she is unfairly "sexualizing" him. I wouldn't be surprised if this happened, as language and concepts coined to critique social inequities are often flipped by those who wish to perpetuate them (as seen in claims of "reverse" sexism and racism). So allow me to preemptively address this matter. For starters, there is an obvious difference between stereotyping an entire marginalized group en masse as "sexual predators" and highly specific claims about how person X carried out an act of sexual violence against person Y. While the en masse claim is clearly baseless and defamatory, the specific claim attempts to communicate an incident that has actually occurred. Furthermore, if the specific claim that person Y has made about person X is true, then it's misleading to say that Y has "sexualized" X. Rather, person X is the one who has sexualized person Y (by perpetrating sexual violence against them), and person Y is simply holding person X accountable for that act.

Individuals who are sexually harassed or assaulted generally experience sexual stigma as a result, as it's their boundaries that are crossed and their bodily autonomy that is violated. In contrast, the perpetrator typically does not experience sexual stigma. However, this may change if they are ultimately found out. For instance, during Me Too, I often heard people derisively refer to various bad actors as "perverts," even though this strikes me as an odd choice of words. After all, "pervert" has historically been used to smear people who have atypical sexual interests, whereas most of the Me Too–era bad actors had fairly conventional sexual interests (in that they were male "sexual aggressors" pursuing female "sexual objects"). However, this word choice makes some sense if we realize that "pervert" functions primarily as a sexualizing slur here, not unlike how slurs such as "slut" or "faggot" are often hurled at people regardless of their actual sexual behaviors.

As a society, we often stigmatize people who commit atrocities, so I can understand why someone might want to do the same in the case of these bad actors. But I encourage people to think twice about using these particular slurs. For one thing, "pervert" has long been used to demonize queer people and others who engage in solitary and consensual sexual acts, so there's no need to additionally conflate us with rapists. But more to the point, the power behind sexualizing slurs is that they invoke the idea that sex itself is "dirty" and "disgusting." While the sexual violence perpetrated by these bad actors was horrific, it's not because these acts were "sexual" per se, but rather because they were *violent*—they involved wielding power over another person, and violating their bodily autonomy. In future considerations of such acts, we should center the fact that they are nonconsensual rather than irredeemably "sexual." And there are plenty of alternative descriptors that we can use that do just that: "perpetrator," "assailant," "violator," "harasser," "abuser," and so on.

Dropping Science

There are some people—okay, probably many people—who upon reading my guidelines on how to be ethically sexual, going off script, and working to bring an end to sexual violence, are now thinking, "But Julia, women and men have been evolutionarily programmed to behave in these ways. We can't do anything to change it, as it's in our very nature!"

With regards to sexual violence, there is significant evidence demonstrating that its prevalence varies across cultures and environments, and is often influenced by ideology and social norms.[9] Indeed, the fact that only 5–11 percent of men in the United States resort to rape shows that it's not a ubiquitous male trait by any means. A glance at history might also suggest that humans are potentially predisposed toward war, murder, slavery, torture, oppression, and a host of other atrocities. We could haggle over the extent to which biology influences these phenomena (or not) until we're blue in the face. Or instead, we could focus our attention on doing everything we can to try to eliminate them inasmuch as possible.

As a biologist, I believe that the scientific method provides a powerful tool to better understand the world around us. But I'm also aware of its limitations. I believe that data obtained from a well-designed experiment may offer insight into what is actually taking place. But I also know that humans are fallible, and we're the ones who ultimately interpret that data. We may be fairly objective in some contexts—such as poring over a math problem, since it's just numbers to us. But when it comes to sex and sexuality, we are heavily invested parties and chock-full of biases. On top of that, when it comes to examining human sex differences, there are no truly well-designed experiments, as they all lack proper controls. There is no way to untangle the social and experiential from the biological, as they all interact with one another, and all influence the final outcome.

I'm not saying that it's pointless to scientifically study human sex, gender, and sexuality. I'm just saying that the results—and especially our interpretations of said results—should be taken with an as yet to be determined number of grains of salt.

Earlier, I described late-nineteenth-century scientific researchers who purportedly "proved" that European men were evolutionarily superior to everybody else and that people could evolutionarily "degenerate" if they had the wrong kind of sex, or sex with the wrong type of person, or even if they simply masturbated. In retrospect, knowing how wildly incorrect they were, it's easy for us to see how these researchers were mostly making the available evidence fit their worldview.

Nowadays, we have a brand-new evolutionary theory of human sexuality! Actually, it's not all that new. It started to congeal in the 1970s when biologist Robert Trivers expanded upon Darwin's original claims that, sexually speaking, males are "eager," while females are "coy." Even if you're not a biologist, you're probably familiar with Trivers's "parental investment" theory. It goes something like this: Since sperm are inexpensive to produce, males must be programmed to have as much sex as possible with as many females as they can mate with. In contrast, since eggs (not to mention pregnancy) are very resource heavy, females are evolutionarily programmed to be very picky, and to only mate with males who have "good genes." I am oversimplifying this a bit, but then again, nearly everybody oversimplifies this theory.

This isn't a biology book, so I'm not going to get into the weeds about the pros and cons of this theory other than to mention that there are plenty of exceptions to it, as well as contradictory evidence.[10] But what is astounding to me is how ardently both scientists and laypeople alike try to shoehorn any and all observations about human sexuality into this narrative, even when the evidence doesn't really fit, and when nonbiological explanations make far more sense. Sure, it could be that the parental investment theory is largely correct. Or, alternatively, it could be that the Predator/Prey mindset leads us to *expect* males to be "eager" and females to be "coy." The very fact that we, as a society, stigmatize people who fail to live up to these ideals, or else erase them via straight assumption, suggests to me that we are once again attempting to make the evidence fit our worldview.

Elsewhere I have detailed how both sides of ye olde Nature versus Nurture debate fail to adequately explain the existence of people who are atypical with regards to their genders and sexualities, such as bisexual trans women like me.[11] Researchers used to insist that queer people were extraordinarily rare—a maneuver that enabled them to hand-wave us away as anomalies, rather than take us seriously as exceptions that potentially disprove the rule. But as anti-queer stigma has gradually decreased over the decades, the percentage of LGBTQIA+ people in the population has correspondingly increased.[12] Some anti-LGBTQIA+ campaigners have tried to blame this increase on "social contagion" (because of course they did). A more apt explanation is that this demographic change parallels the sharp increase in left-handedness that occurred in Western countries once they stopped forcing all children into being right-handed.[13] If you're searching for evidence that our genders and sexualities can be influenced by social norms and stigma, it doesn't get much more obvious than this.

Because gender and sexual minorities of various persuasions have long been stigmatized and excluded from the mainstream, we have gradually "evolved" our own sexual subcultures, some of which bear little resemblance to Predator/Prey. I can tell you firsthand that going off script works because most people in the sex-positive communities that I inhabit are already doing it. And many of them strive to be ethically sexual as well. I get that some of the ideas that I have presented here may be new for some readers, but I didn't invent them out of whole cloth. Just because they don't jibe with the human sexuality theories and narratives that most people are familiar with doesn't mean that they aren't possible or cannot work.

Sexual Dystopias and Utopias

Upon considering the many work-related incidents that came to light during Me Too, one often proposed way to curb sexualization is to remove all discussions or insinuations of "sex" from the workplace. While this might seem like a reasonable solution—especially for those of us who'd prefer to keep our work lives and sex lives entirely separate—it's important to view this reaction in a broader context. For instance, this approach is not all that dissimilar from anti-pornography feminist campaigns to prohibit objectifying depictions of women in the hope that this might reduce sexualization. I've come to think of this more generally as the "hiding sex" strategy for ending sexualization. And it seems to make superficial sense. After all, if we remove all signs of sex, then sexualization should go away too. Right?

Well, not necessarily. People will continue to have sexual thoughts and fancy other people even if we remove all indications or expressions of sex from those settings. If anything, "hiding sex" may make those sexual thoughts seem even more taboo, thus leading some people to develop unhealthy relationships with their own desires. In fact, the veneer of a "sex-free" environment can create a cover for sexual indiscretions to fester unabated—

look no further than the child sexual abuse scandals of the Catholic Church or within certain Evangelical communities. In other words, "hiding sex" doesn't make sexualization go away; it simply forces it underground.

As a crucial aside, those who favor "hiding sex" strategies will often try to justify them via "but think about the children"–type pleas. According to such arguments, we must protect children's "innocence" by shielding them from the "corruptive" influence of "sex"—where the latter is often broadly interpreted to include sex education, non-explicit media that touches on sexual themes, and marginalized individuals who are stereotyped as "excessively sexual" (LGBTQIA+ folks and people of color in particular). But in reality, this "protecting innocence" strategy can do more harm than good, as it often prevents children who are actually sexually abused from coming forward, and denies them the language to describe and process what has happened to them.[14] The same holds true for adults: The reason why we are even able to have discussions about sexualization and sexual violence is because of decades of past feminist work making it possible for us to speak openly about these previously suppressed topics.

There is yet another problem with the "hiding sex" strategy; namely, it fails to account for double standards in our perception and interpretations of sex and sexuality. I have already provided countless examples of how certain subpopulations are "marked by sex" and viewed as "excessively sexual" in many people's eyes. A man who walks down the street topless is not considered "sexual," whereas a woman who does the same is. A heterosexual couple who engages in public hand-holding or kissing is not considered "sexual," but a same-sex couple doing the same is. If a billboard ad featured a white, cisgender, thin, able-bodied woman wearing a sexy outfit, many passersby wouldn't even notice it, but if the model were Black, or transgender, or fat, or disabled, or some combination thereof, it might strike them as "sexually inappropriate." In other words, the "hiding sex" strategy will inevitably police some people's bodies and behaviors far more than others, thereby perpetuating pre-existing social and sexual inequities.

For the record, I don't think there's anything fundamentally wrong with having *some* spaces be relatively "sex-free," provided that there's at least some attempt to address the aforementioned discrepancies. But as a society-wide strategy, "hiding sex" will ultimately lead us down a path toward sexual dystopia.

So if a fully realized "hiding sex" strategy is dystopian, then what might a sexual utopia look like? Well, given the diversity of sexual desires and meanings, I'm pretty sure that every person would have somewhat different ideas about this. Over the years, I've seen various types of porn and read numerous genres of erotica, and I can tell you that *I wouldn't want to live in most of y'all's sexual utopias!* And you might feel the same way about mine!

Given this, my working premise is that a so-called sexual utopia would have to accommodate our sexual differences. And upon contemplating what that might look like, I keep returning to our previous food/taste analogy. People experience a diversity of gustatory pleasures, sometimes in our very presence, yet we usually don't feel the need to police or suppress them. If I were out in public and saw someone eating a sandwich, I wouldn't find it offensive, even if it was a type of sandwich that I personally find disgusting. But there are some limits to this. For instance, if the sandwich eater spit the food they were chewing onto me, then everyone would agree that I had been wronged by them. Or if they tried to force me to take a bite of their sandwich or to share a meal with them—that is, to *directly involve me* in their eating practices—then that would also clearly cross a line. In other words, while we are fairly open about eating food in our culture, we nevertheless recognize the importance of boundaries, bodily autonomy, and consensuality.

Since we are generally fine with public displays of food eating and enjoyment, provided that they don't cross the aforementioned lines, then why don't we extend this tolerance to public expressions of sexuality? I'm pretty sure that the answer here relates to sexual stigma. In our sex-negative culture, this stigma is often invoked anytime we confront anything that is deemed "sexual" in nature (whereas eating a sandwich doesn't typically invoke stigma). And we are taught to detest stigma, to avoid it at all costs for fear of becoming "contaminated" ourselves. This explains why most of us prefer it when sex that we are not personally interested in remains out of sight and out of mind. This is yet another reason why the "hiding sex" strategy tends to resonate with us.

Some might be inclined to describe a public expression of sexuality that they accidentally come across as "offensive," or "gross," or "immoral," or "despicable"—these are all words we often use in reference to stigmatized behaviors, thus supporting the idea that stigma is driving our reactions here. A few people might describe this public expression as "nonconsensual." I've heard this "nonconsensual" claim made in other contexts too, including ones I find particularly disturbing, so I want to take a moment to interrogate it. For example, I've heard anti-trans campaigners make the case that, because trans women are "perverts" who are constantly aroused by wearing women's clothing in their eyes, our very presence in public spaces is tantamount to a "nonconsensual" sexual act that ropes in anyone we encounter. I've heard similar claims that people who wear a BDSM collar or an item of fetishwear in public are "nonconsensually" involving other people in their kink or scene. I must point out that these assertions are but a small step away from me claiming that people who publicly wear wedding rings are "nonconsensually" involving me in their relationships.

Or claiming that women who wear short skirts are "nonconsensually" exposing me to their "sexual" bodies. Oh, wait, people actually do say that last one, sometimes to compel the woman to cover herself up, other times to invoke the victim-blaming trope "she was asking for it."

We all possess sexed bodies. We all wear various outfits and accessories in public, many of which are sex-coded in some way or other. And most of us, on occasion, have sexual thoughts in front of other people—we might find someone we see attractive, or be lost in one of our own sexual fantasies. None of these things are inherently harmful to anyone. As with our earlier sandwich-eating example, they do not cross into the realm of nonconsensuality unless we *directly involve* other people in them.

What I believe is happening in the case of coming across a public expression of sexuality, or a trans woman in a dress, or someone wearing a BDSM collar, or a woman in a short skirt is that these things will strike some people as inherently "sexual" in ways that other things (such as topless men and wedding rings) do not. And things that strike us as "sexual" may evoke sexual stigma in our minds. And this experience of sexual stigma—which can act indirectly and from a distance, as we've seen with all the fears of "contagiousness"—can make us feel as if we are being "nonconsensually" implicated in a "sexual" activity, even though no boundaries have actually been breached, and the supposed act may not even be sexual for the other party. Such overreaches are worrisome, not only because they further marginalize those who are already unfairly "marked by sex" in our culture, but also because they can dilute or weaken legitimate claims of nonconsent in cases where actual sexual violence has been perpetrated.

Returning to the question "What would a sexual utopia look like?," two things seem clear to me. First, it would involve having an open attitude toward sex and sexuality rather than constantly forcing them into hiding. I'm not saying that we would treat sex in the exact same way that we treat eating. But we would certainly be more open to the reality of sex and sexuality than we are today. Second, due to the current pervasiveness of sexual stigma, I can't envision this sexual utopia coming to fruition anytime soon. Sexual stigma poses at least two obstacles here—let's call them the "us" problem and the "them" problem. The "us" problem is more tractable, as it involves us as individuals learning to "sever sex from stigma." It may be difficult and gradual work, but it's nevertheless achievable for us to largely overcome the sex-related stigma that emanates from within us. But even once we've personally moved beyond it, we still have to contend with the "them" problem: the fact that other people still subscribe to sexual stigma and may continue to invoke and wield it to invalidate and punish others.

Here's an example that highlights the complications that can arise from both the "us" and "them" problems: Many of my friends are queer women, and we often talk quite candidly about sex and sexuality. This is partly because, as queer people who grew up in a fiercely anti-LGBTQIA+ world, we've all had to eventually overcome our "us" stigma in order to persevere. And because we are all currently active in sex-positive and social justice–oriented communities, we would never think of leveraging sexual stigma over others, such as by judging their sexual bodies, policing their solitary and consensual sexual activities, or outright sexualizing them. While we may not be perfect, we have all at least striven to overcome our "them" problem. I believe that it's this combination of having eliminated both the "us" stigma (so the subject of sex doesn't distress us as individuals) and the "them" stigma (so we're not constantly worried about others leveraging sexual stigma against us) that allows us to speak frankly about sexual matters with one another. It also helps that none of us buys into the Predator/Prey script, in which an openness to discussing sex is sometimes (mis)read as an expression of sexual interest in the other party.

Now, imagine that my friends and I are joined by a few social conservatives. I'm pretty sure that they would feel scandalized by our candid sexually themed discussions. The topic is bound to evoke sexual stigma in them (as they haven't worked on their "us" problem), and they would likely chide us because, in their minds, sex should be kept "hidden" in polite conversation. Alternatively, imagine that my friends and I were dropped into a stereotypical straight-male-dominated conversation about sex, one in which "confused slut" attitudes abound. Speaking for myself, I'd feel extremely uncomfortable engaging in such conversations, but not because of any "us" stigma on my part. Rather, I'd be worried that queer-phobic and misogynistic stigma might be leveraged against me, or that if I talked openly about sex, some of these men might misinterpret that as a sign of my sexual interest (or perhaps even "sluttiness"). In other words, I would not feel comfortable talking openly about sex with these guys because they haven't yet worked on their "them" problem.

So long as there are people who haven't bothered to work on their "us" problem, there will always be complaints about how a more open or permissive atmosphere regarding sex will potentially cause "harm" and "corrupt" others, even if said sex does not directly involve them. And so long as there are people who haven't bothered to work on their "them" problem, these same attempts to create a more open or permissive atmosphere will be hindered by bad actors who will attempt to take advantage of the situation and champion their own sexual interests over those of others. True progress toward an imagined sexual utopia will only come if we work on all these fronts simultaneously.

Destigmatizing Sex and Sexuality

In the previous chapter, I shared some of my thoughts on how we can sever sex from stigma. Those suggestions were offered in the context of how we as individuals may become more ethically sexual. But as we saw in the previous example, some people take sexual stigma for granted, and may be less inclined to do the self-work to address their "us" and "them" problems. Therefore, if we wish to destigmatize sex and sexuality, then we must also incite broad shifts in social attitudes regarding these issues.

While daunting, I believe that such shifts are possible. In my own lifetime, I've witnessed transgender people go from being fully stigmatized to now being increasingly tolerated or even legitimized in some segments of society. This progress has largely followed a standard destigmatization playbook previously used by other marginalized groups. Such strategies may include emphasizing our humanity; debunking negative stereotypes; making resources and information about us more accessible; increasing visibility and authentic media representations; highlighting more positive aspects of our experiences and communities; garnering allies, including influential ones (politicians, celebrities); and revamping laws, policies, and norms to discourage anti-trans discrimination. Analogous efforts have been employed by other sexual minorities, and they may be utilized to destigmatize sex and sexuality more generally.

If we choose to use this playbook, then we should also be aware of the potential pitfalls. I've previously discussed the dilemma of how respectability politics can lead to "desexualized" depictions of LGBTQIA+ people. On the other extreme, many ostensibly sex-positive portrayals of sexual diversity sensationalize our supposedly taboo or transgressive nature. While I understand why some people gravitate toward these themes, in the long run, we would be best served by more realistic and ambivalent considerations of these matters.

A major obstacle in destigmatizing trans people, or any minority group for that matter, is that the dominant majority has little personal investment in our social progress. Destigmatizing sex is strikingly different in this regard, as it's an issue that touches nearly everybody. Such a movement could draw from all marginalized groups, including women, as well as men who fail or refuse to live up to Predator/Prey roles and ideals. Together, we comprise a majority. And if we were all to work together to condemn sexualization and to destigmatize sex and sexuality, then there's a good chance that we would ultimately succeed. We simply need to recognize that it's in our mutual interests to do so.

Researchers who have studied destigmatization have observed that the process is greatly facilitated when there are obvious connections and shared experiences between both stigmatized and non-stigmatized populations.[15] This certainly holds true in the case of sex, as every single one of us is susceptible to being smeared as a "slut," "faggot," "pervert," etc. at the drop of a hat, regardless of our sexual histories, simply because the stigma associated with these labels makes them such powerful weapons. However, if we all were to unilaterally "disarm"—to refuse to sexualize other people's bodies and their solitary and consensual behaviors—then these charges would gradually lose their impact, and the stigma associated with them would dissipate accordingly. And if we were to shift societal norms so that the act of sexualizing another person was viewed far more negatively than being the target of sexualization, then there would be little to no incentive for people to continue propagating this stigma.

When I first began working on this book, I wasn't aware that stigma would play such a central role in it. I knew that I wanted to share the dramatic differences in how my body, behaviors, and desires were perceived and interpreted by others upon my transition from male to female, and once people started viewing me as transgender rather than cisgender. I knew that I wanted to discuss the many unconscious assumptions and meanings that people projected onto my body and sexuality, how they sometimes differed from person to person, and how we can alter or revise these meanings once we become consciously aware of them. I knew that I wanted to talk about the various forms of sexualization that I've experienced: being sexually harassed by men as a young woman; being deemed an "exotic other" and "fetish object" as a trans woman; being called a "pervert," "deviant," "deceiver," or "predator" as a queer person; and being sexualized in all these various ways while simultaneously being discounted as "undesirable." I knew that I wanted to draw connections between my own personal anecdotes and the many analogous stories of sexualization told by people who are marginalized in other ways. I initially tried to make sense of all this through existing frameworks, such as objectification or dehumanization, but those constructs fell short. Eventually, I realized that sexual stigma was the through line that seemed to link together all these disparate experiences.

Back in the Introduction, I stressed that this book would paint an incomplete picture, as is the case for all books that tackle the topics of sex and sexuality. Admittedly, there is more to this subject than perception, interpretation, and the imagined contagion of sexual stigma. But hopefully, some of you will find what I've shared here useful as you attempt to solve your own personal puzzles. And perhaps we can all strive to apply some of these ideas to creating a world where sexual equity and diversity are finally able to thrive.

NOTES

INTRODUCTION

1. Leonore Tiefer, *Sex Is Not a Natural Act & Other Essays* (Boulder, CO: Westview Press, 2004), 2–4.

2. I discuss my experiences with hormonal transition in Julia Serano, *Whipping Girl: A Transsexual Woman on Sexism and the Scapegoating of Femininity* (Berkeley, CA: Seal Press, 2016), 65–76.

3. Hana Lango Allen et al., "Hundreds of Variants Clustered in Genomic Loci and Biological Pathways Affect Human Height," *Nature* 467 (2010): 832–838.

4. Janet Shibley Hyde, Rebecca S. Bigler, Daphna Joel, Charlotte Chucky Tate, and Sari M. van Anders, "The Future of Sex and Gender in Psychology: Five Challenges to the Gender Binary," *American Psychologist* 74, no. 2 (2019): 171–193.

5. Claire Ainsworth, "Sex Redefined," *Nature* 518 (2015): 288–291.

6. William G. Reiner and John P. Gearhart, "Discordant Sexual Identity in Some Genetic Males with Cloacal Exstrophy Assigned to Female Sex at Birth," *The New England Journal of Medicine* 350, no. 4 (2004): 333–341; John Colapinto, *As Nature Made Him: The Boy Who Was Raised as a Girl* (New York: HarperCollins, 2000).

7. Julia Serano, *Excluded: Making Feminist and Queer Movements More Inclusive* (Berkeley, CA: Seal Press, 2013), 8–10, 138–168.

8. Serano, *Whipping Girl*, 95–113; Hyde et al., "The Future of Sex and Gender in Psychology."

9. Joan Roughgarden, *Evolution's Rainbow: Diversity, Gender, and Sexuality in Nature and People* (Berkeley: University of California Press, 2004). Additional references in Serano, *Excluded*, 308, note 4.

10. "LGBTQIA+" stands for lesbian, gay, bisexual, transgender, queer/ questioning, intersex, asexual (respectively), with "+" signifying related identities that may not be explicitly denoted. All these labels, as well as the word "queer," are contested to various degrees; I discuss such debates and my own usage of these terms in Serano, *Excluded*, 8–14; see also Julia Serano, *Outspoken: A Decade of Transgender Activism and Trans Feminism* (Oakland, CA: Switch Hitter Press, 2016), 244–251.

11. A comprehensive bibliography of my writings can be found at http://juliaserano.com/writings.html.

CHAPTER 1: THE TWO FILING CABINETS IN OUR MINDS

1. Asia Friedman, *Blind to Sameness: Sexpectations and the Social Construction of Male and Female Bodies* (Chicago: University of Chicago Press, 2013).

2. Reviewed in Suzanne J. Kessler and Wendy McKenna, *Gender: An Ethnomethodological Approach* (Chicago: University of Chicago Press, 1978); Sandra Lipsitz Bem, "Genital Knowledge and Gender Constancy in Preschool Children," *Child Development* 60, no. 3 (1989): 649–662; Carol Lynn Martin, Diane N. Ruble, and Joel Szkrybalo, "Cognitive Theories of Early Gender Development," *Psychological Bulletin* 128, no. 6 (2002): 903–933; and Anne A. Fast and Kristina R. Olson, "Gender Development in Transgender Preschool Children," *Child Development* 89, no. 2 (2018): 620–637.

3. Kessler and McKenna, *Gender*, 107–108; and Bem, "Genital Knowledge and Gender Constancy in Preschool Children."

4. Fast and Olson, "Gender Development in Transgender Preschool Children."

5. Kessler and McKenna, *Gender*, 101–111, 142–153.

6. Ibid., 111; Friedman, *Blind to Sameness*, 60–63.

7. Kessler and McKenna, *Gender*, 103–111.

8. Ibid.; Friedman, *Blind to Sameness*.

9. Kessler and McKenna, *Gender*, 142–153. See also Frederike Wenzlaff, Peer Briken, and Arne Dekker, "If There's a Penis, It's Most Likely a Man: Investigating the Social Construction of Gender Using Eye Tracking," *PLoS One* 13, no. 3 (2018); e0193616 (and references therein).

10. I discuss my experiences performing (and transitioning) in Bitesize in Serano, *Outspoken*, 11–13. See also http://www.bitesize.net.

11. *Gender dissonance* is my preferred term for what's commonly called *gender dysphoria*; see Serano, *Whipping Girl*, 27–29, 85–89.

12. I have described "the look" elsewhere; see Serano, *Excluded*, 27; and Serano, *Whipping Girl*, 171–172.

CHAPTER 2: OPPOSITES

1. Serano, *Whipping Girl*, 286.

2. Ibid., especially 13–15, 104–111.

3. Reviewed in Julia Serano, "What Is Transmisogyny?," *Medium*, May 24, 2021, https://juliaserano.medium.com/what-is-transmisogyny-4de92002caf6.

4. Kimberlé Crenshaw, "Demarginalizing the Intersection of Race and Sex: A Black Feminist Critique of Antidiscrimination Doctrine, Feminist Theory and Antiracist Politics," *University of Chicago Legal Forum* 139 (1989): 139–167.

5. I forwarded this idea in Serano, *Excluded*, 200–215. An analogous approach can be found in Erika V. Hall, Alison V. Hall, Adam D. Galinsky, and Katherine W. Phillips, "MOSAIC: A Model of Stereotyping Through Associated and Intersectional Categories," *Academy of Management Review* 44, no. 3 (2019): 643–672.

6. Chronicled in Serano, *Excluded*, especially in Part 2.

7. This mindset has historically been described in terms of "binary oppositions," as reviewed in Hans Bertens, *Literary Theory: The Basics*, 2nd ed. (New York: Routledge, 2008), 41–60, 91–134.

8. Perry R. Hinton, *Stereotypes, Cognition and Culture* (Hove, East Sussex, UK: Psychology Press, 2000), 96–97, 111–115; Lee Jussim, Lerita M. Coleman, and Lauren Lerch, "The Nature of Stereotypes: A Comparison and Integration of Three Theories," *Journal of Personality and Social Psychology* 52, no. 3 (1987): 536–546; and David J. Schneider, *The Psychology of Stereotyping* (New York: Guilford Press, 2004), 229–265.

9. bell hooks, *Feminist Theory: From Margin to Center* (Boston: South End Press, 1984).

10. George Yancey and Michael O. Emerson, "Does Height Matter? An Examination of Height Preferences in Romantic Coupling," *Journal of Family Issues* 37, no. 1 (2016): 53–73.

11. I originally introduced the idea of gender being *socially exaggerated* (as opposed to being wholly constructed) in Serano, *Whipping Girl*, 65–76.

12. Jonathan B. Freeman and Kerri L. Johnson, "More Than Meets the Eye: Split-Second Social Perception," *Trends in Cognitive Sciences* 20, no. 5 (2016): 362–374.

13. Kerri L. Johnson, Jonathan B. Freeman, and Kristin Pauker, "Race Is Gendered: How Covarying Phenotypes and Stereotypes Bias Sex Categorization," *Journal of Personality and Social Psychology* 102, no. 1 (2012): 116–131; Adam D. Galinsky, Erika V. Hall, and Amy J. C. Cuddy, "Gendered Races: Implications for Interracial Marriage, Leadership Selection, and Athletic Participation," *Psychological Science* 24, no. 4 (2013): 498–506; and Hall et al., "MOSAIC."

CHAPTER 3: UNWANTED ATTENTION

1. Carol Brooks Gardner, "Passing By: Street Remarks, Address Rights, and the Urban Female," *Sociological Inquiry* 50, no. 3–4 (1980): 328–356; and Carol Brooks Gardner, *Passing By: Gender and Public Harassment* (Berkeley: University of California Press, 1995), 91–94.

2. Gardner calls this the "romanticized" interpretation of male-on-female street remarks, and she explains why it's an insufficient explanation in Gardner, *Passing By: Gender and Public Harassment*, 158–198.

3. Ibid., 146–147.

4. Ibid., 135.

5. Serano, *Whipping Girl*.

6. Serano, *Outspoken*, 83–86.

7. This phenomenon is more generally described in Christian S. Crandall and Amy Eshleman, "A Justification-Suppression Model of the Expression and Experience of Prejudice," *Psychological Bulletin* 129, no. 3 (2003): 414–446; and Peter Hegarty and Anne M. Golden, "Attributional Beliefs About the Controllability of Stigmatized Traits: Antecedents or Justifications of Prejudice?," *Journal of Applied Social Psychology* 38, no. 4 (2008): 1023–1044.

8. I debunk these particular attributions in Serano, *Whipping Girl*, especially in Chapter 7.

9. Julia Serano, "Transgender Agendas, Social Contagion, Peer Pressure, and Prevalence," *Medium*, November 27, 2017, https://juliaserano.medium.com/transgender-agendas-social-contagion-peer-pressure-and-prevalence-c3694d11ed24.

10. Erving Goffman, *Stigma: Notes on the Management of Spoiled Identity* (Englewood Cliffs, NJ: Prentice-Hall, 1963).

11. Reviewed in Wayne Brekhus, "A Sociology of the Unmarked," *Sociological Theory* 16, no. 1 (1998): 34–51; Linda R. Waugh, "Marked and Unmarked: A Choice Between Unequals in Semiotic Structure," *Semiotica* 38 (1982): 299–318; and Eviatar Zerubavel, *Taken for Granted: The Remarkable Power of the Unremarkable* (Princeton, NJ: Princeton University Press, 2018).

12. Serano, *Excluded*, 169–199.

13. While this has historically been the dominant view, in certain activist settings, "reverse discourses" may lead to reciprocal claims that cis men are the ones who are inherently biased; this issue is discussed more in Serano, *Outspoken*, 269–282 (accessible online at http://juliaserano.blogspot.com/2014/11/cissexism-and-cis-privilege-revisited.html).

14. See Serano, *Excluded*, 171–174, and references therein.

CHAPTER 4: THE PREDATOR/PREY MINDSET

1. I previously introduced the Predator/Prey mindset in Serano, *Whipping Girl*, 253–271; and Julia Serano, "Why Nice Guys Finish Last," in *Yes Means Yes: Visions of Female Sexual Power and a World Without Rape*, ed. Jaclyn Friedman and Jessica Valenti (Berkeley, CA: Seal Press, 2008), 227–240. While many of the social dynamics discussed in this chapter have been described by others, "Predator/Prey" represents my synthesis of these perceptions and attitudes.

2. Hannah Frith and Celia Kitzinger, "Reformulating Sexual Script Theory: Developing a Discursive Psychology of Sexual Negotiation," *Theory & Psychology* 11, no. 2 (2001): 209–232; and Michael W. Wiederman, "The Gendered Nature of Sexual Scripts," *Family Journal* 13, no. 4 (2005): 496–502.

3. Leora Tanenbaum, *Slut! Growing Up Female with a Bad Reputation* (New York: Seven Stories Press, 1999); and Emily White, *Fast Girls: Teenage Tribes and the Myth of the Slut* (New York: Scribner, 2002).

4. Elizabeth A. Armstrong, Laura T. Hamilton, Elizabeth M. Armstrong, and J. Lotus Seeley, "'Good Girls': Gender, Social Class, and Slut Discourse

on Campus," *Social Psychology Quarterly* 77, no. 2 (2014): 100–122; Regina Rahimi and Delores D. Liston, "What Does She Expect When She Dresses Like That? Teacher Interpretation of Emerging Adolescent Female Sexuality," *Educational Studies* 45, no. 6 (2009): 512–533; Tanenbaum, *Slut!*; and White, *Fast Girls*.

5. Claire R. Gravelin, Monica Biernat, and Caroline E. Bucher, "Blaming the Victim of Acquaintance Rape: Individual, Situational, and Sociocultural Factors," *Frontiers in Psychology* 9 (2019): 2422.

6. Charlene L. Muehlenhard and Carie S. Rodgers, "Token Resistance to Sex: New Perspectives on an Old Stereotype," *Psychology of Women Quarterly* 22, no. 3 (1998): 443–463; and Michael S. Kimmel, *Guyland: The Perilous World Where Boys Become Men* (New York: Harper, 2008), 225–228.

7. The complex relationship between testosterone and libido is examined in Sari M. van Anders, "Testosterone and Sexual Desire in Healthy Women and Men," *Archives of Sexual Behavior* 41, no. 6 (2012): 1471–1484.

8. Serano, *Whipping Girl*, 65–76.

9. Mary Crawford and Danielle Popp, "Sexual Double Standards: A Review and Methodological Critique of Two Decades of Research," *Journal of Sex Research* 40, no. 1 (2003): 13–26.

10. RAINN (Rape, Abuse & Incest National Network), "Perpetrators of Sexual Violence: Statistics," accessed June 16, 2021, https://www.rainn.org/statistics/perpetrators-sexual-violence.

11. Serano, *Whipping Girl*, 17–20, 319–343; Serano, *Excluded*, 48–69; Julia Serano, "Empowering Femininity," *Ms.*, July 28, 2014, https://msmagazine.com/2014/07/28/empowering-femininity.

12. Serano, *Outspoken*, 137–141.

13. Monique Wittig, *The Straight Mind and Other Essays* (Boston: Beacon Press, 1992), 8.

14. Ann J. Cahill, *Overcoming Objectification: A Carnal Ethics* (New York: Routledge, 2012), 56–83. See also Chapter 6, note 4.

CHAPTER 5: CONFUSED SLUTS

1. C.J. Pascoe, "'Dude, You're a Fag': Adolescent Masculinity and the Fag Discourse," *Sexualities* 8, no. 3 (2005): 329–346; Kimmel, *Guyland*, 55–59; White, *Fast Girls*, 116–117.

2. Discussed more in Serano, *Whipping Girl*, 77–89.

3. I first introduced this concept in Serano, *Whipping Girl*, 290–294.

4. Wiederman, "The Gendered Nature of Sexual Scripts."

5. David Futrelle, "We Hunted the Mammoth: The FAQ-ening," https://wehuntedthemammoth.com/faq/; Donna Zuckerberg, *Not All Dead White Men: Classics and Misogyny in the Digital Age* (Cambridge, MA: Harvard University Press, 2018).

6. Serano, *Outspoken*, 5–8.

7. Julia Serano, *99 Erics: A Kat Cataclysm Faux Novel* (Oakland, CA: Switch Hitter Press, 2020). The specific chapter I reference in this paragraph ("Ethical Slut vs. Confused Slut") can be read online at https://juliaserano.medium.com/ethical-slut-vs-confused-slut-b820a674c503.

8. Dossie Easton and Catherine A. Liszt (aka Janet Hardy), *The Ethical Slut: A Guide to Infinite Sexual Possibilities* (San Francisco: Greenery Press, 1997), 19.

9. Serano, "Why Nice Guys Finish Last."

10. *Geek Feminism Wiki*, "Nice Guy Syndrome," accessed November 18, 2020, https://geekfeminism.wikia.org/wiki/Nice_Guy_syndrome.

11. Lara Stemple, Andrew Flores, and Ilan H. Meyer, "Sexual Victimization Perpetrated by Women: Federal Data Reveal Surprising Prevalence," *Aggression and Violent Behavior* 34 (2017): 302–311.

12. Sharon G. Smith, Xinjian Zhang, Kathleen C. Basile, Melissa T. Merrick, Jing Wang, Marcie-jo Kresnow, and Jieru Chen, *The National Intimate Partner and Sexual Violence Survey: 2015 Data Brief–Updated Release* (Atlanta, GA: National Center for Injury Prevention and Control, Centers for Disease Control and Prevention, 2018).

13. Steve Krakauer, "Column: Statutory Rape Treatments Shouldn't Change With Gender," *The Daily Orange*, March 29, 2006, http://dailyorange.com/2006/03/column-statutory-rape-treatments-shouldn-t-change-with-gender/.

14. Dara Lind, "What We Know About False Rape Allegations," *Vox*, June 1, 2015, https://www.vox.com/2015/6/1/8687479/lie-rape-statistics.

15. Serano, "Why Nice Guys Finish Last," 230–232.

16. Daisy Hernández, "Becoming a Black Man," *Colorlines*, January 7, 2008, https://www.colorlines.com/articles/becoming-black-man.

17. Nelson O. O. Zounlome, Y. Joel Wong, Elyssa M. Klann, and Jessica L. David, "'I'm Already Seen as a Sexual Predator from Saying Hello': Black Men's Perception of Sexual Violence," *Journal of Interpersonal Violence* 36, no. 19–20 (2021): NP10809–10830.

CHAPTER 6: SEXUALIZATION, OBJECTIFICATION, AND STIGMA

1. Joyce E. Williams, "Rape Culture," *The Blackwell Encyclopedia of Sociology* (2015), https://doi.org/10.1002/9781405165518.wbeosr019.pub2.

2. Reviewed in American Psychological Association Task Force on the Sexualization of Girls, *Report of the APA Task Force on the Sexualization of Girls* (Washington, DC: American Psychological Association, 2007); and L. Monique Ward, "Media and Sexualization: State of Empirical Research, 1995–2015," *Journal of Sex Research* 53, no. 4–5 (2016): 560–577.

3. Nick Haslam and Steve Loughnan, "Dehumanization and Infrahumanization," *Annual Review of Psychology* 65 (2014): 399–423.

4. Reviewed in Philippe Bernard, Sarah J. Gervais, and Olivier Klein, "Objectifying Objectification: When and Why People Are Cognitively Reduced to Their Parts Akin to Objects," *European Review of Social Psychology* 29, no. 1 (2018): 82–121.

5. Ciro Civile and Sukhvinder S. Obhi, "Power, Objectification, and Recognition of Sexualized Women and Men," *Psychology of Women Quarterly* 40, no. 2 (2016): 199–212.

6. Barbara L. Fredrickson and Tomi-Ann Roberts, "Objectification Theory: Toward Understanding Women's Lived Experiences and Mental Health Risks," *Psychology of Women Quarterly* 21, no. 2 (1997): 173–206.

7. Overviews of feminist theorizing and debates about objectification can be found in Martha C. Nussbaum, "Objectification," *Philosophy & Public Affairs* 24, no. 4 (1995): 249–291; Lina Papadaki, "What Is Objectification?," *Journal of Moral Philosophy* 7, no. 1 (2010): 16–36; and Cahill, *Overcoming Objectification*.

8. Goffman, *Stigma*, 30.

9. Gregory M. Herek, "Beyond 'Homophobia': Thinking About Sexual Prejudice and Stigma in the Twenty-First Century," *Sexuality Research & Social Policy* 1, no. 2 (2004): 6–24.

10. Gregory M. Herek, "AIDS and Stigma," *American Behavioral Scientist* 42, no. 7 (1999): 1106–1116; and Adina Nack, "Bad Girls and Fallen Women: Chronic STD Diagnoses as Gateways to Tribal Stigma," *Symbolic Interaction* 25, no. 4 (2002): 463–485.

11. Cecilia Benoit, S. Mikael Jansson, Michaela Smith, and Jackson Flagg, "Prostitution Stigma and Its Effect on the Working Conditions, Personal Lives, and Health of Sex Workers," *Journal of Sex Research* 55, no. 4–5

(2018): 457–471; and Ronald Weitzer, "Resistance to Sex Work Stigma," *Sexualities* 21, no. 5–6 (2018): 717–729.

12. Armstrong et al., "'Good Girls'"; Crawford and Popp, "Sexual Double Standards"; and Terri D. Conley, Ali Ziegler, and Amy C. Moors, "Backlash from the Bedroom: Stigma Mediates Gender Differences in Acceptance of Casual Sex Offers," *Psychology of Women Quarterly* 37, no. 3 (2013): 392–407.

13. Tanenbaum, *Slut!*; and White, *Fast Girls*.

14. Ibid.

15. Joan C. Chrisler, "Leaks, Lumps, and Lines: Stigma and Women's Bodies," *Psychology of Women Quarterly* 35, no. 2 (2011): 202–214.

16. The relationship between stigmatization and dehumanization is explored in Aniuska M. Luna, Emily Jurich, and Francisco Quintana, "Thwarting Stigma and Dehumanization Through Empathy," in *Teaching Empathy in Healthcare*, ed. Adriana E. Foster and Zimri S. Yaseen (Cham, Switzerland: Springer, 2019), 251–267. I agree with their assessment that "dehumanization does not create the rejective boundary that stigma creates; it informs, shapes, enforces, and justifies it" (p. 254).

17. I address the "Stockholm syndrome" and "false consciousness" charges in Serano, *Whipping Girl*, 330–343; and Serano, *Excluded*, 252–255. The possibilities for nonharmful and even pleasurable instances of objectification are explored in Nussbaum, "Objectification."

CHAPTER 7: INTERSECTIONALITY AND HYPERSEXUALIZATION

1. Armstrong et al., "'Good Girls'"; Rahimi and Liston, "What Does She Expect When She Dresses Like That?"; Tanenbaum, *Slut!*; and White, *Fast Girls*.

2. Mary Elizabeth Williams, "Brock Turner's Victim Has Dreams and a Future, Too: Sympathy for Convicted Sex Offender Is Grossly Misplaced," *Salon*, June 7, 2016, https://www.salon.com/2016/06/07/brock_turners _victim_has_dreams_and_a_future_too_sympathy_for_convicted_sex _offender_is_grossly_misplaced.

3. Kate Manne, *Down Girl: The Logic of Misogyny* (New York: Oxford University Press, 2018), 197–198.

4. Schneider, *The Psychology of Stereotyping*, 455–461; and Andrew R. Todd, Kelsey C. Thiem, and Rebecca Neel, "Does Seeing Faces of Young

Black Boys Facilitate the Identification of Threatening Stimuli?," *Psychological Science* 27, no. 3 (2016): 384–393.

5. Kelsey C. Thiem, Rebecca Neel, Austin J. Simpson, and Andrew R. Todd, "Are Black Women and Girls Associated with Danger? Implicit Racial Bias at the Intersection of Target Age and Gender," *Personality and Social Psychology Bulletin* 45, no. 10 (2019): 1427–1439; Galinsky, Hall, and Cuddy, "Gendered Races"; and Johnson, Freeman, and Pauker, "Race Is Gendered."

6. Megan Stevenson and Sandra Mayson, "The Scale of Misdemeanor Justice," *Boston University Law Review* 98 (2018): 731–777 (especially Figs. 13 and 14); rights4girls, "Racial & Gender Disparities in the Sex Trade," May 1, 2019, https://rights4girls.org/wp/wp-content/uploads/r4g/2019/05/Racial-Disparity-fact-sheet-May-2019-1.pdf; and Joey L. Mogul, Andrea J. Ritchie, and Kay Whitlock, *Queer (In)Justice: The Criminalization of LGBT People in the United States* (Boston: Beacon Press, 2012).

7. Matthew Barry Johnson, *Wrongful Conviction in Sexual Assault: Stranger Rape, Acquaintance Rape, and Intra-Familial Child Sexual Assaults* (New York: Oxford University Press, 2021), 9.

8. These developments are chronicled in Ladelle McWhorter, *Racism and Sexual Oppression in Anglo-America: A Genealogy* (Bloomington: Indiana University Press, 2009).

9. This account is largely drawn from ibid. See also Christian Klesse, "Race and Sexology," *The International Encyclopedia of Human Sexuality* (2015): 1059–1114; Siobhan Somerville, "Scientific Racism and the Emergence of the Homosexual Body," *Journal of the History of Sexuality* 5, no. 2 (1994): 243–266; Nancy Leys Stepan, "Race and Gender: The Role of Analogy in Science," *Isis*, 77, no. 2 (1986): 261–277; and Merl Storr, "The Sexual Reproduction of 'Race': Bisexuality, History and Racialization," in *Queer Feminist Science Studies: A Reader*, ed. Cyd Cipolla, Kristina Gupta, David A. Rubin, and Angela Willey (Seattle: University of Washington Press, 2017), 56–67.

10. Klesse, "Race and Sexology"; and Stepan, "Race and Gender."

11. Storr, "The Sexual Reproduction of 'Race.'"

12. McWhorter, *Racism and Sexual Oppression in Anglo-America*; Klesse, "Race and Sexology"; and Stepan, "Race and Gender."

13. McWhorter, *Racism and Sexual Oppression in Anglo-America*; and Stepan, "Race and Gender."

14. McWhorter, *Racism and Sexual Oppression in Anglo-America*, 179–181.

15. Ibid.; and Somerville, "Scientific Racism and the Emergence of the Homosexual Body."

16. The words "contaminate," "corrupt," "pollute," and "contagion" occur repeatedly throughout McWhorter's account of this era—these are all hallmarks of stigma, as I discuss in other chapters.

17. McWhorter, *Racism and Sexual Oppression in Anglo-America*, 172.

18. Such paternalistic attitudes toward middle- and upper-class white women and children are described throughout ibid.

19. This account is drawn from Patricia Hill Collins, *Black Feminist Thought: Knowledge, Consciousness and the Politics of Empowerment* (New York: Routledge, 2000), 123–148; Sander L. Gilman, *Difference and Pathology: Stereotypes of Sexuality, Race and Madness* (Ithaca, NY: Cornell University Press, 1985); Rachel A. Feinstein, *When Rape Was Legal: The Untold History of Sexual Violence During Slavery* (New York: Routledge, 2019); bell hooks, *Ain't I a Woman? Black Women and Feminism* (Boston: South End Press, 1981); and Johnson, *Wrongful Conviction in Sexual Assault*, 57–104.

20. Johnson, *Wrongful Conviction in Sexual Assault*, 59–60.

21. Collins, *Black Feminist Thought*, 129.

22. Joel R. Anderson, Elise Holland, Courtney Heldreth, and Scott P. Johnson, "Revisiting the Jezebel Stereotype: The Impact of Target Race on Sexual Objectification," *Psychology of Women Quarterly* 42, no. 4 (2018): 461–476.

23. Noah Berlatsky, "The Imagined Sex Worker," *Pacific Standard*, September 22, 2014, https://psmag.com/social-justice/black-female-sex-work-prostitution-police-arrest-jail-lapd-daniele-watts-90974.

24. Feinstein, *When Rape Was Legal*, 79–86.

25. Angela Y. Davis, *Women, Race, and Class* (New York: Random House, 1983), 172–201. See also Collins, *Black Feminist Thought*, 146–148; Johnson, *Wrongful Conviction in Sexual Assault*, 60–74; and McWhorter, *Racism and Sexual Oppression in Anglo-America*, 153–162.

26. Johnson, *Wrongful Conviction in Sexual Assault*, 61–64.

27. Ibid., 81–83.

28. Mary Romero, "State Violence, and the Social and Legal Construction of Latino Criminality: From El Bandido to Gang Member," *Denver Law Review* 78 (2001): 1081–1118; and Johnson, *Wrongful Conviction in Sexual Assault*, 9.

29. Cindy Casares, "Trump's Repeated Use of the Mexican Rapist Trope Is as Old (and as Racist) as Colonialism," NBCNews.com, April 7, 2018,

https://www.nbcnews.com/think/opinion/trump-s-repeated-use-mexican
-rapist-trope-old-racist-colonialism-ncna863451.

30. Małgorzata Martynuska, "The Exotic Other: Representations of
Latina Tropicalism in U.S. Popular Culture," *Journal of Language and Cultural Education* 4, no. 2 (2016): 73–81.

31. Stacy Smith, Marc Choueiti, and Katherine Pieper, *Race/Ethnicity in 600 Popular Films: Examining On Screen Portrayals and Behind the Camera Diversity* (Los Angeles: Media, Diversity, & Social Change Initiative, 2014),
https://annenberg.usc.edu/sites/default/files/MDSCI_Race_Ethnicity
_in_600_Popular_Films.pdf.

32. Irvin C. Schick, *The Erotic Margin: Sexuality and Spatiality in Alteritist Discourse* (London: Verso, 1999), 105–173 (quotation on 13).

33. Klesse, "Race and Sexology."

34. This account is drawn from Alexandra (Sandi) Pierce, "'Sexual Savages': Christian Stereotypes and Violence Against North America's Native Women," in *Religion and Men's Violence Against Women*, ed.
Andy J. Johnson (New York: Springer, 2015), 63–97; Rayna Green,
"The Pocahontas Perplex: The Image of Indian Women in American Culture," *Massachusetts Review* 16, no. 4 (1975): 698–714; S. Elizabeth Bird, "Gendered Construction of the American Indian in Popular Media," *Journal of Communication* 49, no. 3 (1999), 61–83; and Roxanne Dunbar-Ortiz and Dina Gilio-Whitaker, "Busting Stereotypes: Native American Women Are More Than Princesses and Squaws," *Bitch Media*, September 19, 2017, https://www.bitchmedia.org/article/whats
-problem-thinking-indian-women-princesses-or-squaws.

35. Bird, "Gendered Construction of the American Indian in Popular Media."

36. Pierce, "Sexual Savages," 68–69.

37. Ibid., 80–86.

38. Chiung Hwang Chen, "Feminization of Asian (American) Men in the U.S. Mass Media: An Analysis of *The Ballad of Little Jo*," *Journal of Communication Inquiry* 20, no. 2 (1996): 57–71; see also Chapter 2, note 13.

39. Aki Uchida, "The Orientalization of Asian Women in America," *Women's Studies International Forum* vol. 21, no. 2 (1998): 161–174 (quotation on 162).

40. Ibid., 163–167; see also Sunny Woan, "White Sexual Imperialism: A Theory of Asian Feminist Jurisprudence," *Washington and Lee Journal of Civil Rights and Social Justice* 14 (2008): 275–301.

41. Uchida, "The Orientalization of Asian Women in America," 169.

42. Armstrong et al., "'Good Girls'"; Tanenbaum, *Slut!*; Bev Skeggs, "The Making of Class and Gender Through Visualizing Moral Subject Formation," *Sociology* 39, no. 5 (2005): 965–982; and Bettina Spencer, "The Impact of Class and Sexuality-Based Stereotyping on Rape Blame," *Sexualization, Media, & Society* 2, no. 2 (2016): 1–8.

43. Alison Phipps, "Rape and Respectability: Ideas about Sexual Violence and Social Class," *Sociology* 43, no. 4 (2009): 667–683 (quotation on 669–670).

44. Anna Mollow, "Is Sex Disability? Queer Theory and the Disability Drive," in *Sex and Disability*, ed. Robert McRuer and Anna Mollow (Durham, NC: Duke University Press, 2012), 285–312 (quotation on 286).

45. Ibid.

46. McWhorter, *Racism and Sexual Oppression in Anglo-America*, 172 (see also 125–140, 162–168); and Estelle B. Freedman, "'Uncontrolled Desires': The Response to the Sexual Psychopath, 1920–1960," *Journal of American History* 74, no. 1 (1987): 83–106.

47. Hind Khalifeh et al., "Domestic and Sexual Violence Against Patients with Severe Mental Illness," *Psychological Medicine* 45, no. 4 (2015): 875–886; and Kathleen C. Basile, Matthew J. Breiding, and Sharon G. Smith, "Disability and Risk of Recent Sexual Violence in the United States," *American Journal of Public Health* 106, no. 5 (2016): 928–933.

48. Christina E. Wells and Erin Elliott Motley, "Reinforcing the Myth of the Crazed Rapist: A Feminist Critique of Recent Rape Legislation," *Boston University Law Review* 81 (2001): 127–198 (quotation on 154).

CHAPTER 8: QUEER AS A THREE-DOLLAR BILL

1. *Dictionary.com*, s.v. "Straight," accessed August 27, 2020, https://www.dictionary.com/browse/straight. While some people use the term "straight" as shorthand for "heterosexual," I am using it here in reference to all people whom society deems "not queer"; my rationale for doing so is explained in Serano, *Excluded*, 8–14.

2. Gary J. Gates, "LGBT Data Collection amid Social and Demographic Shifts of the U.S. LGBT Community," *American Journal of Public Health* 107 (2017): 1220–1222. Intersex and asexual people have each been estimated to constitute about 1 percent of the population; see Ainsworth, "Sex Redefined"; and Anthony F. Bogaert, "Asexuality: Prevalence and

Associated Factors in a National Probability Sample," *Journal of Sex Research* 41, no. 3 (2004): 279–287.

3. Emma Mishel, "Intersections Between Sexual Identity, Sexual Attraction, and Sexual Behavior Among a Nationally Representative Sample of American Men and Women," *Journal of Official Statistics* 35, no. 4 (2019): 859–884.

4. Gallup, "Gay and Lesbian Rights," accessed October 9, 2020, https://news.gallup.com/poll/1651/gay-lesbian-rights.aspx (see May 2020 response to "Do you think gay or lesbian relations between consenting adults should or should not be legal?"); and Anna Brown, "Republicans, Democrats Have Starkly Different Views on Transgender Issues," Pew Research Center, November 8, 2017, https://www.pewresearch.org/fact-tank/2017/11/08/transgender-issues-divide-republicans-and-democrats.

5. *Dictionary.com*, s.v. "Queer," accessed August 27, 2020, https://www.dictionary.com/browse/queer.

6. *TheFreeDictionary.com*, s.v. "Queer as a three-dollar bill," accessed September 29, 2020, https://idioms.thefreedictionary.com/queer+as+a+three-dollar+bill.

7. Various aspects of "straight assumption" are discussed further in Serano, *Whipping Girl*, 161–193; and Serano, *Excluded*, 110–117, 181–182, 194–196.

8. Kessler and McKenna, *Gender*, 142–153; and Wenzlaff, Briken, and Dekker, "If There's a Penis, It's Most Likely a Man."

9. For more on my views about penises and "bottom surgery" (which in my case involved reconfiguring my penis into a clitoris, vagina, etc.), see Serano, *Whipping Girl*, 229–231; and Serano, *Outspoken*, 35–37, 98–105.

10. Reviewed in Gary Gute, Elaine M. Eshbaugh, and Jacquelyn Wiersma, "Sex for You, but Not for Me: Discontinuity in Undergraduate Emerging Adults' Definitions of 'Having Sex,'" *Journal of Sex Research* 45, no. 4 (2008): 329–337.

11. Talia Mae Bettcher, "Getting 'Naked' in the Colonial/Modern Gender System: A Preliminary Trans Feminist Analysis of Pornography," in *Beyond Speech: Pornography and Analytic Feminist Philosophy*, ed. Mari Mikkola (Oxford, UK: Oxford University Press, 2017), 157–176 (quotation on 164).

12. Alaa Elassar, "8 of Last Year's 10 Most Challenged Books Had One Thing in Common: LGBTQ Content," CNN, April 21, 2020, https://www.cnn.com/2020/04/21/us/top-challenged-books-2019-lgbtq-trnd/index.html.

13. Mary E. Kite and Kay Deaux, "Gender Belief Systems: Homosexuality and the Implicit Inversion Theory," *Psychology of Women Quarterly* 11, no. 1 (1987): 83–96.

14. Stephanie L. Budge, Joe J. Orovecz, Jesse J. Owen, and Alissa R. Sherry, "The Relationship Between Conformity to Gender Norms, Sexual Orientation, and Gender Identity for Sexual Minorities," *Counselling Psychology Quarterly* 31, no. 1 (2018): 79–97; and William T. L. Cox, Patricia G. Devine, Alyssa A. Bischmann, and Janet S. Hyde, "Inferences About Sexual Orientation: The Roles of Stereotypes, Faces, and the Gaydar Myth," *Journal of Sex Research* 53, no. 2 (2016): 157–171.

15. Robert W. Mitchell and Alan L. Ellis, "In the Eye of the Beholder: Knowledge That a Man Is Gay Promotes American College Students' Attributions of Cross-Gender Characteristics," *Sexuality & Culture* 15, no. 1 (2011): 80–99.

16. Elizabeth Armstrong, "Traitors to the Cause? Understanding the Lesbian/Gay 'Bisexuality Debates,'" in *Bisexual Politics: Theories, Queries, and Visions*, ed. Naomi Tucker (New York: Haworth Press, 1995), 199–217.

17. Armstrong, "Traitors to the Cause?"; Sarah Boeshart, "Hate Crimes and Corrective Rape," in *Encyclopedia of Rape and Sexual Violence*, vol. 1, ed. Merril D. Smith (Santa Barbara, CA: ABC-CLIO, 2018), 175–189; and Dominique Mosbergen, "Battling Asexual Discrimination, Sexual Violence and 'Corrective' Rape," *HuffPost*, June 20, 2013, https://www.huffpost.com /entry/asexual-discrimination_n_3380551.

18. Julie Sondra Decker, *The Invisible Orientation: An Introduction to Asexuality* (New York: Skyhorse Publishing, 2015), 91–136.

19. Shiri Eisner, *Bi: Notes for a Bisexual Revolution* (Berkeley, CA: Seal Press, 2013), 37–49, 137.

20. Ibid., 141–234. The bisexual rape statistic is from Mikel L. Walters, Jieru Chen, and Matthew J. Breiding, *The National Intimate Partner and Sexual Violence Survey (NISVS): 2010 Findings on Victimization by Sexual Orientation* (Atlanta, GA: National Center for Injury Prevention and Control, Centers for Disease Control and Prevention, 2013).

21. Miki R., "Phallocentrism and Bisexual Invisibility," in *Recognize: The Voices of Bisexual Men: An Anthology*, ed. Robyn Ochs and H. Sharif Williams (Boston: Bisexual Resource Center, 2014), 170–173.

22. Julia Serano, "Transgender People, 'Gay Conversion,' and 'Lesbian Extinction': What the Data Show," *Medium*, December 28, 2020,

https://juliaserano.medium.com/transgender-people-gay-conversion-and
-lesbian-extinction-what-the-data-show-dea2a3e70174.

23. I make this argument more thoroughly in Serano, *Whipping Girl*,
35–52, 253–271; and Serano, *Outspoken*, 136–144.

24. Joanne Meyerowitz, *How Sex Changed: A History of Transsexuality in
the United States* (Cambridge, MA: Harvard University Press, 2002), 168–
170, 196–207.

25. Ibid., 197–198.

26. Ibid., 206.

27. Serano, *Whipping Girl*, 261–262, plus 381n3. See also Matt Kane,
"GLAAD Examines Ten Years of Transgender Images on Television;
More than Half Were Negative or Defamatory," November 20, 2012,
https://www.glaad.org/blog/glaad-examines-ten-years-transgender-images
-television-more-half-were-negative-or-defamatory.

28. Serano, *Whipping Girl*, 35–52.

29. Talia Mae Bettcher, "Evil Deceivers and Make-Believers: On Transphobic Violence and the Politics of Illusion," *Hypatia: A Journal of Feminist
Philosophy* 22, no. 3 (2007): 43–65.

30. Ray Blanchard, "The Classification and Labeling of Nonhomo-
sexual Gender Dysphorias," *Archives of Sexual Behavior* 18, no. 4 (1989):
315–334 (quotation on 322). Evidence contradicting the theory is reviewed in Julia Serano, "The Case Against Autogynephilia," *International
Journal of Transgenderism* 12, no. 3 (2010), 176–187; Julia Serano, "Autogynephilia: A Scientific Review, Feminist Analysis, and Alternative
'Embodiment Fantasies' Model," *Sociological Review* 68, no. 4 (2020):
763–778; and Julia Serano, "Autogynephilia, Ad Hoc Hypotheses, and
Handwaving," *Medium*, March 31, 2020, https://juliaserano.medium
.com/autogynephilia-ad-hoc-hypotheses-and-handwaving-cecca4f6563d.

31. Elizabeth Reis, *Bodies in Doubt: An American History of Intersex* (Bal-
timore, MD: Johns Hopkins University Press, 2009).

32. Kristen Schilt and Laurel Westbrook, "Doing Gender, Doing
Heteronormativity: 'Gender Normals,' Transgender People, and the Social Maintenance of Heterosexuality," *Gender & Society* 23, no. 4 (2009):
440–464 (quotation on 457). That research also shows that many people
who claim to have been "sexually deceived" were aware at the time that
the person was transgender but pled ignorance afterward in order to save
face or avoid prosecution; see also Serano, *Whipping Girl*, 247–251. For

further consideration of this issue, see Alex Sharpe, *Sexual Intimacy and Gender Identity 'Fraud': Reframing the Legal and Ethical Debate* (New York: Routledge, 2018).

33. Kane, "GLAAD Examines Ten Years of Transgender Images on Television"; *Disclosure: Trans Lives on Screen*, directed by Sam Feder (Field of Vision; Bow and Arrow Entertainment; Level Forward, 2020); Jennifer Lee, "Mainstream Fictional Depictions of Intersex Experience: Representations and Real Lives," *International Journal of the Humanities* 8, no. 11 (2011): 169–184; and Phoebe Hart, "Writing Characters with Intersex Variations for Television," *Journal of Screenwriting* 7, no. 2 (2016): 207–223.

34. This "worst of both worlds" model was influenced by Talia Bettcher's writings on this matter, particularly Bettcher, "Evil Deceivers and Make-Believers"; and Talia Mae Bettcher, "Full-Frontal Morality: The Naked Truth about Gender," *Hypatia* 27, no. 2 (2012): 319–337.

35. Reviewed in Rebecca L. Stotzer, "Violence Against Transgender People: A Review of United States Data," *Aggression and Violent Behavior* 14, no. 3 (2009): 170–179; and Jane M. Ussher, Rosie Charter, Virginia Schmied, and Alexandra Hawkey, "Sexual Violence," and Rebecca L. Stotzer, "Violence," both in *The SAGE Encyclopedia of Trans Studies*, vol. 2, ed. Abbie E. Goldberg and Genny Beemyn (Thousand Oaks, CA: SAGE Publications, 2021), 772–776 and 898–903, respectively. The experiences of transgender students are found in Emily A. Greytak, Joseph G. Kosciw, and Elizabeth M. Diaz, *Harsh Realities: The Experiences of Transgender Youth in Our Nation's Schools* (New York: GLSEN, 2009); and Gabriel R. Murchison, Madina Agénor, Sari L. Reisner, and Ryan J. Watson, "School Restroom and Locker Room Restrictions and Sexual Assault Risk Among Transgender Youth," *Pediatrics* 143, no. 6 (2019): e20182902.

36. "Brandon Teena," *Wikipedia*, accessed January 3, 2021, https://en .wikipedia.org/wiki/Brandon_Teena; and "Murder of Gwen Araujo," *Wikipedia*, accessed January 3, 2021, https://en.wikipedia.org/wiki/Murder_of _Gwen_Araujo.

37. Ussher et al., "Sexual Violence"; and Stotzer, "Violence."

38. Janae L. Teal, "'Black Trans Bodies Are Under Attack': Gender Non-conforming Homicide Victims in the US, 1995–2014" (master's thesis, Humboldt State University, 2015), http://humboldt-dspace.calstate .edu/handle/10211.3/143682. The quotation about "overkill" is from Stotzer, "Violence," 900.

39. Jordan Blair Woods, Brad Sears, and Christy Mallory, *Model Legislation for Eliminating the Gay and Trans Panic Defenses* (Los Angeles: Williams Institute, UCLA School of Law, 2016).

40. Katherine Farrimond, "'Stay Still So We Can See Who You Are': Anxiety and Bisexual Activity in the Contemporary Femme Fatale Film," *Journal of Bisexuality* 12, no. 1 (2012): 138–154; Jonathan David White, "Bisexuals Who Kill: Hollywood's Bisexual Crimewave, 1985–1998," *Journal of Bisexuality* 2, no. 1 (2001): 39–54; and Vito Russo, *The Celluloid Closet: Homosexuality in the Movies*, rev. ed. (New York: Harper & Row, 1987), 122–179.

41. McWhorter, *Racism and Sexual Oppression in Anglo-America*, 182–193; Fred Fejes, *Gay Rights and Moral Panic: The Origins of America's Debate on Homosexuality* (New York: Palgrave Macmillan, 2008), 11–27; and Michele Eliason, Carol Donelan, and Carla Randall, "Lesbian Stereotypes," *Health Care for Women International* 13, no. 2 (1992): 131–144.

42. Andrea Dworkin, *Right-Wing Women* (New York: Perigee Books, 1983), 32.

43. Jane Ward, "Bad Girls: On Being the Accused," *Bully Bloggers*, December 21, 2017, https://bullybloggers.wordpress.com/2017/12/21/bad-girls-on-being-the-accused/.

44. This scene is analyzed in Feder, *Disclosure*.

45. Nancy J. Knauer, "Homosexuality as Contagion: From *The Well of Loneliness* to the Boy Scouts," *Hofstra Law Review* 29, no. 2 (2000): 401–501; Serano, *Outspoken*, 198–200; and McWhorter, *Racism and Sexual Oppression in Anglo-America*, 182–194.

46. Gregory M. Herek, "Facts About Homosexuality and Child Molestation," *Sexual Orientation: Science, Education, and Policy* (2012), https://lgbpsychology.org/html/facts_molestation.html.

47. Warren J. Blumenfeld, "How LGBTQ People and Jews Were Stereotyped as Violent Predators," *LGBTQ Nation*, December 31, 2016, https://www.lgbtqnation.com/2016/12/lgbtq-people-jews-stereotyped-violent-predators/.

48. Gillian Frank, "Rethinking Bussing in the 1970s: The Sexual Politics of School Integration in the United States," *Notches*, July 1, 2014, https://notchesblog.com/2014/07/01/rethinking-bussing-in-the-1970s-the-sexual-politics-of-school-integration-in-the-united-states/; and Gillian Frank, "The Anti-Trans Bathroom Nightmare Has Its Roots in Racial Segregation," *Slate*, November 10, 2015, https://slate.com/human-interest

/2015/11/anti-trans-bathroom-propaganda-has-roots-in-racial-segregation
.html. See also Fejes, *Gay Rights and Moral Panic.*

49. Amy L. Stone, "Frame Variation in Child Protectionist Claims: Constructions of Gay Men and Transgender Women as Strangers," *Social Forces* 97, no. 3 (2019): 1155–1176.

50. Reviewed in Julia Serano, "Transgender People, Bathrooms, and Sexual Predators: What the Data Say," *Medium*, June 7, 2021, https:// juliaserano.medium.com/transgender-people-bathrooms-and-sexual -predators-what-the-data-say-2f31ae2a7c06.

51. Ibid.

52. RAINN (Rape, Abuse & Incest National Network), "Children and Teens: Statistics," accessed May 30, 2021, https://www.rainn.org/statistics /children-and-teens.

53. Amy L. Stone, "Gender Panics About Transgender Children in Religious Right Discourse," *Journal of LGBT Youth* 15, no. 1 (2018): 1–15; and Jessica Fields, "'Children Having Children': Race, Innocence, and Sexuality Education," *Social Problems* 52, no. 4 (2005): 549–571.

CHAPTER 9: YOU MAKE ME SICK

1. Jacqueline Howard, "The History of the 'Ideal' Woman and Where That Has Left Us," CNN, March 9, 2018, https://www.cnn .com/2018/03/07/health/body-image-history-of-beauty-explainer-intl /index.html.

2. Hanne Blank, *Big Big Love, Revised: A Sex and Relationships Guide for People of Size (and Those Who Love Them)* (Berkeley, CA: Celestial Arts, 2011); Kate Harding, "How Do You Fuck a Fat Woman?," in *Yes Means Yes*, ed. Friedman and Valenti, 67–75; Eli Clare, *Exile and Pride: Disability, Queerness, and Liberation* (Durham, NC: Duke University Press, 2009), 119–141; and Alison Kafer, "Desire and Disgust: My Ambivalent Adventures in Devoteeism," in *Sex and Disability*, ed. McRuer and Mollow, 331–354. See also Cahill, *Overcoming Objectification*, 84–93.

3. Serano, *Outspoken*, 148–150, 204–214.

4. Ray Blanchard and Peter I. Collins, "Men with Sexual Interest in Transvestites, Transsexuals, and She-Males," *Journal of Nervous and Mental Disease* 181, no. 9 (1993): 570–575.

5. See "abasiophilia," "acrotomophilia," and "gerontophilia" in "List of Paraphilias," *Wikipedia*, accessed February 8, 2021, https://en.wikipedia .org/wiki/List_of_paraphilias.

6. Blank, *Big Big Love*, 8–9; Harding, "How Do You Fuck a Fat Woman?"; and Kafer, "Desire and Disgust."

7. Weitzer, "Resistance to Sex Work Stigma."

8. Julia Serano, "Prejudice, 'Political Correctness,' and the Normalization of Donald Trump," *Medium*, November 22, 2016, https://juliaserano.medium.com/prejudice-political-correctness-and-the-normalization-of-donald-trump-28c563154e48.

9. Paul Rozin, Jonathan Haidt, and Clark R. McCauley, "Disgust," in *Handbook of Emotions*, 3rd ed., ed. Michael Lewis, Jeannette M. Haviland-Jones, and Lisa Feldman Barrett (New York: Guilford Press, 2008), 757–776; Martha C. Nussbaum, *Hiding from Humanity: Disgust, Shame, and the Law* (Princeton, NJ: Princeton University Press, 2004); and Daniel Kelly, *Yuck! The Nature and Moral Significance of Disgust* (Cambridge, MA: MIT Press, 2011).

10. Paul Rozin, "Technological Stigma: Some Perspectives from the Study of Contagion," in *Risk, Media, and Stigma: Understanding Public Challenges to Modern Science and Technology*, ed. J. Flynn, P. Slovic, and H. Kunreuther (London: Earthscan, 2001), 31–40; and Carol Nemeroff and Paul Rozin, "Back in Touch with Contagion: Some Essential Issues," *Journal of the Association for Consumer Research* 3, no. 4 (2018): 612–624.

11. Nussbaum, *Hiding from Humanity*; Gordon Hodson, Becky L. Choma, Jacqueline Boisvert, Carolyn L. Hafer, Cara C. MacInnis, and Kimberly Costello, "The Role of Intergroup Disgust in Predicting Negative Outgroup Evaluations," *Journal of Experimental Social Psychology* 49, no. 2 (2013): 195–205. See also notes 15 and 16 below.

12. Joshua Rottman, "Evolution, Development, and the Emergence of Disgust," *Evolutionary Psychology* 12, no. 2 (2014): 417–433; and Rozin, Haidt, and McCauley, "Disgust."

13. Nussbaum, *Hiding from Humanity*; and Kelly, *Yuck!*, 137–152.

14. Rozin, Haidt, and McCauley, "Disgust."

15. Breanna Maureen O'Handley, Karen L. Blair, and Rhea Ashley Hoskin, "What Do Two Men Kissing and a Bucket of Maggots Have in Common? Heterosexual Men's Indistinguishable Salivary α-Amylase Responses to Photos of Two Men Kissing and Disgusting Images," *Psychology & Sexuality* 8, no. 3 (2017): 173–188.

16. Mark J. Kiss, Melanie A. Morrison, and Todd G. Morrison, "A Meta-Analytic Review of the Association Between Disgust and Prejudice Toward Gay Men," *Journal of Homosexuality* 67, no. 5 (2020): 674–696.

17. Serano, *Whipping Girl*, 277–281.

18. Cahill, *Overcoming Objectification*, 32.

19. bell hooks, *Black Looks: Race and Representation* (Boston: South End Press, 1992), 21–39.

20. Ibid., 21–22.

21. Denton Callander, Christy E. Newman, and Martin Holt, "Is Sexual Racism Really Racism? Distinguishing Attitudes Toward Sexual Racism and Generic Racism Among Gay and Bisexual Men," *Archives of Sexual Behavior* 44, no. 7 (2015): 1991–2000; Gilbert Caluya "'The Rice Steamer': Race, Desire and Affect in Sydney's Gay Scene," *Australian Geographer* 39, no. 3 (2008): 283–292; Chong-suk Han and Kyung-Hee Choi, "Very Few People Say 'No Whites': Gay Men of Color and the Racial Politics of Desire," *Sociological Spectrum* 38, no. 3 (2018): 145–161; and Niels Teunis, "Sexual Objectification and the Construction of Whiteness in the Gay Male Community," *Culture, Health & Sexuality* 9, no. 3 (2007): 263–275.

22. Robin Zheng, "Why Yellow Fever Isn't Flattering: A Case Against Racial Fetishes," *Journal of the American Philosophical Association* 2, no. 3 (2016): 400–419.

23. Julia Serano, "Autogynephilia and Anti-transgender Activism," *Medium*, October 26, 2021, https://juliaserano.medium.com/autogynephilia -and-anti-trans-activism-23c0c6ad7e9d. See also Chapter 8, note 30.

CHAPTER 10: FANTASIES AND HIERARCHIES

1. Charles Moser and Peggy J. Kleinplatz, "DSM-IV-TR and the Paraphilias: An Argument for Removal," *Journal of Psychology & Human Sexuality* 17, no. 3–4 (2006): 91–109. Other critiques of the concept can be found in notes 6, 8, and 11 below.

2. BDSM is an umbrella acronym intended to include consensual acts that involve bondage/discipline, dominance/submission, and/or sadism/ masochism.

3. Quotation from subsection 302.89 (F65.89), "Other Specified Paraphilic Disorder," within the "Paraphilic Disorders" section of American Psychiatric Association, *Diagnostic and Statistical Manual of Mental Disorders*, 5th ed. (*DSM-5*) (Washington, DC: American Psychiatric Association, 2013).

4. "List of Paraphilias," *Wikipedia*. See also John Money, *Lovemaps: Clinical Concepts of Sexual/Erotic Health and Pathology, Paraphilia, and Gender Transposition in Childhood, Adolescence, and Maturity* (New York: Irvington Publishers, 1986), 257–273.

5. Money, *Lovemaps*, 266.

6. Quotation from "Paraphilic Disorders" section of *DSM-5* (full citation in note 3 above). For critiques of this definition, see Andrew C. Hinderliter, "Defining Paraphilia in *DSM-5*: Do Not Disregard Grammar," *Journal of Sex and Marital Therapy* 37, no. 1 (2011): 17–31; and Charles Moser, "Yet Another Paraphilia Definition Fails," *Archives of Sexual Behavior* 40 (2011): 483–485.

7. Laura Cameron, "How the Psychiatrist Who Co-wrote the Manual on Sex Talks About Sex," *Motherboard*, April 11, 2013, https://www .vice.com/en/article/ypp93m/heres-how-the-guy-who-wrote-the-manual -on-sex-talks-about-sex.

8. Christian C. Joyal, "How Anomalous Are Paraphilic Interests?," *Archives of Sexual Behavior* 43, no. 7 (2014): 1241–1243; Christian C. Joyal, Amélie Cossette, and Vanessa Lapierre, "What Exactly Is an Unusual Sexual Fantasy?," *Journal of Sexual Medicine* 12, no. 2 (2015): 328–340; Christian C. Joyal and Julie Carpentier, "The Prevalence of Paraphilic Interests and Behaviors in the General Population: A Provincial Survey," *Journal of Sex Research* 54, no. 2 (2017): 161–171; Debby Herbenick, Jessamyn Bowling, Tsung-Chieh Fu, Brian Dodge, Lucia Guerra-Reyes, and Stephanie Sanders, "Sexual Diversity in the United States: Results from a Nationally Representative Probability Sample of Adult Women and Men," *PLoS One* 12, no. 7 (2017): e0181198; and Justin J. Lehmiller, *Tell Me What You Want* (New York: Da Capo Press, 2018).

9. For instance, the arousal associated with "transvestic fetishism" and "autogynephilia" are commonly reported to diminish or completely disappear over time; reviewed in Serano, "The Case Against Autogynephilia."

10. Christian C. Joyal, "Defining 'Normophilic' and 'Paraphilic' Sexual Fantasies in a Population-Based Sample: On the Importance of Considering Subgroups," *Sexual Medicine* 3, no. 4 (2015): 321–330.

11. Charles Moser and Peggy J. Kleinplatz, "Does Heterosexuality Belong in the *DSM*?," *Lesbian & Gay Psychology Review* 6, no. 3 (2005): 261–267.

12. Reviewed in Toni O. L. Brown, "'If Someone Finds Out You're a Perv': The Experience and Management of Stigma in the BDSM Subculture" (master's thesis, Ohio University, Columbus, 2010), http://rave .ohiolink.edu/etdc/view?acc_num=ohiou1279225927; and Serano, "Autogynephilia and Anti-transgender Activism."

13. Alain Giami, "Between DSM and ICD: Paraphilias and the Transformation of Sexual Norms," *Archives of Sexual Behavior* 44, no. 5 (2015): 1127–1138.

14. Serano, "The Case Against Autogynephilia"; Charles Moser, "A Response to Lawrence's (2009) Erotic Target Location Errors," *Journal of Sex Research*, 46, no. 5 (2009): 383–384; and Talia Mae Bettcher, "When Selves Have Sex: What the Phenomenology of Trans Sexuality Can Teach About Sexual Orientation," *Journal of Homosexuality* 61, no. 5 (2014): 605–620.

15. Joyal, Cossette, and Lapierre, "What Exactly Is an Unusual Sexual Fantasy?" and other studies cited in note 8; Lehmiller, *Tell Me What You Want*; Emily Dubberley, *Garden of Desires: The Evolution of Women's Sexual Fantasies* (Croydon, UK: Black Lace, 2013).

16. Lehmiller, *Tell Me What You Want*, 82–83; Harold Leitenberg and Kris Henning, "Sexual Fantasy," *Psychological Bulletin* 117, no. 3 (1995): 469–496; and Anthony F. Bogaert, Beth A. Visser, and Julie A. Pozzebon, "Gender Differences in Object of Desire Self-Consciousness Sexual Fantasies," *Archives of Sexual Behavior* 44, no. 8 (2015): 2299–2310.

17. Dubberley, *Garden of Desires*, 152 (examples of such fantasies can be found throughout Chapters 3 and 5).

18. Bettcher, "Full-Frontal Morality," provides an illuminating discussion of such boundaries.

19. Bettcher, "When Selves Have Sex"; and Talia Mae Bettcher, "Trans Women and 'Interpretive Intimacy': Some Initial Reflections," in *The Essential Handbook of Women's Sexuality: Diversity, Health, and Violence*, vol. 2, ed. Donna Castañeda (Santa Barbara, CA: Praeger, 2013), 51–68.

20. Leitenberg and Henning, "Sexual Fantasy"; Joyal, Cossette, and Lapierre, "What Exactly Is an Unusual Sexual Fantasy?"; and Lehmiller, *Tell Me What You Want*, 84–86.

21. Jenny Bivona and Joseph Critelli, "The Nature of Women's Rape Fantasies: An Analysis of Prevalence, Frequency, and Contents," *Journal of Sex Research* 46, no. 1 (2009): 33–45; and Dubberley, *Garden of Desires*, 81–124.

22. Bivona and Critelli, "The Nature of Women's Rape Fantasies"; Joseph W. Critelli and Jenny M. Bivona, "Women's Erotic Rape Fantasies: An Evaluation of Theory and Research," *Journal of Sex Research* 45, no. 1 (2008): 57–70; Donald S. Strassberg and Lisa K. Locker, "Force in

Women's Sexual Fantasies," *Archives of Sexual Behavior* 27, no. 4 (1998): 403–414; and Julie L. Shulman and Sharon G. Home, "Guilty or Not? A Path Model of Women's Sexual Force Fantasies," *Journal of Sex Research* 43, no. 4 (2006): 368–377.

23. Joyal, Cossette, and Lapierre, "What Exactly Is an Unusual Sexual Fantasy?," reported that 64.6 percent of women and 53.3 percent of men in their sample responded affirmatively to the statement "I have fantasized about being dominated sexually"; conversely, 46.7 percent of women and 59.6 percent of men responded affirmatively to "I have fantasized about dominating someone sexually." Lehmiller, *Tell Me What You Want* (p. 27), stated that nearly two-thirds of women and more than one-half of men in his study fantasized about being forced to have sex.

24. Lehmiller, *Tell Me What You Want*, 66. I discuss these various "cross-sex" fantasies in more depth in Serano, "Autogynephilia: A Scientific Review, Feminist Analysis, and Alternative 'Embodiment Fantasies' Model."

25. Dubberley, *Garden of Desires*, 158–159, 164–167, 218–232.

26. Ibid., 92–93.

27. Ibid., 122–123.

28. Lehmiller, *Tell Me What You Want*, 11.

29. Dubberley, *Garden of Desires*, 233–249.

30. Kristina Gupta, "Compulsory Sexuality: Evaluating an Emerging Concept," *Signs: Journal of Women in Culture and Society* 41, no. 1 (2015): 131–154.

31. Lori A. Brotto and Morag Yule, "Asexuality: Sexual Orientation, Paraphilia, Sexual Dysfunction, or None of the Above?," *Archives of Sexual Behavior* 46, no. 3 (2017): 619–627.

32. Elizabeth Wilson, "The Context of 'Between Pleasure and Danger': The Barnard Conference on Sexuality," *Feminist Review* 13, no. 1 (1983): 35–41.

33. Melissa Gira Grant, "The Truth About Trafficking: It's Not Just About Sexual Exploitation," *Guardian*, October, 24, 2012, https://www.theguardian.com/commentisfree/2012/oct/24/truth-about-trafficking-sexual-exploitation.

34. Diverse perspectives on such claims can be found in Mikkola, *Beyond Speech*.

35. David Speed, Jordan MacDonald, Alyssa Parks, Hannah Doucette, and Keerthana Munagapati, "Pornography Consumption and Attitudes Towards Pornography Legality Predict Attitudes of Sexual Equality,"

Journal of Sex Research 58, no. 3 (2021): 1–13 (quotation on 2); and Martin Barker, "The 'Problem' of Sexual Fantasies," *Porn Studies* 1, no. 1–2 (2014): 143–160.

36. R. Danielle Egan and Gail L. Hawkes, "Endangered Girls and Incendiary Objects: Unpacking the Discourse on Sexualization," *Sexuality & Culture* 12, no. 4 (2008): 291–311; and Kari Lerum and Shari L. Dworkin, "'Bad Girls Rule': An Interdisciplinary Feminist Commentary on the Report of the APA Task Force on the Sexualization of Girls," *Journal of Sex Research* 46, no. 4 (2009): 250–263.

37. Serano, *Excluded*, 67, 81–82, 110–137, 196–199, 254–256.

38. Ibid., 188–193.

39. Ibid., 257–262.

40. Joshua B. Grubbs and Samuel L. Perry, "Moral Incongruence and Pornography Use: A Critical Review and Integration," *Journal of Sex Research* 56, no. 1 (2019): 29–37. I further analyze why stigmatized desires are often viewed as "compulsive" in section 5 of Serano, "Autogynephilia, Ad Hoc Hypotheses, and Handwaving."

41. Terri D. Conley, Amy C. Moors, Jes L. Matsick, and Ali Ziegler, "Sexuality-Related Risks Are Judged More Harshly than Comparable Health Risks," *International Journal of Sexual Health* 27, no. 4 (2015): 508–521.

42. *TV Tropes*, accessed May 10, 2021, http://tvtropes.org/pmwiki /pmwiki.php/Main/DeathBySex; https://tvtropes.org/pmwiki/pmwiki.php /Main/DownfallBySex; https://tvtropes.org/pmwiki/pmwiki.php/Main /BuryYourGays; and https://tvtropes.org/pmwiki/pmwiki.php/Main /DisposableSexWorker.

CHAPTER 11: RETHINKING SEX AND CHALLENGING SEXUALIZATION

1. I review the many flaws inherent in such claims in Serano, *Excluded*, 117–168.

2. Ibid., 263–280.

3. Reviewed in Joseph J. Fischel, *Screw Consent: A Better Politics of Sexual Justice* (Oakland: University of California Press, 2019).

4. Thomas MacAulay Millar, "Toward a Performance Model of Sex," in *Yes Means Yes*, ed. Friedman and Valenti, 29–40.

5. David Lisak and Paul M. Miller, "Repeat Rape and Multiple Offending Among Undetected Rapists," *Violence and Victims* 17, no. 1 (2002):

73–84; John D. Foubert, Angela Clark-Taylor, and Andrew F. Wall, "Is Campus Rape Primarily a Serial or One-Time Problem? Evidence from a Multicampus Study," *Violence Against Women* 26, no. 3–4 (2020): 296–311; and Kevin M. Swartout, Mary P. Koss, Jacquelyn W. White, Martie P. Thompson, Antonia Abbey, and Alexandra L. Bellis, "Trajectory Analysis of the Campus Serial Rapist Assumption," *JAMA Pediatrics* 169, no. 12 (2015): 1148–1154.

6. Julia Serano, "He's Unmarked, She's Marked," in *Believe Me: How Trusting Women Can Change the World*, ed. Jessica Valenti and Jaclyn Friedman (New York: Seal Press, 2020), 51–63.

7. Reviewed in Fischel, *Screw Consent*, 172–182; and Elena Nicolaou and Courtney E. Smith, "A #MeToo Timeline to Show How Far We've Come—& How Far We Need to Go," *Refinery29*, October 5, 2019, https://www.refinery29.com/en-us/2018/10/212801/me-too-movement -history-timeline-year-weinstein.

8. Dara Lind, "What We Know About False Rape Allegations," and Sandra Newman, "What Kind of Person Makes False Rape Accusations?," *Quartz*, May 11, 2017, https://qz.com/980766/the-truth-about-false-rape -accusations.

9. Williams, "Rape Culture."

10. Roughgarden, *Evolution's Rainbow*; Patricia Adair Gowaty, "Sexual Natures: How Feminism Changed Evolutionary Biology," *Signs: Journal of Women in Culture and Society* 28, no. 3 (2003): 901–921; Zuleyma Tang-Martínez, "Rethinking Bateman's Principles: Challenging Persistent Myths of Sexually Reluctant Females and Promiscuous Males," *Journal of Sex Research* 53, no. 4–5 (2016): 532–559; and Malin Ah-King and Patricia Adair Gowaty, "A Conceptual Review of Mate Choice: Stochastic Demography, Within-Sex Phenotypic Plasticity, and Individual Flexibility," *Ecology and Evolution* 6, no. 14 (2016): 4607–4642.

11. Serano, *Excluded*, 138–168.

12. Gates, "LGBT Data Collection amid Social and Demographic Shifts of the U.S. LGBT Community."

13. Serano, "Transgender Agendas, Social Contagion, Peer Pressure, and Prevalence." The history of claims that "social contagion" turns people gay or transgender is described in Knauer, "Homosexuality as Contagion"; and Julia Serano, "Origins of 'Social Contagion' and 'Rapid Onset Gender Dysphoria,'" February 20, 2019, https://juliaserano.blogspot.com /2019/02/origins-of-social-contagion-and-rapid.html.

14. Jenny Kitzinger, "Who Are You Kidding? Children, Power, and the Struggle Against Sexual Abuse," in *Constructing and Reconstructing Childhood*, 2nd ed., ed. Allison James and Alan Prout (London: Routledge, 2005), 161–185.

15. Matthew Clair, Caitlin Daniel, and Michèle Lamont, "Destigmatization and Health: Cultural Constructions and the Long-Term Reduction of Stigma," *Social Science & Medicine* 165 (2016): 223–232.

JULIA SERANO is the author of four books, including the acclaimed modern classic *Whipping Girl*. Her writing has been published in the *New York Times*, the *Guardian*, *Time*, *Salon*, the *Daily Beast*, *Out*, *Bitch*, and *Ms.* Julia holds a PhD in biochemistry from Columbia University. Her current solo music project is *soft vowel sounds*. She lives in Oakland, California.